Educating the Gifted

Volumes based on the annual Hyman Blumberg Symposia
on Research in Early Childhood Education

Julian C. Stanley, general series editor

Educating the Gifted
ACCELERATION AND ENRICHMENT

Revised and Expanded Proceedings of the Ninth Annual
Hyman Blumberg Symposium
on Research in Early Childhood Education, 9th,
Johns Hopkins University, 1977.

Edited by William C. George,
Sanford J. Cohn, and Julian C. Stanley

The Johns Hopkins University Press
Baltimore and London

The Johns Hopkins University Press, Baltimore, Maryland 21218
The Johns Hopkins Press Ltd., London

Library of Congress Cataloging in Publication Data
Hyman Blumberg Symposium on Research in Early
    Childhood Education, New York, 1977.
    Educating the gifted.

    Includes index.
    1. Gifted children—Education—Congresses.
2. Educational acceleration—Congresses.
3. Education, Preschool—Congresses. I. George,
William C. II. Cohn, Sanford J. III. Stanley,
Julian C. IV. Title.
LC3992.H95 1977   371.9′5   79-7559
ISBN 0-8018-2260-2
ISBN 0-8018-2266-1 (pbk.)

To Sidney L. Pressey, Dean A. Worcester, and James R. Hobson, strong proponents of educational acceleration for intellectually talented youths, and to the great founders of the gifted-child movement, Lewis M. Terman and Leta S. Hollingworth, who stressed both acceleration and enrichment, we dedicate this first volume to treat both alternatives extensively.

CONTENTS

IV. Symposium

TABLES

FIGURE

CONTRIBUTORS

Sanford J. Cohn is a faculty member in special education at Arizona State University, Tempe, Arizona 85281.

Stephen P. Daurio is an assistant professor of psychology at St. Johns University, Staten Island, New York, New York 10301.

Lynn H. Fox is the coordinator of the Intellectually Gifted Child Study Group (IGCSG) and an associate professor of education in the Evening College and Summer Session of The Johns Hopkins University, Baltimore, Maryland 21218.

William C. George is the associate director of the Study of Mathematically Precocious Youth (SMPY) and director of the Office of Talent Identification and Development (OTID) at The Johns Hopkins University, Baltimore, Maryland 21218.

James R. Hobson is the retired coordinator of Pupil Personnel Services, Public Schools of Brookline, Massachusetts, currently residing at 463 Boyleston Street, Newton Center, Massachusetts 02159.

Morris Meister is a former principal of the [Bronx] High School of Science, New York, New York 10468.

Harold A. Odell is a former principal of Princeton High School, Princeton, New Jersey 08540.

Melita H. Oden is a former member of the Psychology Department at Stanford University, Stanford, California 94305.

Sidney L. Pressey, born in 1888, taught for many years at The Ohio State University, where he advocated educational acceleration. Dr. Pressey died in July, 1979.

Joseph S. Renzulli is a professor of educational psychology at the University of Connecticut, Storrs, Connecticut 06268.

Julian C. Stanley is the director of the Study of Mathematically Precocious Youth (SMPY) and a professor of psychology at The Johns Hopkins University, Baltimore, Maryland 21218.

Lewis M. Terman (1877–1956) was the internationally eminent professor of psychology at Stanford University who in 1921 launched the *Genetic*

Studies of Genius that provided the empirical foundation for the "gifted-child movement."

Dean A. Worcester is a professor emeritus of educational psychology at the University of Nebraska, currently residing at 1050 Arapahoe, Boulder, Colorado 80302. Dr. Worcester, born in 1889, also taught for a number of years at the Universities of Wisconsin and Arizona.

PREFACE

The acceleration versus enrichment controversy has existed virtually for as long as there have been sizable schools. Early entrance and "double promotions" seemed more natural in the context of the one-room schoolhouse than they do today. The issue has led to a great deal of argument, most of it unsupported by firm empirical evidence. Seldom is it even recognized explicitly that there are about as many different ways to speed up the educational progress of an intellectually talented youth as there are ways to "enrich" his or her educational experiences (e.g., see Stanley 1978 for a list of the former). It was the purpose of the 1977 American Educational Research Association symposium, on which this book is based, to explore the situation from many points of view and to see what studies thus far indicate. We were fortunate to assemble an outstanding panel and to provide its members in advance with some of the most relevant literature, including a rather thorough survey prepared by Stephen P. Daurio especially for this symposium. We hope that this volume will steady the keel a bit by counteracting unsupported statements that favor either point of view. This does not mean we are neutral, however. In our opinion, empirical evidence strongly supports the value of letting intellectually brilliant youths move ahead educationally at *their own* preferred rates, rather than being held to the lock step age-in-grade pace that characterizes most schools.

The three editors collaborated closely from the inception of the idea for the symposium through the publication of this volume. The symposium itself was organized by Julian Stanley, managed by William George, and supervised technically by Sanford Cohn. Preparing the manuscript itself was the responsibility of Messrs. George, Cohn, and Stanley, in that order. Considerable assistance was provided by Camilla P. Benbow, Catherine M. G. Cohn, Lynn M. Daggett, Ann R. Eisenberg, Karen J. Feinstein, and Lauren B. Mardell. Typing was done expertly by Lois S. Sandhofer and Laura M. Thommen.

This is the ninth volume based on the annual Hyman Blumberg Symposia on Research in Early Childhood Education. The symposia are supported by income from a $110,000 endowment given to The Johns Hopkins University in 1969 by the Amalgamated Clothing Workers of America. The late Mr. Blumberg was the executive vice president of ACWA. Financial support for this particular project of the Study of Mathematically Precocious Youth (SMPY) at The Johns Hopkins University also came from the Spencer Foundation of Chicago.

I
Acceleration and Enrichment: A Controversy in Perspective

1

ACCELERATION AND ENRICHMENT: DRAWING THE BASE LINES FOR FURTHER STUDY

Sanford J. Cohn

THE CONTROVERSY IN PERSPECTIVE

For nearly forty years prior to 1970, the acceleration versus enrichment argument lay dormant as far as the public was concerned. The Great Depression had eliminated the prerogative for public-interested disagreement for all but a few educational and psychological investigators. Before that time, however, there had been proponents of educational acceleration and others who favored enrichment. Each group considered its own a singularly appropriate underlying strategy for educating intellectually gifted youngsters. But with few jobs waiting for graduates after 1929, there seemed to be no reason or purpose even for brilliant students to finish their formal schooling. In the ensuing absence of public debate, the unrivaled assumptions implied, and even voiced, by advocates for enrichment became entrenched firmly in the nation's public consciousness. Some of these assumptions were clear expressions of the mythology that had developed in regard to great intellectual talent and precocity. "Early ripe, early rot" was but one epigram that encouraged educators of the mid-1900s to suppress actively the rapid intellectual development experienced by some youths. Parents of such children were counseled to avoid even considering accelerative educational plans for their children. The price one "surely" would have to pay for moving more rapidly through the educational lock step than did one's age mates was his or her "social and emotional adjustment." Counselors predicted lives characterized by loneliness and despair for these children if they chose to skip a grade in school or even to move ahead more quickly in certain subjects. Montour (1977b) has explored this theme expertly.

We cannot doubt that these counselors were acting in good faith by voicing their professional concerns, inasmuch as similar feelings were voiced by many other professionals throughout the hierarchy of educational practitioners. After all, America of the early 1900s was considered a "melting pot" culture. Social pressure to conform added to the depression's economic realities. Sameness and assimilation were thought to lead to social acceptance and therefore to be basic among the attitudes needed by the many then-recent immigrants to the United States. Counseling intellectually gifted children toward programs that would "enrich" or broaden their cultural assimilation (via academic experiences) was consistent with these outlooks. Enrichment seemed to offer less conspicuous methods for teachers and administrators to deal with the special educational needs of these children. Accusations of "elitism" thereby could be avoided.

The year 1971 saw a resurgence of public debate about the relative merits of enrichment over acceleration. In that year Julian C. Stanley, a noted educational measurement specialist, formed his actively interventional Study of Mathematically Precocious Youth (SMPY) at The Johns Hopkins University with substantial support from the Spencer Foundation of Chicago. Stanley chose to continue the empirical study of strategies for educating gifted youths that had been begun implicitly by Lewis M. Terman in his *Genetic Studies of Genius* series and carried out more explicitly by Leta S. Hollingworth (1942) in her studies and counseling efforts based at Teachers College of Columbia University. The empirical evidence gathered by SMPY since its inception has formed the basis of outspoken advocacy by Stanley and his associates for educationally accelerative techniques to help those mathematically brilliant youngsters who are eager to proceed quickly and to excel in high-level mathematics curricula.

Not only has SMPY worked with thousands of youths who reason extremely well mathematically, but also it has served as a training ground for a number of educational and developmental psychologists under the mentorship of its founder. New programs for studying specific issues concerning educationally accelerative techniques have been created by these and other SMPY-trained personnel. (Once such methods are developed, they are validated first; only then are they applied to the education of mathematically gifted youths.) Lynn H. Fox's Intellectually Gifted Child Study Group, for example, directs its energies primarily toward the study of sex differences among mathematically talented youths and of ways to minimize their effects among gifted girls.

In less than a decade a small but vociferous group of professionals has become the national advocate for educational acceleration. Practitioners and other investigators who either actively or quietly support the use of accelerative techniques have rallied to join forces with this group. Still, champions of acceleration represent a tiny minority among educational specialists interested in gifted students. Because many of these advocates come from the tradition of empirical study in education and psychology, they have made an effort to substantiate their claims with fairly rigorously determined evidence. Professionals at SMPY and at projects stimulated by it have published numerous books and articles. They and their former prodigies have received considerable attention in the press and electronic communications media, even to the extent that several states, counties, regional units, and localities, to say nothing of one South American country, have begun programs using the SMPY strategies as their model. Such projects, which replicate the continuing string of SMPY pilot studies, eventually will serve to help the public assess the value of accelerative techniques for mathematically brilliant youths, and perhaps for children with other talents as well.

The major point of this brief perspective is that a controversy presently exists—perhaps even rages! Even a naïve spectator attending one of the national association conferences for the gifted would notice the incipient, but growing, dialogue.

The purpose of this book, the fifth volume in the SMPY *Studies of Intellectual Precocity* series, is to set forth clearly the positions of the partisans in the acceleration-enrichment debate. In order to accomplish this end, the editors have chosen, first, to place the argument in historical perspective by tracing it through the educational and psychological literature; second, to provide the reader with several glimpses or highlights of relevant literature espousing each viewpoint; and third, to recapitulate the present status of the dialogue as expressed in an eighteen-member symposium. Since SMPY is intended as a series of longitudinal investigations into the effects of accelerative intervention in the education of mathematically brilliant youths, we hope that this volume will serve to mark the base lines against which the results of these long-term efforts eventually will be judged.

THE STRUCTURE OF THIS VOLUME

In his review of 182 books and articles (chapter 2), Stephen P. Daurio identifies four sources of problems that enter into the acceleration-enrichment controversy: (1) the tradition of the age-grade lock step in the American educational system; (2) resistance among the populace to the use of standardized tests that are appropriate for identifying talented youths; (3) practitioners' selective recall of social adjustment problems among those children who have accelerated through the formal schooling process; and (4) confusion over the definitions of the terms enrichment and acceleration. Daurio treats each of the first three issues in turn. First, he reviews the history of chronological age grading in America. Second, he discusses the use of tests in identifying intellectually talented youths. And third, he offers an analysis of educators' "selective" versus "representative" biases against acceleration. The major portion of his paper, however, traces the development of and conclusions drawn from observations of programs and reports on studies that favor either enrichment or acceleration as an appropriate strategy for educating intellectually gifted students. It is in this section that Daurio addresses the definitional problems regarding the terms *enrichment* and *acceleration*.

Daurio delineates two kinds of enrichment. The first type, called "lateral, nonaccelerative enrichment," is traced chronologically via programs developed in school systems throughout the country. Little empirical evidence exists that substantiates the appropriateness of such programs. Then Daurio differentiates a second type of enrichment, "relevant academic enrichment," into three sub-classifications: special schools, special programs within schools, and fast-paced classes.

Daurio's treatment of relevant enrichment techniques in chapter 2 makes special note of two inherent problems. First, "relevant" enrichment generally exposes students to curricula they typically would encounter later in their educational careers; hence it often results only in postponing boredom. Second, enrichment programs proved beneficial not only for intellectually gifted students but also for students of more average ability. Consequently, such strategies could not be described as "qualitatively differentiated" for gifted students, an important evaluative criterion suggested in guidelines provided by national legislation (Federal Register 1976).

Chapter 3 of this volume is a reprint of the 1951 article by Meister and Odell entitled "What Provisions for the Education of Gifted Students?" It appeared originally in the *National Association of Secondary School Principals* (NASSP) *Bulletin*. Meister and Odell provide a glimpse of educators' arguments that offer social and emotional maladjustment as justification for counseling students to avoid breaking the educational lock step.

A more up-to-date definition of enrichment is provided in chapter 4, which is excerpted from Joseph S. Renzulli's *The Enrichment Triad Model: A Guide for Developing Defensible Programs for the Gifted and Talented,* published in 1977. In this brief article *enrichment* is defined, assumptions underlying its utility are outlined, and several specific enrichment activities are introduced.

In chapter 5, "Career Education for Gifted Preadolescents," Lynn H. Fox offers an example of relevant academic enrichment that avoids both of the problems mentioned above. In the programs that Fox describes the student is provided with information relevant to planning his or her educational future. Such information generally is not offered elsewhere in the typical schooling process. As a result boredom in the class or at some later point in time is an unlikely consequence. Moreover, the types of careers discussed are geared to the completion of a considerable amount of formal education. Most of her procedures involve accelerative strategies to complete such schooling rapidly and well. Since only persons of exceptionally high ability are advised to consider these strategies, such programs do offer "qualitatively differentiated" training for gifted young-sters.

The problems that enrichment strategies seek to avoid (especially social and/or emotional maladjustment due to displacement from one's age peers) must be considered in the light of the problems such methods create (e.g., the stigma of segregated age grouping by ability without subsequent programs that are appropriately challenging).

Empirical evaluation of these techniques has advanced little since Dean Worcester addressed them in his 1956 monograph, *The Education of Children of Above-Average Mentality.* (The section of that monograph entitled "Enrichment'' has been reprinted as chapter 6 in this volume.) Worcester examined the practical issues relevant to enrichment programs: the time during which they should be given; their advantages and disadvantages; and variables such as class size for segregated groups and the social adjustment of students in these highly differentiated situations. In his summary he compared acceleration and enrichment. He maintained that through 1956 ''no good studies'' had been conducted that compared the relative merits of the two strategies. It appeared that *any* method aimed at meeting the special needs of the gifted had value. However, Worcester concluded that ''We do know that the accelerated students have saved time.''

Since 1956 only one substantial study has been made (Goldberg, Passow, Camm, and Neill 1966) that compares the respective techniques. Although it is not reprinted in this volume, its method and conclusions are summarized below. In brief, enriched and accelerated programs were wedded with specific curricula for mathematics instruction (contemporary versus standard) for seventh-grade students chosen on the basis of high general intelligence (IQ over 120). Fifty-one classes (about 1,500 pupils) comprised the initial population sample. After the three-year duration of the study, however, only thirty-seven classes remained (868 pupils). Although a number of other problems involved with longitudinal field research were encountered in addition to loss of subjects, several conclusions were suggested. In simplified form they were as follows: (1) contemporary mathematics appeared to produce better results than did standard mathematics; (2) accelerated programs were better than enriched ones; and (3) contemporary-accelerated programs produced the best results of all.

In his literature survey Daurio found a considerable number of studies that offered empirical evidence supporting claims for the relative benefits of educational acceleration. Inasmuch as concern for the gifted student's social and emotional development forms the justification for caution against accelerative options, Daurio traces the evolution of this argument carefully. The practice of past educators, and even present ones, has been to exercise extraordinary restraint in applying accelerative techniques. Such caution was offered in spite of considerable evidence reported by Terman and his associates that there was a positive relationship between mental development and social and emotional adjustment.

In volume 4 of the *Genetic Studies of Genius* Lewis M. Terman and Melita H. Oden address directly ''The Problem of School Acceleration.'' Their essay is reprinted as chapter 7 of this volume. The evidence provided is encouraging and the conclusions drawn support the use of accelerative techniques. The authors argue that conservative applications of accelerative strategies such as skipping a single grade often were insufficient to meet the actual needs of brilliant youngsters. In their opinion several grade skips might be more appropriate if spaced properly throughout a youth's educational years (e.g., fifth to seventh grade, eighth to tenth grade, or eleventh grade to college, in a kindergarten through six, seven through nine, and ten through twelve grade setting, respectively).

Daurio breaks down evidence regarding accelerative techniques into three broad categories: studies of early entrance to college, rapid completion of the bachelor's degree, and acceleration prior to college entrance. Within the first class, he cites the importance of biographical case histories. An early associate of Terman, Catharine M. Cox, based the second volume of the *Genetic Studies of Genius* series (1926) on a review of biographical data concerning the early lives of 300 "geniuses." About the same time Leta S. Hollingworth employed case history techniques in gathering evidence to support her development of special schools for the gifted and counseling strategies for intellectually prodigious youngsters. More recently, Kathleen Montour, a former SMPY project associate who received her baccalaureate from The Johns Hopkins University in 1976, traced the lives of a rather large number of prodigies, many of them still living. She emphasizes the necessity for excellent detective work and discusses some secrets of her research techniques (Montour 1978a). In an impressively detailed article about the tragic case of William James Sidis (Montour 1975a, 1977b), she traces the well-publicized decline of this once famous mathematical prodigy and compares his sad circumstances with those of the magnificently successful Norbert Wiener. She also has scrutinized the later lives of a number of prodigies identified in the past. Leta S. Hollingworth served as the source of some case studies (Montour 1976d, 1977c), as did the famous 1940s radio show "Quiz Kids" (Montour 1975b). Montour used a more nearly pure retrospective method (similar to Cox's technique) in tracking down the early experiences of a number of more modern intellectual *Wunderkinder,* including Merrill Kenneth Wolf, who earned his bachelor's degree at age 14 (Montour 1976a), and Charles Louis Fefferman, who at age 22 became the youngest American full professor (Montour 1976b). She also performed retrospective analyses of such outstanding present-day scientific personalities as Wernher von Braun, Harold Brown, and Robert Burns Woodward (Montour 1977d). Several historically eminent prodigies who lived in prerevolutionary America (Paul Dudley, Cotton Mather, and John Trumbull) underwent her detective-like scrutiny as well (Montour 1976c). Computational skill was contrasted with mathematical reasoning ability in her comparative study of the early lives of Zerah Colburn and Carl Friedrich Gauss (Montour 1976g). A problematic literary genius, Thomas Chatteron, was studied against the backdrop of a socially manipulated mathematical prodigy, Evariste Galois (Montour 1978b). Montour has carried her passionate interest in ferreting out early facts about prodigious children into areas other than the intellectual, among them talent in the drama (1976e), in the opera (1978c), in the world of finance (1976f), and even in gymnastics (1978d).

  With the exceptions of Sidis and Colburn, whose childhoods were exploited ruthlessly by their parents, the early and rapid educational development experienced by these prodigies demonstrated no consistent relationship to social maladjustment or emotional problems. Family dynamics were found to be at the root of the serious problems and maladjustments that have occurred in a few prodigies, even in the extremely morbid case of the brilliant youthful murderers, Leopold and

Loeb (Montour 1977a). For those whose lives were problematic, possessing extraordinary intellectual abilities served to help them survive.

These glimpses into the past have been corroborated in a preliminary fashion by recent prospective evidence gathered among SMPY's hundreds of early entrants to college, as well as from The Johns Hopkins University's own experience in this area (Eisenberg and George 1979). Most of these youngsters appear remarkably well adjusted and successful, both academically and socially. But anecdotal evidence cannot stand alone. Daurio also reviews a number of data-based studies of younger-than-average-aged college entrants. Among these studies, the 1949 monograph entitled *Educational Acceleration: Appraisals and Basic Problems* by Sidney L. Pressey has become a classic work on investigating the relationship between entrance age and pace through college and the effects such variables have on subsequent academic and personal success. Chapter 4 of that monograph, "Outcomes and Concomitants of Acceleration in College," has been reprinted as chapter 8 of this volume.

Other social experiments focusing on early entrants to twelve major U.S. colleges or universities were performed during the early 1950s. Sponsored by the Ford Foundation's Fund for the Advancement of Education, these studies were distinguished not only by their attention to the social and emotional adjustments of the participants, but also by the fact that they represented the first *prospective* studies of acceleration. Results from the follow-ups of the younger-than-average-aged college entrants overwhelmingly supported the use of early entrance as a viable technique for meeting the educational needs of intellectually brilliant youngsters. This support was based on the observation that the social and/or emotional maladjustment predicted for the early entrants occurred no more frequently than it did among college students of typical age. This observation and other conclusions have been recapitulated in detail in chapter 9, "A Summing Up." The essay is taken from *They Went to College Early,* the second evaluation report issued in April 1957 by the fund.

In his classification of studies on accelerative techniques, Daurio includes "acceleration prior to college" last. Several methods for bridging the transition from high school to college are discussed. Besides the retrospective assessment of acceleration conducted by Terman and Oden as part of their 40-year follow-up of high-IQ youths, several other investigations into the use of accelerative methods at the secondary level are reviewed. Included in this section is the extensive evidence gathered by SMPY in implementing its "smorgasbord" of educationally accelerative options for the intellectually talented, especially for youths of junior high school age.

Similar techniques for early entrance and rapid transit through elementary school form the substance of the final category of evidence regarding acceleration that Daurio offers. A particularly outstanding example of longitudinal research concerning accelerative methods employed among children of elementary school age is James R. Hobson's 1963 article from *Educational and Psychologi-*

cal Measurement entitled "High School Performance of Underage Pupils Initially Admitted to Kindergarten on the Basis of Physical and Psychological Examinations." The conclusions that Hobson draws from his data form a bulwark of support for the use of these strategies among young children. This article is reprinted as chapter 10 of this volume.

Daurio made no attempt to evaluate the relative balance of evidence supporting enrichment as opposed to accelerative strategies for educating gifted youngsters. The excerpts and articles, their number and content, speak for themselves. The present status of the enrichment/acceleration controvery is summarized well and the case for acceleration is articulated clearly in Julian C. Stanley's 1976 article from the *Phi Delta Kappan* entitled "Identifying and Nurturing the Intellectually Gifted." The article appears as chapter 11 of this volume.

THE CONTROVERSY TODAY

The controversy today stands approximately as follows: accelerative strategies have achieved maximal support from the results of experimental and quasi-experimental studies but only minimal acceptance among educational practitioners. That the debate continues is illustrated adequately in the final chapter of this volume, "Educational Acceleration of Intellectually Talented Youths: Prolonged Discussion by a Varied Group of Professionals." Position statements in the debate are offered here by eighteen professionals: program directors, practitioners, and educational psychologists. These discussions among symposium participants were designed to clarify or amplify specific points, as were the interactions with the audience attending the symposium held at the 1977 annual meeting of the American Educational Research Association in New York City.

Although she was unable to attend the symposium, Dr. Dorothy A. Sisk, then director of the National Office of Gifted and Talented, U.S. Office of Education, was asked to add her comments. Her statement closes the discussion and the volume. In it she warns of the dangers of enrichment alone, as well as the dangers of inadequately planned and unbridled acceleration. She suggests instead sensible plans that stress meeting the needs of individual students, both in terms of timing their identification and pacing their facilitation in terms of instructional style and curricular content for enrichment. She concludes that a rapprochement between acceleration and enrichment may be the solution.

It is interesting that the single experimental study (Goldberg, Passow, Camm, and Neill 1966) comparing enrichment with accelerative options for mathematics instruction provided results that indicated a combination of strategies as the most effective technique. In a sense, this three-year study sets the stage for a number of multigenerational longitudinal studies, only some of which have begun. Following the example set by exponents of controversial issues in psychology and education, perhaps we need to look at the more complex interactions. How might the type of strategy be varied to achieve the most appropriate program for a gifted youngster according to his or her ability, age, or sex? The base lines have been drawn for several studies that address but a few of these specific questions, namely talent in mathematical and verbal reasoning. The ground is broken, but the field barely has been touched.

REFERENCES

Cox, C. M. 1926. The early mental traits of three hundred geniuses. *Genetic studies of genius,* vol. II. Stanford, Calif.: Stanford University Press.

Eisenberg, A. R., and George, W. C. 1979. Early entrance to college: The Johns Hopkins experience. *College and University* 54(2): 109–18.

Federal Register. 6 May 1976. HEW/OE final regulations governing programs and projects for special educational needs; effective 6-21-76. 41(89): 18643–780.

Goldberg, M. L., Passow, A. H., Camm, D. S., and Neill, R. D. 1966. A comparison of mathematics programs for able junior high school students (Volume 1—Final report). Washington, D.C.: U.S. Office of Education, Bureau of Research (Project No. 3-0381).

Hollingworth, L. S. 1942. *Children above 180 IQ Stanford-Binet: Origin and development.* Yonkers-on-Hudson, N.Y.: World Book.

Montour, K. M. 1975a. Success vs. tragedy. *Intellectually Talented Youth Bulletin* 1 (9, 15 May): 3.

———. 1975b. Two men who were mathematically talented boys. *Intellectually Talented Youth Bulletin* 2(3, 15 Nov.): 2.

———. 1976a. Merrill Kenneth Wolf: A bachelor's degree at 14. *Intellectually Talented Youth Bulletin* 2(7, 15 Mar.): 1.

———. 1976b. Charles Louis Fefferman: Youngest American full professor. *Intellectually Talented Youth Bulletin* 2(8, 15 Apr.): 2.

———. 1976c. American pre-revolutionary prodigies. *Intellectually Talented Youth Bulletin* 2(9, 15 May): 1.

———. 1976d. Three precocious boys: Where are they now? *Gifted Child Quarterly* 20(2, Summer): 173–79.

———. 1976e. Precocity and the juvenile actor. *Intellectually Talented Youth Bulletin* 3(1, 15 Sept.): 3.

———. 1976f. An example of precocity in finance. *Intellectually Talented Youth Bulletin* 3(2, 15 Oct.): 4.

———. 1976g. Skill vs. genius. *Intellectually Talented Youth Bulletin* 3(4, 15 Dec.): 3–4.

———. 1977a. The infamous wonders: Leopold and Loeb. *Intellectually Talented Youth Bulletin* 3(8, 15 Apr.): 2–3.

———. 1977b. William James Sidis, the broken twig. *American Psychologist* 32(4, Apr.): 265–79.

———. 1977c. Accelerated growing pains and later success. Unpublished manuscript, Study of Mathematically Precocious Youth, The Johns Hopkins University, Baltimore, Md. 21218.

———. 1977d. An engineer, a physicist, and a chemist. Unpublished manuscript, Study of Mathematically Precocious Youth, The Johns Hopkins University, Baltimore, Md. 21218.

————. 1978a. Calling all teachers: Have you seen a genius? *G/C/T* 1(1, Jan.–Feb.): 52–53.

————. 1978b. The marvelous boys: Thomas Chatterton, Evariste Galois and their modern counterparts. *Gifted Child Quarterly* 22(1, Spring): 68–78.

————. 1978c. The unsinkable Beverly Sills. *G/C/T* 1(2, Mar.–Apr.): 24–25.

————. 1978d. Nadia Comaneci, a champion. *G/C/T* 1(3, May–June): 42–44.

2

EDUCATIONAL ENRICHMENT VERSUS ACCELERATION: A REVIEW OF THE LITERATURE

Stephen P. Daurio

INTRODUCTION

The impetus for this report stems from current controversy over whether "enrichment" or "acceleration" is better suited to meet the special educational needs of intellectually able students. Of course, there are those who question the validity of *any* type of intervention designed especially for a subsample of the educable population. Vociferous claims of "antidemocratic" or "antiegalitarian" are raised by parents and educators who believe equality of educational opportunity implies equal experiences during equal lengths of school time for all children and adolescents. On this point, however, the U.S. Office of Education recently reported to the Congress that "We are increasingly being stripped of the comfortable notion that a bright mind will make its own way. Intellectual and creative talent cannot survive educational neglect and apathy" (1972, p. 1). Thus, in the present review it is assumed that educational intervention on behalf of the intellectually able indeed is appropriate. Consequently, evidence related to the specific type of intervention, namely enrichment or acceleration, is reviewed.

Problems in the controversy over enrichment versus acceleration stem from at least four sources. First, age segregation in American education has been a "tradition" for only little more than one hundred years (cf. Kett 1974). Second, there remains opposition to the use of tests to identify promising talent at young ages. This opposition exists despite a sixty-year tradition, beginning with the work of Lewis Terman (1916), which has shown the high reliability and validity underlying psychometric tests of intelligence. Third, educators' perceptions of the ensuing effects of acceleration often are biased through "selective" rather than "representative" recall of adjustment problems following such intervention (see Laycock 1964). Fourth, confusion over definitions of enrichment and acceleration often blinds educators to the communality of both interventions, that is, the desire to improve the quality of education for bright children and adolescents.

This introduction describes briefly the first three aforementioned problems for two reasons. First, it is believed that certain misconceptions concerning education of intellectually able youths are pervasive enough to warrant focusing upon these areas. Second, evaluation of the efficacy of different types of educational interventions for the gifted depends upon the delineation of certain assumptions and the elimination of common pitfalls. Following these remarks, this report focuses at length on a variety of enrichment and acceleration strategies implemented primarily during the past half century. Within these two major sections, the definitional problems are discussed.

History of Chronological Age Grading in America

In a recent report to the President's Science Advisory Committee, Joseph Kett (1974) expertly outlined the evolution of chronological age-grade grouping in America. Prior to 1860, heterogeneity in the schools was the rule. This was a simple extension of the age mixture characteristic of children's social and work experience. Concerning education around 1830 Kett wrote, "Few educators found the association of boys of 12 with young men of 20 in academics or college anomalous, perhaps because age heterogeneity in the schools reflected the more fundamental age heterogeneity of the family and the peer group" (ibid., p. 11).

According to Kett, age segregation was a by-product of the educational reform movement led by Horace Mann and Henry Barnard. Similarly, age segregation was contemporary with industrialization and preceded the rising tide of immigration by only a few years. Thus, the structured school experience that resulted from "enlightened ideas about childhood" (ibid., p. 18) after 1820 also served the economic and political needs of a society transformed by industrialization. Age-grade grouping was well suited to the Americanization of immigrants. Moreover, the elementary schools and later the high schools provided the practical training that was necessitated by the increased specialization of industry.

Chronological age-grade grouping initially affected elementary school children aged 7 to 14 years. Yet as early as 1890 there was a substantial rise in the high school population. Kett offered two possible reasons for this. First, greater family affluence permitted extended schooling for children who no longer had to work. Second, educational certification provided an opportunity for poor children to be upwardly mobile. It was the Depression of the 1930s, however, that solidified age-grade grouping in the high schools as an American institution. This was because " . . . the high school was defended in the 1930s more explicitly than ever before as a 'cure' for unemployment" (ibid., p. 27).

Thus, age-grade grouping is a relatively recent phenomenon of the past 100 years or less, depending on the geographical region being considered. Although based upon well-intentioned concern for educational reform, the practice initially was well suited to the political and economic needs of the nation; however, age-grade grouping survives to this day essentially unchanged. Therefore, it is important to underscore both the relative brevity of this "tradition" and the multifaceted considerations underlying age homogeneity in order to provide needed perspective for this literature survey. In addition, an objective evaluation of enrichment and acceleration as educational methods depends upon the elimination at the outset of unwarranted assumptions concerning chronological age-grade grouping.

Use of Tests in Identifying Intellectual Talent

A second problematic area involves selection strategies for the identification of precocious intellectual ability. These strategies are necessary precursors for assignment to either enrichment or acceleration programs. According to the 1972 Office of Education report, "Types of screening procedures commonly employed in identifying the gifted included teacher nomination and group tests. Both means have about the same level of accuracy, and both fail to identify large numbers of gifted children" (U.S. Office of Education, p. 18). Nearly three-quarters of a century of evidence, however, supports the notion that intelligence test scores actually are valid indices of scholastic aptitude and that they usually are superior to teachers' judgments.

Two classic longitudinal investigations initiated during the 1920s attest to the reliability and predictive validity of intelligence test data. First, Terman's retrospective account of more than 1,000 gifted California children unequivocally underscored the value of test scores in the identification of unusually high intellectual ability at young ages (see Oden 1968; Terman 1925, 1931, 1954; and Terman and Oden 1947, 1959). Second, Hollingworth's independent investigations, conducted at about the same time but in the New York City public schools, corroborated Terman's findings (see, e.g. Hollingworth 1942, Lorge and Hollingworth 1936). In addition, related research conducted during the Second World War reported results consistent with Terman and Hollingworth (Hildreth 1943, Witty 1940). Recent investigations have provided further evidence that tests of intellectual ability and intellectual aptitude indeed are valid predictors of precocious intellectual ability (see Chauncey 1958; Chauncey and Hilton 1965; MacDonald, Gammie, and Nisbet 1964; Mauger and Kolmodin 1975).

Perhaps the most convincing evidence in support of the validity of *group* measures of intellectual ability follows a series of recent investigations being conducted by the Study of Mathematically Precocious Youth (SMPY) at The Johns Hopkins University (Keating 1976; Stanley, Keating, and Fox 1974). SMPY researchers emphasize the importance of using appropriately difficult tests for the most intellectually able students. This use mitigates common "ceiling effect" problems associated with the use of conventional tests designed for less gifted agemates (Keating 1976, Keating and Stanley 1972). Adherence to this testing strategy has led to the outstandingly successful identification of large numbers of precocious mathematical reasoners who, as junior high school students, perform as well as or better than high school seniors on the College Board Scholastic Aptitude Test. Even more surprising have been results from two SMPY studies in which group tests were found to be far *better* predictors than teachers in the identification of mathematical talent (Stanley 1976c, 1976d).

Educators' "Selective" versus "Representative" Biases

Excessive concern that potential social and emotional maladjustment will follow the acceleration of intellectually able youths represents the third problem area. Contemporary sentiment reflects a conservative educational perspective analogous to that which presupposes that teachers are as good as tests in identifying intellectual talent, despite evidence to the contrary. Moreover, educators' perceptions of chronological age-grade grouping as traditional and purposive do little to countermand widespread zealous caution regarding acceleration.

In an important monograph Pressey (1949) posed an interesting historico-political analysis of the antiacceleration sentiment that was prevalent following World War II. According to Pressey, the 1920s and the 1940s were similar in that during both decades acceleration was rather widely implemented, although certainly for different reasons:

> Twice in recent educational history, efforts to vary the rates of progress through educational programs according to ability have been aborted by an inadequacy of method plus a handicapping circumstance. In the twenties, there was much interest in the ways of adjusting progress to ability, and in the gifted child. However, social maladjustment was not adequately guarded against and became unduly feared, and the depression made the hope of early graduation into employment seem futile. The second world war brought sweeping practical experiments in acceleration. However, the burdensomeness of the lengthened school year as a method, plus the apparent unwisdom of accelerating young persons straight from high school into collegiate or vocational competition with the great number of older veterans, brought a reaction against rapid progress. Instead, the tendency has been to lengthen professional programs and to emphasize the value of maturity because of the admirable record of the veterans in college. Educators, believing as they do in the great worth of their work, have an understandable hesitancy about plans which deliberately seek to reduce the total time the ablest students have to profit from their schooling. Furthermore, the unfortunate custom of expressing amounts of education in terms of time taken leads to the implication that shortening time inevitably reduces value. (ibid., pp. 140–41)

Pressey's remarks reflect an "interactive trichotomy" of sorts. Note that he reported that the acceleration interventions of the 1920s and the 1940s were curtailed through an "inadequacy of method plus a handicapping circumstance." However, it is impossible to separate the "method" and "circumstance" problems from what Pressey called the "unfortunate custom of expressing amounts of education in terms of time taken." Put differently, the educational "lock step," an intrinsic component of chronological age segmentation, provided only tenuous support for the acceleration efforts of the twenties and forties. Consequently, these efforts faltered, probably due more to the "handicapping circumstance" than to the "inadequacy of methods."

There are at least two other reasons for contemporary antiacceleration sentiment among educators. First, it seems that a disproportionate amount of caution against acceleration stems from the unfortunate case of William James Sidis (see Montour 1977). Yet, according to Stanley, "For every William Sidis who renounces intellectual pursuits because of extreme—and apparently quite unwise—parental pressure, there are many persons . . . who benefit greatly from the time saved, frustration avoided, and stimulation gained" (1976e, p. 237).

The second point regards what some researchers have called educators' stereotypes of gifted youths (e.g., Solano 1976) and, by extension, of gifted accelerants. According to Laycock, this stereotyping represents a problem in perception, what he terms educators' "selective" use of evidence despite psychologists' "representative" research concerning the effects of acceleration. "Administrators have reported the cases they remember best, while psychologists have insisted upon good samples. . . . It is particularly disquieting to realize that more administrators these days have at least had token exposure to survey methods, experimental-logic, and statistical reasoning" (Laycock 1964, p. 1006). In other words, administrators' reluctance to endorse acceleration, despite evidence supporting the intervention procedures simply may reflect these individuals' *choice* to overlook such evidence.

In this report, research is reviewed concerning enrichment and acceleration as educational interventions appropriate for the needs of intellectually able youths. Laycock's point, however, is intended to denote a common pitfall; namely, some educators tend to disregard empiricism when the issue of acceleration arises. Moreover, the question of socioemotional adjustment following acceleration is perhaps the most typical point of disagreement among proponents of acceleration or enrichment. Therefore, throughout the report close attention is directed to data bearing on this issue.

ENRICHMENT

Lateral, Nonaccelerative Enrichment

This section reviews so-called lateral enrichment (cf. Havighurst, Stivers, and De Haan 1955). Stanley (1976e) uses two terms to describe this type of intervention: *irrelevant academic enrichment,* and *cultural enrichment.* According to Stanley, "Irrelevant academic enrichment . . . consists of setting up a special subject or activity meant to enrich the educational lives of some group of intellectually talented students. It pays no attention to the specific nature of their talents" (ibid., p. 234). Notice that this designation disregards the question of segregation based on ability. That is, it makes no difference whether the special activity occurs within the regular classroom (heterogeneously grouped), or within an ability-segregated classroom (homogeneously grouped). The *nature* of the intervention actually is appropriate for most students—if not presently, then perhaps in a year or so.

Three criteria characterize lateral, nonaccelerative enrichment as discussed in this report. First, the intervention is *claimed* to be appropriate for individuals with superior intellectual ability. Second, there is great likelihood that such an enrichment intervention also is appropriate for less intellectually precocious individuals. Third, lateral, nonaccelerative enrichment maintains the individual's age-in-grade status; that is, no attempt is made to accelerate the educational pace of the students.

The Havighurst, Stivers, and De Haan (1955) definition of lateral enrichment corresponds to our definition: *lateral enrichment* is "encouraging older children to broaden their experience by working in areas not explored by the average student" (p. 21). According to Havighurst, lateral enrichment includes training in the following areas: art, music, drama, creative writing, and foreign language, provided such language is studied at an unusually young age, for example, during one's elementary school years.

The lateral, nonaccelerative enrichment literature reported in this section is divided chronologically into four subsections: pre-1950, 1950 to 1959, 1960 to 1969, and 1970 to the present. Additional reference lists, including citations to review articles, follow each subsection; in all, seventy references are cited.

Pre-1950.   One of the earliest interventions (Danielson 1929) described an attempt to group homogeneously students at or above Stanford-Binet IQ 125 for a reading course in general literature. Separate special classes for bright students in California in the 1930s have been reported (Addicott 1930, Goddard 1933, and Gould 1939). Dransfield (1933) cited the administration of an in-class enrichment program for students of above-average ability. In addition, Osburn and Rohan (1931) noted that activities clubs were organized for the gifted in Wisconsin; such clubs were intended for individuals interested in radio, newspapers, forestry, mechanics, and arts and crafts.

During the 1940s considerable attention was paid to the formation of special enrichment classes for the mentally gifted (see, e.g., Brown 1949, Handy and Lindstrom 1944, Mosso 1945, Nelson and Carlson 1945, Shearer and Fannin 1949). For communities too small in population to offer special classes, Thorndike (1941) suggested the provision of a room where gifted children might work independently in order to avoid the repetition of classroom instruction. Mosso (1944) suggested starting a "library corner" for students of over 120 IQ in which they could engage in independent study or hold seminars. Seegers (1949) emphasized investigation, reading, and creative work within the heterogeneously grouped class for the child with an IQ above 135. Similarly, a national survey following World War II found strong support for within-class enrichment (Wilson 1949). Additional references on this topic are Cook (1948), Jensen (1927), Miles (1946), Newland (1941), Witty (1940), and Woods (1944).

1950 to 1959.   During the early 1950s a number of reports called for special enrichment programs to meet gifted students' needs (Anderson 1954, Hayes 1954, Shufele 1953). Bowman surveyed twenty-four California school systems concerning provisions for gifted students. Enrichment in the regular classroom was cited most often, followed by elementary school "grade-skipping" in eleven of twenty-four California cities. Nevertheless, "double promotion," as this type of acceleration sometimes was called, was much less common in the secondary schools. Bowman suggested that this circumstance was due to decreased need because of "wider course offerings" in high school (1955, p. 199).

Three years prior to the Soviet launching of Sputnik, Oliver (1954) suggested the following five enrichment devices that fit the criteria for inclusion in the category "lateral, nonaccelerative enrichment":

1. Have gifted children do more toward planning, carrying out, and evaluating of their own work.
2. Expand the range of interests and experiences, especially through the activity program calling for full development of creative abilities.
3. Set high standards of accomplishment. . . . The gifted should become ready to prove their points.
4. Enlarge firsthand experiences through trips, excursions, construction activities, and supplementary reading. While it may be pointed out that such experiences are valuable for all pupils, again it is a matter of degree, of realizing that superior pupils "take away" much more from such experiences.
5. Develop civic responsibility through extra school projects. (Oliver 1954, p. 321)

Indeed, these activities inherently are worthwhile "for all pupils," yet they certainly are irrelevant for furthering skill in a particular area for which a youngster is exceptionally talented. Moreover, these suggestions seem better suited as principles of general education, rather than special education.

Blaudauf (1959) reported an evaluation of an in-class enrichment program in three Cedar Rapids, Iowa, schools for students of IQ 125 or higher. Slight overall differences between control and experimental groups prompted him to suggest, "The enriched curriculum may not have supplied a sufficient challenge to mentally advanced pupils, constituting a kind of interesting or uninteresting busy work" (p. 183). However, Blaudauf noted that teachers in the experiment had not been blind to subjects' group membership and "may have unconsciously and informally enriched their program" (ibid., p. 183); therefore, results from this study are inconclusive.

Additional references include the following: Fliegler and Bish (1959), Gilfoy (1958), Lesse (1957), McWilliams and Birch (1957), Newland (1953), Powell (1954), West (1958), Williams (1958), and Witty (1956).

1960 to 1969.   California's educational intervention for the gifted in the 1950s included enrichment in the regular classes, acceleration, and special grouping at the elementary and secondary levels (Martinson 1960). These programs received positive evaluations; according to Martinson, "[Those students] who started the program year with high achievements, good attitudes and motivation, and high status with their classmates, made striking gains academically with no penalty to themselves in personal-social areas" (1960, p. 343).

Gallagher et al. (1960) attempted to adapt educational programming to meet the individual needs of elementary school children. They reported positive subjective attitude changes, although objective tests failed to demonstrate program efficacy. Nine years later, Plowman (1969) reported the trend concerning individualized instruction in the education of gifted children to be as follows: "In general, enrichment programs in regular classes should provide greater breadth and depth of learning, more opportunities for developing creative behaviors, increased emphasis on rich social experiences, and ample freedom to pursue independent study" (ibid., p. 548). It would seem, however, that the individualized approach reserved for education of the gifted, like Oliver's five enrichment strategies cited above, ought to be incorporated within the aims of general education.

Gross and Sabatino (1965) indicated positive gains in general reading ability for gifted first and second graders enrolled in an experimental class. According to Birch and Reynolds (1963), however, this has been the exception, since "Very little work [was] described in the literature which could be classified as research, as field testing, or as demonstration with built-in evaluation devices" (p. 93). The dearth of curriculum research contrasts markedly with developments in modern mathematics and physics as reported four years earlier by Fliegler and Bish (1959).

Perhaps the single most important shift since Terman's work on educating the gifted followed major contributions in the area of creativity and intelligence (Torrance 1962, Getzels and Jackson 1962). Torrance and Myers (1962) succeeded in teaching gifted grade-school children research skills and concepts. They used the Torrance Tests of Creative Thinking, which have not been restricted solely to use with intellectually precocious children (nor should they be).

Shouksmith and Taylor (1964) and Ewing and Gilbert (1967) reported positive effects on academic performance resulting from high-ability intermediate-school pupils in Great Britain and high-ability college students in the United States. Despite the appropriate use of high-ability, noncounseled control groups in both studies, the question remains as to whether counseling alone might improve the academic performance of *less able* students as well. More research is needed to answer this question.

Additional references: Braunstein (1968), Enzmann (1963), Frierson (1969), Gallagher and Rogge (1966), Gowan (1961), Hanson (1968), Hausdorff and Far (1965), Rippin (1969), and Rowe (1967).

1970 to the Present.   Frierson (1969) reviewed the literature on the gifted and the talented and reported that "Since 1965, research related to the gifted has indeed shifted dramatically from a concern for the gifted child to a concern for the creative process" (p. 25). Continuing this trend was Torrance (1970), wh advocated inclusion of creativity within a broader definition of giftedness. Gowan (1971) recommended lowering conventional IQ cutoffs for inclusion within the gifted child category because it was maintained that creativity and intelligence correlated substantially below IQ 120. Other researchers reported a continuation of lateral, nonaccelerative creativity training for the gifted (e.g., Bachtold and Werner 1970; Bachtold 1974; Wilson, Greer, and Johnson 1973).

Ryder (1972) reported enriching the lives of gifted fifth graders through museum study. Similarly, Isaacs (1971) suggested the use of Greek mythology in the education of the gifted. Toomin and Toomin (1973) recommended biofeedback as a potential means of enhancing the gifted child's self-discovery, self-awareness, and self-determination. Martinson, Hermanson, and Banks (1972) described an independent study program for gifted students covering a wide range of course materials. Finally, Dunn's (1972) evaluation of one-day excursions for gifted sixth and eighth graders to a college campus was negative mainly because of the time that was wasted on the bus and because of the late hour associated with termination of the excursion.

Each of these interventions—museum trips, courses in mythology, biofeedback, independent study, and one-day excursions—undoubtedly are broadening experiences in and of themselves. They exemplify the kinds of lateral nonaccelerative enrichment advocated for intellectually precocious youths. However, no research has demonstrated the suitability of such enrichment solely for those individuals gifted in mental ability. A need exists for systematic evaluation of lateral, nonaccelerative enrichment of the type described in this section—an evaluation involving use of matched control groups of average and below-average ability.

Additional references on this topic include Feldman and Bratton (1972); Crockenberg (1972); Isaacs (1973); Lazar, Gensley, and Gowan (1972); Sato (1974); and Stanley, George, and Solano (1978).

Relevant Academic Enrichment

This section reviews the literature termed *relevant academic enrichment* (Stanley 1976e, p. 235). The term *relevant* is intended to connote the idea that this type of enrichment fits the special educational needs of students with specific superior intellectual abilities. In contrast with lateral enrichment, relevant academic enrichment is appropriate solely for intellectually precocious youths because it acknowledges the inadequacy of conventional education, given the above-average special talents of a small number of students. Relevant academic enrichment contrasts with outright acceleration because it maintains the age-in-grade lock step discussed earlier. Therefore, if one endorses the notion that individual differences in mental ability exist but agrees with the relatively recent tradition of age segmentation in schools, then one probably would advocate some type of relevant academic enrichment.

One problem arises upon completion of such an enrichment program. According to Stanley, "The more relevant and excellent the enrichment program, the more it calls for acceleration of subject-matter or grade placement later. Otherwise, it just puts off the boredom awhile and virtually guarantees that eventually it will be more severe" (1976e, p. 235).

It is not difficult to discover why educators are reluctant to follow up true enrichment with acceleration (see Keating 1976). In 1951 the principal of the Princeton (New Jersey) High School commented:

> By his very nature, the gifted child has an enriched life in his experiences, insights, and appreciations. But the child cannot grow to his potential with self-direction only. He needs planned enrichment. The enrichment of subject matter and other educational experiences seems to have the advantage of adopting the material and teaching to the individual without the accompanying possible danger of social maladjustment involved in "skipping." (Meister and Odell 1951, p. 43)

According to Odell (1933), educators' concern over acceleration's potentially detrimental social effects warranted maintenance of chronological age-grade grouping within enrichment programs. Yet such programs were designed initially for students of superior *mental* ability in order that such students could progress at rates appropriate to their ability. Undoubtedly, such contradictory educational practices engender academic boredom for gifted students, if not in the short term, then, ultimately at some point in time when education appropriate to their abilities terminates.

In the following sections, three types of relevant academic enrichment implemented during approximately the last forty years are presented.

Special Schools.   Hollingworth (1936) described a newly opened, unique elementary school designed for children with a tested Stanford-Binet IQ of at least 130. Speyer School was based on the principle that intellectually superior children could master regular curricula in half the time it takes average-ability students. However, in contrast to the special Terman classes reported elsewhere (Lamson 1930, Hollingworth 1929), Speyer School was designed for nonaccelerative enrichment during the time saved by acceleration in the regular course material. In other words, students at Speyer School worked through the ordinary curricular materials at a faster pace, then participated in courses which they otherwise would not have found in New York schools. The course enrichment areas included French, art, nutrition, music appreciation, elementary science, and the history of civilization (Hollingworth 1936, p. 87).

Over the years New York City was foremost in the establishment of special schools for intellectually precocious students. Since the 1940s Hunter College Elementary School had provided special education for students of superior ability (Braumbaugh 1944, Hildreth 1952). Meister and Odell (1951) noted that four New York secondary schools were designed specially for high-level ability: Brooklyn Technical High School, High School of Music and Art, Bronx High School of Science, and Stuyvesant High School. Since all of the above schools employed curricula appropriate to the superior ability of their students, presumably progress through such schools could be accelerated. Instead, these schools endorsed qualitative enrichment while preserving the chronological age-in-grade lock step.

Special Within-School Programs.   Two well-known examples of special within-school enrichment programs for intellectually superior students are the Cleveland Major Work Classes (e.g., Goddard 1928) and the Colfax Plan in Pittsburgh (Pregler 1954). One evaluation of the former project matched equally bright graduates of the Regular Work Classes with Major Work Classes alumni (Sumption 1941). Based on results from a questionnaire, Sumption reported significant differences in favor of the Major Work graduates in areas of leadership, reading activities, sense of social responsibility, and development of individual attitudes.

Barbe's (1954, 1955) evaluation of the Cleveland project reported a 77 percent return from a questionnaire sent to persons who had been graduated from the program between 1938 and 1952. Among those responding, slightly under one-half voiced approval of the program, while a little over one-third approved with hesitancy. In contrast to Sumption (1941), Barbe had not matched Major Work alumni with equally bright graduates of the regular course program. Therefore, there remained some question about the overall efficacy of the Cleveland Major Work Classes. Since the evaluation of a similar program, the Detroit Major Works Project (Fine 1953), likewise failed to include a control group, conclusions about such projects remain incomplete.

Parker (1956) reported a relevant academic enrichment program for bright (IQ above 125) elementary school children in Iowa. Both experimental *and* control groups were in the same classroom. Parker concluded the following:

(1) Normal achievement of mentally advanced pupils was not disturbed adversely by the provision of curricular enrichment, and in many cases significant favorable differences in achievement were shown.
(2) According to the measuring instruments used, the provision of curricular enrichment caused no detrimental effect on pupil adjustment and personality. . . .
(3) The data indicate that in the majority of cases curricular enrichment, when offered to mentally advanced pupils in the regular classrooms, proved to be beneficial to the average students in the classroom. (Parker 1956, p. 24)

Parker's first two conclusions supported notions of the efficacy of the Iowa program. However, the third point indicated that what may have been designed initially as enrichment appropriate only for intellectually able students might, in fact, have been interpreted too closely to mean general intellectual ability. If that was the case, then the Iowa intervention for gifted children was in reality another instance of lateral enrichment poorly suited to the specific needs and abilities of the intellectually able.

Fast-Paced Classes.   The third type of relevant academic enrichment, fast-paced classes, also could be described as subject matter enrichment that might or might not be accelerative. During the past thirty years a number of investigations have been conducted on the problem of subject matter enrichment (e.g., Briggs 1947), especially in mathematics (Albers and Seagoe 1947, Fox 1974, George 1976, George and Denham 1976, Stanley 1976b, Wilson 1959). Depending on the use made of time gained through such fast-paced classes, studies of this type were either "terminal (one-course) enrichment" projects or useful enrichment-acceleration combinations.

Wilson (1959) provided an example of nonaccelerative relevant enrichment in which algebra was taught three days per week to gifted junior high school students. During the remaining two days students engaged in activities previously discussed as lateral enrichment, for example, "preparation and presentation of individual research reports, visits to and note-taking at college lecture series [and] field trips to local industries" (p. 157).

In comparison, Briggs (1947) reported a World War II attempt at the Ohio State University in which educational psychology students participated in a fast-paced seminar course. Briggs stated that "When paired with others of equal ability in regular classes, the 'seminar' students scored somewhat higher on objective tests" (p. 214). Presumably the time saved by taking the fast-paced seminar permitted students to graduate early since they were able to take more course work and complete each course in a shorter period of time.

Those conducting SMPY, the Johns Hopkins Study of Mathematically Precocious Youth, have reported outstanding success with fast-paced mathematics instruction for extremely able students of mathematics (Fox 1974; George 1976; George and Denham 1976; and Stanley 1976b, 1977, 1978a, 1978b, 1979). For example, Stanley and colleagues have demonstrated that for very superior students, as few as 100 to 120 hours are sufficient to teach as much as four and one-half years of precalculus mathematics (Fox 1974). If intellectually precocious students avail themselves of the time saved through enrolling in fast-paced courses to study their area of expertise further, then such fast-paced courses stand in marked and obvious contrast to nonaccelerative enrichment (e.g., Wilson 1959). Moreover, a sustained effort, which is possible only through acceleration at some point in an academic career, is less likely to "wash out" over time (see Meeker 1968).

Some additional references are: Glennon (1957), Saslaw (1961), and Williams (1958).

ACCELERATION

Pressey's definition of acceleration presented in the introduction to his classic monograph on that subject is most succinct yet pragmatically objective. According to him, acceleration is "progress through an educational program at rates faster or ages younger than conventional" (Pressey 1949, p. 2). It is important to note, however, that entrance into an educational program—for example, college—at an unusually young age usually implies progression through an earlier phase of the educational "lock step" at a rate faster than conventional. That is, matriculation in college at a younger than conventional age usually means that the individual "skipped a grade" or participated in an accelerated program. For example, a student might complete junior high school in two years, rather than in the standard three years (e.g., Woolf 1957). On the other hand, accelerants who complete a program in less time than usual may *not* necessarily be *younger* than the more conventional graduates. At the time Pressey wrote his monograph there were many World War II veterans either enrolled or planning to enroll in college in order to resume educational programs that the war had interrupted. If, for instance, these veterans were involved in military service for at least two years and in an accelerated college program for three instead of the usual four years, this still would leave the veterans at least one year older than the usual age of persons receiving their baccalaureates.

A second point concerning Pressey's definition is that the specific type of acceleration that qualifies a student for the category "younger-aged accelerant" usually is not specified in the research literature. For example, a student who begins college at age 16 undoubtedly is younger than most college entrants; consequently, he or she is included in an experimental group of younger-aged college entrants. Yet there is usually no mention made concerning *how* this student qualified for college when he or she was one to two years younger than the norm. There are *at least* five possibilities: early admission to primary school at age 5 instead of 6; "grade skipping" in elementary school; "grade skipping" in secondary school; participation in a special accelerative or enrichment program that may have shortened the elementary program by one year; or entering college as a full-time student without completing the twelfth grade. (See Stanley 1979 for a more extensive list.)

Moreover, if one considers younger-aged college *graduates* instead of *entrants,* at least five additional alternatives arise: entrance with sophomore standing based on advanced placement credit; early completion of college with credits earned through examinations and/or heavier-than-average course loads; attendance throughout an extended four-quarter academic calendar; studying for two degrees concurrently (e.g., B.A. and M.A., done fairly often at The Johns Hopkins University); or skipping the baccalaureate and working directly for the doctorate.

Most research on early or younger-aged college entrants fails to distinguish among the *types* of acceleration that enabled students to achieve early entrance status. Such literature does, however, attend very closely to the academic and socioemotional adjustment presumed commensurate with early entrance (e.g., Fund for the Advancement of Education 1957, Keys 1938). Other researchers studying college-level acceleration disregard age at entrance and evaluate, instead, programs of acceleration that enable part of the initial cohort to graduate earlier than is usual (e.g., Flesher 1946). Research concerning elementary and secondary school-aged youths generally reports the effects of moving children at rates faster than conventional, for example, "grade skipping" or "double promotion," as it used to be termed (e.g., Klausmeier 1963). In contrast, at the youngest age of participation in the educational process, considerable research has been undertaken to evaluate the effects of early entrance to school (e.g., Worcester 1956, Hobson 1963).

Finally, research on educational acceleration for the most part reports *retrospective* methodology, usually case studies or group comparisons of accelerants versus nonaccelerants matched on any number of variables from one to many. Two notable *prospective* exceptions involved an experiment at the University of Chicago in the 1930s and 1940s (Bloom and Ward 1952), and an early-entrance program conducted by twelve colleges and universities during the 1950s (Fund for the Advancement of Education 1957). Both types of analyses of acceleration indeed warrant our attention. Moreover, the evidence compiled from successful case histories of acceleration is impressive; several instances will be reported.

In order to look at acceleration more carefully, the following topics are discussed: (1) caution concerning socioemotional adjustment; (2) studies of early entrance to college; (3) research on rapid completion of the bachelor's degree; (4) acceleration at the elementary and secondary school levels; and (5) research on early admission to elementary school.

Caution Concerning Socioemotional Adjustment

A review of the literature concerning recommendations that gifted youths be accelerated revealed countless references advising educators to exercise *extreme caution* with regard to accelerating intellectually able youths. Apprehension stemmed from a belief in the potential hazards of social and/or emotional maladjustment coincidental with acceleration. Most early objections were based on case studies of quite mentally apt children who were *not* necessarily accelerated *or* enriched within the schools (Edelston 1950; Regensberg 1926, 1931; Thom and Newell 1945; Wells 1949, 1950; and Zorbaugh 1937). However, results from these cases are inconclusive, for not a single investigation or article reported *base rates* for socioemotional maladjustment in the juvenile population at large. No attempt was made at matching gifted youngsters who had problems with average-ability control children, similarly plagued, to determine whether unusual intellectual precocity accounted for the socioemotional problems.

In contrast to the overwhelmingly cautious sentiment among psychologists and educators, Hollingworth (1931, 1932, 1936, 1939) was quite reasonable and optimistic in her regard for potential social setbacks among the gifted. Rather than cite instances of social maladjustment, she pointed out that early problems for young gifted children often disappear over time and on their own. On the other hand, Hollingworth advised that there would be problems for *educators* whose responsibility it was to forestall social alienation by the students' less gifted agemates as well as to minimize gifted students' disenchantment with schooling.

Educators continued their cautious refrain about social maladjustment unless acceleration was approved after very careful consideration of multiple factors (Cutts and Moseley 1953a, 1953b; Morgan 1957). At most, educators would recommend only one year of acceleration (Hall 1958). There was no question when it concerned deciding between social adjustment and mental growth (Taylor 1943). This leaning toward a social adjustment policy occurred despite considerable evidence reported by Terman (1925–1959) and his associates that mental growth and social-emotional adjustment generally went hand in hand. In contrast with Taylor (1943), Bonsall (1955) pointed out that, although very bright accelerated children initially felt some socioemotional handicaps, they evaluated the accelerative experience positively. This issue will be discussed further at a later point in this review.

Recent writers still maintain a cautious regard for acceleration (Bridges 1973; Weinstein, Mitchell, Schwartzstein, and Hirschhorn 1966). For the most part, however, these warnings are based more on intuitive than on empirical grounds. All indications point to the maintenance of professional attitudes of excessive concern over potential socioemotional maladjustment among intellectually precocious young accelerates, and too little concern about the probability of maladjusting effects resulting from inadequate intellectual challenge.

Studies of Early Entrance to College

Biographical Case Histories. Three reviews, written approximately twenty years apart, report abundant evidence of outstanding and extreme precocity throughout history (Hollingworth 1929, Miles 1946, Montour 1977). For the most part, these are prodigies who completed college at unusually young ages and continued their success throughout life. We quote at length from each article in order to underscore the extreme break with conventional age-grade grouping practices exemplified by these individuals. First, Hollingworth cites seven instances:

> The following great and long-lived men, as examples representing many others, entered the university as regular students before they were fourteen years old. James Thompson entered at twelve years of age, became a great engineer, and died aged seventy. William Thompson, his brother, who later was made Lord Kelvin, entered at the age of ten years, won fame in the field of physics, and died at eighty-three. The mathematician Gauss went to the university at eleven, won fame in his studies, and lived a long life of intellectual accomplishment. Justice Bennett Van Syckel entered Princeton at thirteen, was graduated at sixteen, and died at ninety-one after a distinguished career, including thirty-five years of service on the bench of the Supreme Court. Judge Lacomb, recently deceased, federal jurist in the United States for

twenty-nine years, was graduated from Columbia College with honors at the age of seventeen. He was so young when he received his degree in law from the same university that he had to wait two years before he could be admitted to practice. He died, aged seventy-nine. Elihu Root was graduated at nineteen from Hamilton College, as valedictorian of his class, and at the age of eighty is actively engaged in such a way to be called "counsel to the world." (Hollingworth 1929, p. 274)

Next, Miles (1946) cites at least eight instances in which a combination of excellent tutors and flexible college admissions policies permitted now-famous individuals to enter college early as well as get a head start on significant careers:

> Karl White, Macaulay, and John Stuart Mill were instructed individually at rates of speed far beyond those of even the most superior of private schools or opportunity classes, and the curricula devised for them were designed to cover by the age of 10 or 12 the elements and many of the higher aspects of liberal education, including the languages, literature, history, mathematics, theoretical science, and philosophy. Many other children besides, including Lord Kelvin, physicist, his brother James Thompson, engineer, Grotius, founder of international law, and the philosophers Bentham and Scheiermacher, were prepared by tutors or under flexible school plans which permitted college or university matriculation at the age of 11 or 12, followed by long careers of brilliant and active accomplishment. Men who achieve the distinction of inclusion in *Who's Who* and the notable group of starred men of science have as a rule passed more rapidly through the elementary and college preparatory school years than the average boy. (Miles 1946, p. 1029)

Third, Montour (1977) focuses on the unfortunate outcome of one man whom she termed "the archetypal father-exploited prodigy," versus the celebrated prodigy Norbert Wiener. In direct contrast with Sidis's case, however— and meant to underscore the infrequency of cases like it—Montour (1976, 1977, 1978) reviews many instances of successful completion of college at ages considerably younger than usual. Two "precocious Harvard alumni" exemplify the degree of eminence associated with those cases cited by Montour:

> Two less familiar figures than the oft-cited cases of Increase and Cotton Mather were even younger than Sidis when they got their degrees from Harvard. Paul Dudley, who was really the youngest man to graduate from Harvard (not Sidis, as claimed), entered at age 10 (class of 1690) and took his first degree at age 14. Dudley led a full life at the college and became an eminent Massachusetts jurist who was appointed Chief Justice in 1745. Andrew Preston Peabody was another youthful Harvard graduate at age 15. Both an academic and a minister, he served as acting president of Harvard College in 1862 and was its overseer for ten years. . . . (1977, p. 276)

Successful prodigies that are more recent include Merrill Kenneth Wolf, who took his bachelor's degree from Yale at barely 14; John Rader Platt, who took his bachelor's degree from Northwestern in 1936 at age 17; and Charles L. Fefferman, who finished college degree requirements at 17 in 1966 at the University of Maryland. Fefferman currently is Princeton's youngest full professor after having become a full professor of mathematics at the University of Chicago at age 24 (Montour 1978, p. 277). In addition, Harold Brown, United States

Secretary of Defense under President Carter, was graduated from the Bronx High School of Science at age 15, completed his bachelor's degree at Columbia at age 18, and earned his Ph.D. in physics at the age of 21 (Walsh 1977).

Recent preliminary follow-ups from the Study of Mathematically Precocious Youth at The Johns Hopkins University (Stanley, Keating, and Fox 1974; Keating 1976) report successful college experiences among over ninety-five young men and women who entered college at least one, and as much as six, years early (Stanley 1976f, p. 41). To date these youths have been remarkably successful academically, socially, and emotionally. For journalistic reports about the vanguard of this group see *Time* (1977) and Nevin (1977).

Early Studies of Younger Aged College Entrants. Two excellent reports reviewed extensively the research literature prior to the mid-1930s. Pressey (1949) cited eleven studies of younger-aged students who completed college early. Seven of these reported results based on young entrants at the following universities: Harvard (Holmes 1913), Columbia (Jones 1916), Minnesota (Pittenger 1917), Dartmouth (Husband 1923), Northwestern (Lloyd-Jones 1929), Columbia and Barnard (Gray 1930), and the City College of New York (Payne 1930). Pressey also cited four review articles in his monograph (Dwyer 1939, Learned and Wood 1938, Odell 1933, and Silverman and Jones 1932). Summarizing the foregoing review literature he concluded:

> Evidence was practically unanimous that younger entrants were more likely to graduate, had the best academic records, won the most honors, and presented the fewest disciplinary difficulties. The evidence is also that the younger entrants are highest in ability; their superior academic record is presumably a product of this attribute. . . . When ability is allowed for, the accelerated students thus still turn out as well as average entrants, or even seem to have profited to some extent by acceleration. (1949, p. 78)

Keys's (1938) review overlooked two studies reported by Pressey (i.e., Pittenger 1917, Lloyd-Jones 1929) but included five additional references. One study, an exception to Pressey's generalization, was reported in a footnote. It noted that at the University of Illinois for the academic year 1909–10 correlations of 0.09 and 0.20 between academic grades and chronological age were reported for samples of men and women, respectively (see Keys 1938, p. 159). Two references reported the success of young entrants to Purdue University (Remmers 1930) and Amherst (Phillips 1934). The remaining two citations (Bear 1926, Whinnery 1926) also reported higher grades among younger entrants when compared with classmates in general (Keys, p. 160).

Keys, an early advocate of the use of controlled investigations in the study of accelerative techniques, cited two studies (Moore 1933, Sarbaugh 1934) as superior examples when compared with previous research because of their inclusion of matched ability comparison results. According to Sarbaugh, fifty-seven University of Buffalo students aged 16 or younger were paired with a control group of equal size on (1) the New York State Regents examinations, (2) approximate class rank, and (3) the American Council Psychological Examination scores. Average freshmen grade point averages and individual subject scores for the two groups were equivalent. Only 5 percent of the young group felt intellectually handicapped in college; however, no comparison data on this point were reported. Moreover, 32 percent of the young group reported some social handicaps because of youth, but again, lack of comparison data renders such percentages difficult to interpret. Undoubtedly, a certain proportion of all college freshmen experience some social and emotional maladjustment. Thus, normative data are essential for valid interpretation of this type of results.

At the University of California at Berkeley during the period from 1922 to 1930 there were 238 entrants who were under 16½ years of age (Keys 1938). In order to assess the academic performance and socioemotional adjustment of these young Berkeley students, Keys selected a control group of students aged 17 and over. However, a comparison of the underaged group with conventional-aged entrants revealed discrepancies in the socioeconomic backgrounds of the two cohorts: "The proportion of students with professional fathers is nearly twice as great among the underaged as in the control group" (ibid., p. 177). Despite this finding, Keys made no attempt to control for these outstanding differences in socioeconomic status. In addition, and, quite surprisingly, Keys made no attempt to match underaged entrants with regular-aged comparisons on the basis of intellectual aptitude. Instead, he assumed the comparison students "were probably persons with records better than the average of their group" (ibid., p. 169).

Based on these two methodological problems vis-à-vis the comparison group, results from the underaged Berkeley students' experience, as reported by Keys (1938), ought to be reconsidered. First, Keys reported "the academic achievement among accelerated students was highly superior to that of the average student, for both men and women" (ibid., p. 261). Since these students were able to enter Berkeley younger than the average college entrance age, there must have been *some* degree of acceleration prior to college entrance, and it is quite likely that such acceleration (for example, "double promotion") had been based on superior intellectual ability. Thus, the fact that the underaged students were successful academically indicated that, *in combination with high intellectual aptitude,* acceleration was appropriate for these students. But no conclusions may be drawn about whether entrance at younger-than-typical ages would have been *more* appropriate for the group when compared with a group exhibiting conventional progress through secondary school and college.

Second, Keys noted "more of the younger entrants at the University of California considered their undergraduate social relations as unsatisfactory" (ibid., p. 263). However, a little later he said, "It seems probable that the 'difference' which troubled one-fourth of those entering at fourteen or fifteen was a penalty of their exceptional intelligence rather than their age" (ibid., p. 264). Being unlike their classmates is what Keys means by "difference." It is likely that comparison of social-emotional adjustment using controls matched on intellectual ability would have attenuated these results and revealed the underaged in a better light than Keys reported.

Table 2.1. Pressey's 1936 early entrants to The Ohio State University

	Ages of entering college					
Item	16	17	18	19	20	+20
1. Number of students	78	624	1,266	488	275	308
2. Percentage of age group entering	3	20	42	16	9	10
3. Percentage of total group graduating	52	51	42	16	9	10
Percentage of each age group:						
4. At 90th percentile or above	28	26	20	16	19	18
5. Below 40th percentile	27	20	26	25	38	26
6. Median O.S.P.E. percentile at entrance[a]	72	70	66	64	61	69

[a]O.S.P.E. refers to Ohio State Psychological Examination. Table 2.1 is adapted from Pressey (1949, p. 49).

Two Experiments: The Ohio State University and the University of Illinois. Four years after the Second World War ended, Pressey reported results based on a study of 3,021 students who had entered The Ohio State University more than ten years earlier. Table 2.1 is adapted from Pressey's 1949 monograph; the first two rows denote sample sizes and percentages of total group comprising each age cohort. Data concerning the percentage of the total group that graduated (row 3) led him to question "whether or not the greater proportion of younger entrants might simply have been the product of superior ability" (Pressey 1949, p. 60). In addition, percentages of each group scoring above the 90th percentile and below the 40th percentile on ability norms (rows 4 and 5) and median ability percentile ranks (row 6) suggested some relation between intellectual ability and academic achievement.

Pressey divided each age cohort into those scoring at or above the 80th percentile and those scoring below the 40th percentile on ability norms at the time of college entrance. "Seventy-five percent of those entering at sixteen years of age who scored at or above the 80th percentile in ability were graduated. However, only 24 percent of the less-able sixteen-year olds . . . obtained a degree" (ibid.). Therefore, Pressey concluded that "Younger able entrants clearly are more likely to graduate . . . and the academic prognosis for the least able is equally poor, whatever the age" (ibid.).

Results from the Ohio State University underaged accelerants were compared with results for a control group matched for intellectual ability, sex, and educational program. According to Pressey, half of those who entered at 16 or younger graduated within six years after entrance compared with 38 percent of the group two years older on the average at entrance to college. In addition, a larger percentage of younger college students were employed part time while in school, and also took part in extracurricular activities.

During World War II the National Educational Association encouraged colleges to accept intellectually able high school seniors as freshmen. In compliance with this federal request, the University of Illinois initiated a program based upon the following selection criteria: (1) faculty referral, (2) minimum acceptable course experience, and (3) evidence of intellectual and socioemotional stability. In 1943 thirty-six students meeting these requirements enrolled one to two semesters before having graduated from secondary school (Berg and Larsen 1945).

Overall academic performance of the Illinois early entrants was quite favorable, that is, defined in terms of at least one standard deviation *above* median achievement norms for the college. In addition, the students made satisfactory personal and social adjustments. However, no data from comparison students, matched on intellectual aptitude, were reported. Thus, the Illinois study was consistent with the Berkeley data reported earlier (Keys 1938); likewise, it failed to answer the question whether or not the same sample would have fared as well without having entered the university at an earlier age than usual.

The University of Chicago Program for Early Admission.   Approximately six years before the University of Illinois initiated its program of early admission and four years before the United States entered World War II, the University of Chicago began an experimental curriculum in general education (Ward 1950). Five years later the university reached a decision that permitted awarding the bachelor's degree upon completion of a four-year program begun after only the tenth year of schooling (Bloom and Ward 1952). Reported elsewhere (Allison and Bloom 1950; Bloom and Allison 1949; Ward 1950), the program of general education at Chicago emphasized the need to demonstrate competence through successful performance on comprehensive examinations. In addition, Chicago introduced survey courses while eliminating compulsory class attendance after the first two years of the program. In fact, the latter innovation generated more unfavorable criticism than the practice of permitting students to enroll after their sophomore year in high school!

In 1952 the University of Chicago responded to the challenges it received for a demonstration of the worth of its bachelor's degree. One-third of the graduating seniors (N = 105) accepted an invitation to take the Graduate Record Examinations (GREs) as part of an "experiment." According to Bloom and Ward (1952), those seniors representing the college did not differ from their classmates in scholastic aptitude, age, comprehensive examinations taken, or number of years of schooling completed prior to graduation. At least 80 percent of the early entrants scored *above median national norms of all GREs taken.* In addition, the University of Chicago seniors' median rank on all eight tests of general education averaged just under the 90th percentile mark, and their median rank on the index of general education was at the 96th percentile. The underaged seniors had demonstrated the unequivocal worth of a Chicago bachelor's degree.

Despite the impressive results reported by Bloom and Ward (1952) the same qualifications concerning the Berkeley (Keys 1938) and Illinois (Berg and Larsen 1945) samples applied for the University of Chicago early entrants. It was reported that the seniors graduating in 1952 averaged two years younger than conventional-aged college graduates that same year. However, the typical University of Chicago undergraduate, who was two years older, scored at the *86th percentile* on the Psychological Examination of the American Council of Education. Thus, the norms against which the underaged seniors' GRE performance were compared must have been considerably *below* those appropriate for such an intellectually able group. Nonetheless, the data were consistent to the extent that the 1940s program at the University of Chicago was, indeed, appropriate for highly intellectually able, younger students.

The Ford Foundation Program of Early Entrance to College.

World War II made unprecedented demands upon American education to produce well trained, educated, competent personnel. But, following the war, interest in early entrance programs at the college level waned until 1951, when our involvement in the Korean conflict replicated wartime demands of the early 1940s. Against this historical and political context emerged the Fund for the Advancement of Education sponsored by the Ford Foundation.

> The project began as a "Pre-Induction Program" involving four universities which were concerned about the problem created for education by the manpower demands of the nation's military services. Under the military draft regulations of early 1951 it appeared that for an indefinite period young men would be drafted at age 18 or shortly thereafter for at least two years of military service, just at the time when they would normally have entered college . . . Discussions of the problem by representatives of four universities—Yale, Chicago, Columbia, and Wisconsin—resulted in a cooperative proposal to the Fund for the establishment of an experimental program of scholarships to enable younger men not older than 16½ to enter college for two years of general education before military service. (Fund for the Advancement of Education 1953, p. 69)

The above rationale differed little from the impetus behind earlier programs of acceleration at, for example, the University of Illinois, The Ohio State University, or the University of Chicago. However, the present investigation contrasted with the earlier studies in two ways. First, the Fund's Program of Early Entrance was designed to attend very carefully to the socioemotional adjustment of the accelerants. Second, the project represented the first *prospective* study of acceleration (with the possible exception of the University of Chicago "experiment"). According to the preliminary report, "Evidence was derived from systematic observation of younger students from the day they entered college" (ibid., p. 70).

Between 1951 and 1954, 1,350 Ford Foundation "Scholars" were awarded scholarships to attend twelve participating colleges and universities. Careful records were kept of a selected group of "Comparison" students who were matched with the Scholars on the basis of academic aptitude (Fund for the Advancement of Education 1957, p. 8). On the average, the accelerants were 16 years old or younger, and only a small minority had completed the conventional twelve years of precollege education.

In general, colleges selected Ford Foundation Scholars on the basis of four criteria: (1) scores above the minimum cutoff for regular entrants; (2) social and emotional adjustment assessed during personal interviews; (3) financial need; and (4) attendance in public schools. For evaluative comparison purposes, the program provided for "carefully selected 'matching' students of comparable aptitude" (ibid., p. 14).[1] Comparison students differed from the Scholars primarily in that they were, on the average, two years older and already had obtained their high school diplomas. In addition, although Comparison students in general were aware of their participation in the project, they were not singled out as distinguished young scholars or "Fordlings" as the group came to be known. Also, the Comparison students may not have been as financially needy as the Ford Scholars (ibid., p. 15).

The Educational Testing Service at Princeton conducted the first evaluation of the Ford Foundation Early Entrance Program. Academic performance and socioemotional adjustment were assessed on the basis of college records, Scholars' self-reports, a psychiatric evaluation, and Scholars' and Comparisons' essays based on their respective four-year experiences. Concerning the academic performance, three results were reported. First, the Scholars exceeded both the Comparison group and the general college population in grade point average and class rank. According to the 1957 report, "Year after year, a higher proportion of the Scholars than the Comparison students ranked in the top tenth, fifth, and third of their classes" (ibid., p. 24). Second, there was variation in the *extent* of acceleration and in its mode of influence on performance: "Scholars with 11 years of schooling tended to do slightly better than those with only 10, but the latter tended to do slightly better than those with 12" (ibid., p. 26). Third, the 1952 Scholar group exceeded Comparison students on area test scores of the Graduate Record Examinations.

Evaluation of the socioemotional adjustment of the Scholars focused on whether or not they had experienced problems directly related to having been accelerated two years on the average. In other words, this evaluation assumed certain base rates of socioemotional maladjustment exist in the general college population, and proceeded to assess whether acceleration contributed disproportionately beyond what might have been expected. All indications reported problems of social maladjustment were not attributable to early entrance status:

> The rate of failure among the first two groups was somewhat higher than that among their Comparison students, but at most of the colleges where comparable data were available it was lower than that among their classmates as a whole. When the reasons for failure were examined, they were found to be no different for the Scholars than for college students in general.

> The Scholars encountered more initial difficulties in adjusting to campus life than

[1]Note that when one matches, for example, a 16-year-old with an 18-year-old on a College Board Scholastic Aptitude Test score such as SAT-V, the former actually is the brighter because at 18 he or she probably will score higher than the latter did at age 18.

their older Comparison students, but most of the difficulties were minor and were soon overcome. (ibid., pp. 9–10)

In 1966, Pressey followed up 87 Scholars and 111 Comparison students who had participated in the Early Entrance Program at Oberlin College ten years earlier. Pressey reported that more than half of both groups later had obtained advanced professional degrees, but that the Scholars had earned certification, on the average, two years earlier than the Comparisons. In addition, accelerants' retrospective accounts coincided with the data reported in the Fund for the Advancement of Education monograph. That is, the early college entrants reported experiencing "initial social difficulty because of youth at entrance but this soon passed" (Pressey 1967, p. 73). Based on Pressey's follow-up then, the 1957 findings appeared to be reliable, at least for the students who attended one of the twelve participating institutions.

Finally, a related study of young college entrants at Harvard (Kogan 1955) compared favorably with the Ford Foundation Early Entrance Program; however, underaged accelerants at Harvard were not supported by the Ford Foundation. Kogan investigated 90 young Harvard undergraduates who were not quite 17 years old by 1 January of their freshmen year. The Harvard students were comparable to the Ford Scholars in age but differed in certification. Ninety percent of the Harvard accelerants had completed *four years* of high school, whereas 42 percent of the Fordlings left high school after only *two* years of secondary education. According to Kogan, this difference probably was due to the Harvard students' having been accelerated at some point prior to high school or having been admitted to elementary school under age.

Kogan's investigation bore more similarity to earlier studies (Berg and Larsen 1945, Keys 1938, Pressey 1949) than to the Ford Foundation Early Entrance Program. This was due to Kogan's having assessed young entrants' academic performance and socioemotional adjustment relative to *all* matriculated Harvard students. Of course, we might reasonably assume the typical Harvard undergraduate at that time was highly intellectually able compared with the average college student. However, we have no way of interpreting how acceleration might have altered the performance and adjustment of the underaged Harvard sample compared with their *not* having been accelerated.

Kogan's results were consistent with the Ford Foundation findings as well as with results reported in other early college entrance literature. The younger Harvard students were "an over-achieving academically superior group.... They did not appear to have more adjustment problems than is characteristic of the college as a whole" (1955, p. 135). Thus, based on numerous *retrospective* accounts of early entrance to college, there appear to be no data reported in the acceleration literature to refute the appropriateness of acceleration for intellectually able students. Furthermore, the single major *prospective* report (Fund for the Advancement of Education 1957) offers considerable positive evidence that acceleration is indeed advantageous for intellectually able and socially mature youths.

Rapid Completion of the Bachelor's Degree

The preceding section reported at length studies of early entrance to college; it should be noted that these types of accelerative strategies generally imply entrance to college at ages younger than conventional. An alternative type of acceleration (cf. Pressey's 1949 definition) appropriate for shortening the time needed to complete bachelor's degree requirements involves academic progress at rates faster than the mode. Both accelerative methods have two points in common: each is designed to shorten time necessary for the baccalaureate; and each is better suited for intellectually precocious youths.

This section reviews the "rates faster" acceleration literature and focuses upon two methods. First, a series of investigations conducted during the 1940s at The Ohio State University (Flesher 1946, Flesher and Pressey 1955, and Pressey 1944a, 1949) described the lengthened school year and heavier course loads as two ways students were able to finish degree requirements rapidly. Second, a few years before the Ohio State University investigations, the University of Chicago initiated a program through which its students could earn credit following successful performance on placement examinations (see Allison and Bloom 1950, Bloom and Allison 1949). In 1953 the Ford Foundation pursued this accelerative method through funding a program for college entrance with advanced placement credit (Fund for the Advancement of Education 1953). In years following, the Educational Testing Service of the College Entrance Examination Board made the Advanced Placement Program a more readily available, viable alternative. More recent experience involves part-time college work for students who are still in high school (see, for example, Solano and George 1976). This approach offers a related accelerative strategy for intellectually talented young adolescents.

World War II Accelerative Strategies at Ohio State University. For over twenty years Sidney Leavitt Pressey (1944a, 1944b, 1944c, 1949, 1955, 1962) has advocated less time-consuming undergraduate, graduate, and professional programs. His 1949 monograph remains a classic in the acceleration literature and provides perhaps the best source for a review of accelerative programs dating back to the mid-nineteenth century in America. According to Pressey (1949), Yale University's Sheffield Scientific School numbered among the earliest prestigious institutions offering a three-year bachelor's program. Prior to 1900, four institutions including Yale had initiated three-year baccalaureate programs: Cornell, Johns Hopkins, and Harvard. In addition, Clark University maintained an accelerated collegiate program from 1902 to 1922. However, these four nineteenth-century three-year programs, like that of Clark University, were relatively short-lived (ibid., p. 10). By the end of the 1930s and the Depression, the University of Chicago apparently was the only major institution to maintain a flexible academic program permitting rapid completion of the bachelor's degree.

The educational lock step with the typical age-grade grouping, even up through the college years, continued to persist until America entered World War

II. At that time, according to Pressey, "The Ohio State University was the only institution anywhere which, upon the outbreak of the war, proceeded systematically to investigate the problem of acceleration and to some extent to direct its practice in the light of its investigation" (ibid., p. 3). Although at least thirty-one professional papers described some aspect of the Ohio State wartime acceleration program, this section focuses upon three major reports (Flesher 1946, Flesher and Pressey 1955, Pressey 1944a).

First, Pressey (1944a) described two Ohio State student groups that were matriculated in 1941–42 and 1942–43. Among the former group (N = 1,122) only 5 percent completed the bachelor's degree in less time than conventional, that is in fewer than three years, nine months. The second cohort (N = 1,030), however, took advantage of the wartime accelerative options, and 33 percent of this group finished in less than the regular time. Therefore, the above figures, including both men and women, describe what Pressey called the "last pre-acceleration and first accelerated graduating class" (1944a, p. 563).

Two reports subsequently were made concerning the 1942–43 accelerated group: a description of methods used, and an evaluation of success (or failure) of these accelerative methods. First, the accelerants' overwhelming choice for rapid completion of bachelor's degree requirements involved yearlong classes during the extended four-quarter academic year. "Sixty-three percent of the acceleration [was] gained simply by attending a fourth quarter, 4 percent by extra load only, and 1 percent by examnation credit alone, while 32 percent of the accelerants used more than one method (ibid., p. 565). These findings led Pressey to term this method "acceleration the hard way."

Pressey was able to assess effects of acceleration in the following way. First, he subdivided the nonaccelerants into two groups: the "regulars" who completed the bachelor's requirements in from three and three-quarters to four years, and the "retardates" who took longer than four years to finish. Then he compared the academic performance and the extracurricular participation of the "accelerates" with each of the nonaccelerated groups. Median ages at time of entrance were comparable for the three groups, but median ages at graduation, although equivalent for the accelerated and regular groups, were reported appreciably higher for the retarded cohort. In addition, the accelerants had an advantage in terms of general ability over the other two groups.

Results were reported as follows: the "accelerants" earned a higher final mean grade point average than either the "regulars" or the "retardates"; and the "accelerants" participated in approximately the same number of nonacademic activities as the "regulars" and the "retardates." In addition, separate analyses of eighteen students completing the program in fewer than three years reported their mean grade point average to be highest among all three groups mentioned above. Moreover, twelve of the eighteen three-year accelerants participated in one or more nonacademic activities (Pressey 1944a, p. 569).

In a second and related study Flesher (1946) reported on seventy-six women in the Ohio State classes of 1944 and 1945 (N = 570) who had been graduated in three years or less. According to Flesher, the seventy-six female accelerants did not differ in age at entrance from their female classmates; however, their group mean for intellectual aptitude exceeded that of the regular students. Flesher reportedly paired each accelerant with a female control matched on ability and age at entrance to college and time of graduation. The accelerants outperformed the paired comparison group (and the class in general) academically. In the extracurricular areas the accelerants were more active than were the regular students but less active compared with the control group. In general, however, (Flesher 1946), these accelerants were matched with 145 graduates of the same erated group.

The third study reported a ten-year follow-up of 145 accelerants who had been graduated from The Ohio State University in three years or fewer between 1941 and 1945 (Flesher and Pressey 1955). As noted in the previous study (Flesher 1946), these accelerants were matched with 145 graduates of the same sex who were of comparable general ability and age at the time of entrance to college and who had taken similar courses of study. Results were based on 81 percent and 71 percent return rates of questionnaires from the accelerated and regular alumnae, respectively. Different response rates were not considered to be due to anything other than chance. Accelerative methods were reported as follows: "Ninety-two percent of the accelerate group, at least once, went four quarters in school; over half took extra heavy schedules; twenty-nine percent got some credit by examination; and over half used two or more methods" (Flesher and Pressey 1955, pp. 321–32). In general, then, the accelerative methods used reflected heavy academic course loads during an extended four-quarter program.

Results of the follow-up of female accelerants may be summarized in five points. First, rates of employment in college for both groups were approximately equal. Second, very few accelerants considered their experiences as having contributed disproportionately to their physical, social, or academic well-being. Third, extracurricular participation in war-related activities was about equal for the two groups; and, given the political and economic conditions generated by participation in the war, Flesher and Pressey considered the accelerants' nonacademic participation quite favorably. Fourth, 24 percent of the accelerants but only 12 percent of the regulars earned degrees above the bachelor's. Fifth, 29 percent of the married accelerants and 16 percent of the regular married alumnae were employed at the time of the survey.

It should be noted that the accelerants studied during the war were not of considerably higher intellectual aptitude than were students who completed the bachelor's at the conventional rate. Flesher and Pressey (1955) reported approximately 10 percentile points were all that differentiated the accelerants from the general, nonaccelerated college students. Therefore, it seems reasonable to conclude that "acceleration the hard way" is perhaps the one method that is least restricted to students of unusually high intellectual aptitude. Hard work and determination would seem equally important for yearlong academic performance. The remaining studies reviewed in this section will consider accelerative methods best suited to the most intellectually able.

Advanced Credit through Examination.   In the preceding section we noted that wartime accelerants at The Ohio State University sometimes received college credit through examination, thereby helping to facilitate completion of the bachelor's degree requirements. One study indicated that only 1 percent of the men and women who were accelerated had taken advantage of earning course credit based on examination performance (Pressey 1944a). A second study (Flesher 1946) reported 29 percent of the female accelerants between 1941 and 1946 had gained credit this way. Despite the relatively low incidence of educational advancement through credit by examination, Pressey was indeed well aware of the method's potential. "Credit by examination has the double merit of placing the student according to ability rather than academic time served (thus preventing able students from learning what they already know) and advancing such students more rapidly toward their educational goals. This method should be more widely used than at present" (1949, p. 132). The phrase "academic time served," in addition to the notion of "acceleration in the hard way" (Pressey 1944a), underscores the idea that wartime accelerative methods might have been better suited to individuals of unusual stamina and/or perseverance rather than to those of unusual intellectual aptitude. Acceleration based on credit by examination, however, denoted a return to the mainstream of accelerative methods, namely, methods appropriate as education individualized for students of unusually high intellectual ability.

Credit by examination was mentioned previously in this report (see "Biographical Case Histories") concerning historical prodigies' early entrance to college. The preindustrialized era was not marked by chronological age-grade segregation at all educational levels, and heterogeneously age-grouped colleges, for example, were not uncommon. The entrance examination indicated the measure of one's intellectual ability, and consequently, assessed one's readiness for college. In most cases readiness for college was considered independent of chronological age. According to Bloom and Allison (1949), in the 1930s the University of Chicago program for general education resumed a long tradition of academic award based on students' having passed comprehensive examinations. The requirement for graduation in the college at the University of Chicago included passing up to fourteen comprehensive examinations. "The principle here places emphasis on the level of achievement rather than on the means of developing such achievement" (ibid., p. 212). Thus, Chicago's program marked the inception of the more recent acceptance of credit through examination.

It is indeed interesting to note that even among underaged University of Chicago scholars who had been admitted after only ten years of schooling (Bloom and Ward 1952), exemption from prerequisite courses by examination did not hinder the students' subsequent course work in the same field. "In 1945, 115 students who had entered at the end of ten years of school were excused from Humanities 1 or Social Sciences 1 comprehensive examinations. On the second year comprehensive examination requirement, Humanities 2 and Social Sciences 2, 35 percent of those students made grades of A or B, while 22 percent made grades of D or F. The corresponding figures for all students taking the comprehensives are 29 percent A or B and 21 percent D or F'' (Allison and Bloom 1950, p. 231). According to this account, underaged University of Chicago students were not handicapped through advanced placement, even though initially they were two years accelerated.

In the early 1950s, the Ford Foundation funded a related project, the "Program for Admission to College with Advanced Standing" (see Fund for the Advancement of Education 1953, chapter 4). According to the preliminary report, the program was begun in order "to enable and challenge the student to proceed at his own best pace . . . here the burden [was] placed on both the high school and college" (ibid., pp. 56–57). The practice of entering college with advanced standing rather than leaving high school without the diploma obviously contrasted with the mechanics of two otherwise quite similar projects, the Program for Early Entrance to College (Fund for the Advancement of Education 1957) and the University of Chicago "practice of general education" (Ward 1950). However, the objectives of all three programs were practically identical: to permit intellectually able students to complete bachelor's degree requirements as rapidly as possible.

In the mid-1950s, the Ford Foundation program for college admission with advanced standing evolved into the College Board's Advanced Placement Program (CEEB 1973, Newland 1976). The procedure for entering college with sophomore standing had been standardized. A student's successful performance on an Advanced Placement Examination (scores of 3 to 5 with a maximum score of 5) could earn him or her up to one full year of college credit, depending on the participating institution. Thus, according to the College Board, the Advanced Placement Program established "an active consortium to which the nation's high schools [could] relate their local programs for thousands of young people demonstrably able to complete a year's worth of college-level studies before progressing from their twelfth to their thirteenth year of formal education" (CEEB 1973, p. *v*). A more recent report (CEEB 1974) cites 136 academic institutions that are prepared "to award immediate Sophomore Standing or its local equivalent to students gaining full Advanced Placement credits."

The following account aptly describes the accelerative potential of the Advanced Placement Program. The student to which the report applies was a participant in the Johns Hopkins Study of Mathematically Precocious Youth (Stanley, Keating, and Fox 1974; Keating 1976):

> The SMPY contestant who in January of 1973 as a 12-year-old public school seventh grader scored 800 on SAT-M managed to earn credit for two semesters of college calculus while still 13 years old and two semesters each of biology, chemistry, and physics while still 15 by making the highest possible grade (5) on each of four APP examinations. Also, while 14 he earned an "A" from a major university by correspondence study in a third-semester college course. And he still has another year in which to take several more APP courses before going off to MIT or Harvard a year early, having skipped the eighth grade. (Stanley 1979, p. 178)

Scoring 800 on the Scholastic Aptitude Test (SAT-M) at age 12 is a remarkable intellectual accomplishment, one of rare occurrence. However, slightly less exceptional aptitude appears more often in the general secondary schools; for such intellectually able groups the Advanced Placement Program provides a realistic opportunity to shorten the bachelor's program by one year.

Finally, the Study of Mathematically Precocious Youth reported that over a five-year period 131 intellectually precocious junior high school youths have taken 277 college courses (Solano and George 1976). The overall grade point average for these courses was 3.59, where A = 4 and B = 3. Recommendations for part-time college level work for 12- and 13-year-olds were based upon their having demonstrated unusually precocious intellectual aptitude as assessed by appropriately difficult tests (Stanley 1976a). For example, College Board Scholastic Aptitude Test scores of at least 550 and 400 on the mathematical and verbal portions, respectively, were guidelines SMPY had established to insure that the young candidates were suited for college work.

SMPY's program for endorsing part-time college courses for intellectually precocious young 12- and 13-year-olds seems appropriate for the unusually high ability of this young group. Yet superior intellectual ability at this young age might be facilitated better through more radical acceleration (for example, see Stanley 1976f, pp. 40–41) some time prior to completion of a conventional four-year secondary school program. It is likely that the usual Advanced Placement Program courses in modern high schools, while appropriate for the needs of bright high school seniors, might very well already be below the level necessary to challenge such intellectually talented youths.

Acceleration Prior to College Entrance

The preceding two sections of this report have focused on accelerative methods designed to bridge the transitional gap between secondary level education and college (cf. Fund for the Advancement of Education 1953). Substantial significant research over the past fifty years has focused upon the evaluation of accelerative methods prior to college matriculation, strategies introduced at various points during the conventional twelve years of elementary and secondary education. In addition, at least four studies reported evaluative research pertinent to the question of the age at which intellectually able students should be admitted to elementary school (e.g., Baer 1958; Birch 1954; Hobson 1948, 1963; and Worcester 1956).

The following section describes important representative acceleration studies conducted during the past fifty years. Our outline divides the research literature into four sections: (1) Terman and Oden's (1947) follow-up of the 1920s California gifted sample; (2) secondary school accelerative methods; (3) elementary school accelerative methods; and (4) studies of early admission to kindergarten or first grade.

The Fulfillment of Promise: Terman and Oden (1947).   Terman's longitudinal investigation (1925–59) of more than one thousand gifted children in

California undoubtedly is the most important study of its kind (see Burks, Jensen, and Terman 1930; Cox 1926; Oden 1968; Sears 1977; Terman 1925; Terman and Oden 1947; Terman and Oden 1959). However, Terman did not intend his study to be an experiment on acceleration of the gifted. Indeed, the investigation is quite unique in its comprehensiveness, and since it fails to fit neatly within our classification of acceleration based on level of education at which the intervention occurs, we have included Terman and Oden's follow-up apart from the other research. According to Stanley, "[Terman's] study was descriptive and observational, not intentionally interventional; he did not attempt to improve the education of the gifted except by trying to modify the attitudes of most adults toward extremely bright youths" (1976d, p. 5). Thus, this section focuses upon chapter 20 in volume 4 of the *Genetic Studies of Genius* series (Terman and Oden 1947, pp. 264–81) in which data concerning the effects of acceleration among a portion of the gifted population are reported relative to those who were not accelerated.

Terman and Oden divided the gifted sample into three separate groups based on chronological age at graduation. Group I included those who were 15.5 years or younger, group II included those who finished between 15.5 and 16.5 years of age, and group III comprised that portion graduating over age 16.5 years. If conventional age-grade grouping practices resulted in graduation at 18 years (plus or minus 6 months), then one might consider groups I, II, and III as having been accelerated 2 to 4 years, 1 to 2 years, and 0 to 1 year, respectively. Terman and Oden reported a mean age at graduation of 15.9 years for a combined sample (I and II) here referred to as the "accelerants." The "nonaccelerants" (III) averaged 17.4 years of age at high school graduation. The sample sizes for the groups are reported in table 2.2. Comparisons between accelerants and nonaccelerants were reported for four categories. First, there was a significant positive correlation between childhood IQ and the degree of acceleration. According to Terman and Oden (1947), however, "The correlation between acceleration and IQ [was] very low, for among the nonaccelerates [there were] 50 men and 39 women in the IQ range 150 to 190. In the schools these subjects attended, IQ's played little part in grade placement" (ibid., p. 268). In other words, despite their superior intellectual ability, approximately 9 percent of group III graduated less than one year younger than the age at which the conventional lock step would have predicted.

Second, a comparison among the groups' levels of academic certification after high school graduation indicated two findings: (1) the greater the degree of acceleration, the greater the likelihood of graduating from college and of remaining for one or more years of graduate work (ibid., p. 270); and (2) Terman reported sex differences indicating that male accelerants demonstrated better scholastic achievement than female accelerants.

Third, greater occupational success was reported for the group I accelerants (42.2 percent) than for the group III nonaccelerants (19.4 percent). That is, 42.2 percent of group I accelerants were employed in professional or upper-level

Table 2.2. Sample sizes for three Terman and Oden groups reported by sex[a]

Group (by age at graduation)	Males	Females	Total
I. Age 15.5 or younger	36	26	62
II. Ages >15.5 to 16.5	181	151	332
III. Older than age 16.5	568	430	998
Total	785	607	1,392

[a]Adapted from Terman and Oden (1947).

business occupations, whereas only 19.4 percent of the group III nonaccelerants were so employed. Moreover, no relation between avocational interests and the degree of acceleration was found.

Fourth, Terman and Oden carefully assessed the socioemotional adjustment differences reported for the accelerated and nonaccelerated groups. Their conclusions substantiated findings of earlier investigations (e.g., Keys 1938). "The influence of school acceleration in causing social maladjustment has been greatly exaggerated. There is no doubt that maladjustment does result in individual cases, but our data indicate that in a majority of subjects the maladjustment consists of a temporary feeling of inferiority which is later overcome" (Terman and Oden 1947, p. 275). In addition, Terman and Oden noted that marital satisfaction was unrelated to acceleration and that no detrimental effects on physical maturation were assessed. On the contrary, "Children most accelerated in school were on the average also accelerated in physical maturation as indicated by age of puberty" (ibid., p. 279). Thus, based on evidence from Terman's gifted sample, acceleration for intellectually able youths, those with an IQ greater than 135, was found to be beneficial academically and vocationally. Only minimal socioemotional maladjustment was reported; moreover, these problems were short-lived.

Accelerative Methods at the Secondary Level.   Most research cited in this section reports evaluation of vertical methods for facilitating the education of intellectually able youths. For the most part, these methods include grade-skipping in junior and senior high schools. For organizational purposes, acceleration at the junior and acceleration at the senior high school levels have been combined under the same heading. In addition, despite the possibility that acceleration sometimes is concurrent with relevant academic enrichment, this section reports only data pertinent to secondary school programs in which rapid progress through school is a primary goal.

Coincidental with the inception of widespread use of intelligence testing in schools (cf. Terman 1916), Alltucker (1924) reported evidence of positive academic performance and good social adjustment among senior high school students who had been accelerated approximately two years. Also, the academic performance in senior high school for a sample of Wisconsin junior high school accelerants who had completed the regular three-year program in two years was reported to be comparable with that of conventional-age high school students (Unzicker 1932). A related study (Houghton and Douglas 1935)[2] revealed that junior high school students' academic achievement was equivalent to that of same-grade comparison students, though the students in the comparison group were slightly abler intellectually and approximately two-thirds of a year older.

Two 1930s studies at the University of Buffalo (Strabel 1936a, 1936b) reported favorable results both for accelerated three-year high school graduates and for younger high school graduates who had not yet reached 16.5 years of age by commencement. Strabel (1936b) paired fifty-five three-year high school graduates with two equal sized groups of four-year high school graduates matched for sex, psychological test scores, class rank, and either age at high school graduation, or age at high school entrance. Results based on freshman academic performance indicated that the latter control group was slightly better in mathematics, while the accelerants had a slight edge in the social sciences. No significant academic indices differentiated the accelerated from the two nonaccelerated control groups.

Wilkins (1936) reported favorable results for 282 high school students who were accelerated approximately one year. The single criterion for inclusion in Wilkins's study was high school graduation before the age of 17. However, Keys (1938) noted Wilkins's unfortunate omission of a control sample with which to compare the accelerants' performance. Herr (1937) followed up junior high school accelerants who had completed a three-year program in two years. Seventy-nine accelerants were paired with an equal number of nonaccelerants on three variables: age at entrance to junior high school, IQ, and mental age derived from the Stanford Achievement Test. According to Herr, the control group included a large number of students whose parents refused permission for their children to enroll in the program. Results during ninth through twelfth grades reported the accelerants' performance as having equaled or exceeded that of the nonaccelerants. Shouse (1937) reported similar findings for social adjustment among accelerated junior high school students in a related study.

Keys's (1938) study of Oakland high school students carefully divided 112 accelerants into two categories. First, 46 underaged students with IQs ranging from 120 to 140 were matched with an equal-sized sample on the basis of comparable IQ, sex, race, and socioeconomic status; however, the comparison students were an average of nineteen months older when they graduated from high school. Second, two groups of students who were accelerated approximately two to five semesters were subdivided according to IQ: (1) the superior ability group (N = 24) had IQs above 136 and (2) the "bright-normal" cohorts (N = 43) had IQs below 120. Therefore, Keys's design permitted analysis of variance among accelerants depending on two factors, chronological age and intellectual ability.

Results may be summarized in four points. First, Keys found significant

[2]Cited in Keys (1938), p. 228.

effects for intelligence that led him to conclude that acceleration of two or more semesters for students below 120 IQ is "seldom advisable" (1938, p. 242). Second, controlling for effects of intelligence among underaged versus regular-rate students, Keys reported the younger group earned more scholarships, had better study habits, participated in a greater number of student activities, and more often held elective offices. Third, according to the Bernreuter Personality Inventory, sociability appeared to be related to differences in intelligence rather than differences in age. Fourth, self-reported estimates of general happiness were highest for the very bright *and* accelerated group.

Following Keys's 1938 report, little evidence of acceleration at the secondary level was reported. Keys had noted previously that most acceleration in California during the 1930s had involved double promotion at the elementary levels. This trend seemed to persist after 1940. In addition, two programs replaced grade-skipping as educational methods for facilitating intellectually able secondary level students. First, programs of "relevant academic enrichment" followed growing sentiment that social maladjustment was due to acceleration (see early discussion on "relevant academic enrichment"). This attitude led to disinterest in high school grade skipping. Second, programs for entrance to college with advanced standing (e.g., Fund for Advancement of Education 1953, CEEB 1973) encouraged development of *potentially* accelerative, relevant academic enrichment programs at the secondary educational level.

Three exceptions during the 1950s contrasted with the enrichment activity schema and provided opportunities for students to save time at the secondary level. Witty (1954) and Woolf (1957) described secondary schools in Baltimore in which one year of acceleration was possible. Jansen (in Havighurst, Stivers, and De Haan 1955) described a related program in New York City in which "some 62 regular junior high schools provide regular progress classes that allow superior students to complete three years' work in two years' time" (p. 70).

More recent research reports successful results for an accelerated high school program in Toronto in which students completed five years' work in four years' time (Adler, Pass, and Wright 1963). However, this kind of intervention is similar to the Advanced Placement Program described earlier in this report in which high school students may earn credit by examination for up to one year's work.

Also, recent extensive evidence from the Study of Mathematically Precocious Youth (SMPY) at The Johns Hopkins University describes successful implementation of a smorgasbord of accelerative educational provisions for intellectually talented junior high school youths who are especially talented in mathematics (Keating 1976; Keating and Stanley 1972; Stanley 1973, 1976d, 1976e, 1976f, Stanley 1977; Stanley, Keating, and Fox 1974; Stanley, George, and Solano 1977). Grade-skipping is but one of at least five accelerative methods employed successfully since 1972. Other methods are reported elsewhere in this paper. These include part-time study in college, credit by examination, early entrance to college, and rapid completion of the bachelor's degree.

Julian Stanley, Director of SMPY since its inception, has reported two necessary conditions for successful acceleration based on his project's experience. First, students must demonstrate unusual intellectual precocity on extremely difficult aptitude and/or achievement tests of the sort usually appropriate for prospective college entrants. Second, students must be willing and eager to progress at rates more rapid than those for which conventional education has been designed. According to Stanley, use of these two criteria h... /e been indeed worthwhile:

> Nearly all of our 44 early entrants to college thus far have done splendidly in their studies and social and emotional development. Compared with the academic and personal record of the typical Johns Hopkins student, the early entrants have been truly outstanding. Only one has performed poorly. He was a brilliant but headstrong 14-year-old who signed up for a heavy load of extremely difficult courses and then would not study enough. By age 15, however, he had earned a year of credit and a high school diploma. (1976d, p. 16)

Two points following this account need clarification. First, SMPY's accelerative strategy primarily relies upon grade-skipping at the secondary education level. However, well-planned educational facilitation for these intellectually precocious youths may *incorporate many alternative methods appropriate for students' intellectual needs*. No rules limit acceleration to any single strategy. In contrast with earlier investigations, SMPY's educative methods for the intellectually able comprise a decidedly eclectic approach. Second, Stanley's reported 98 percent success rate, which is based on only one poor performance among forty-four early entrants, is a reflection of the careful forethought and counseling that are important aspects of SMPY's facilitative methods. In addition, five radical accelerants, each of whom has skipped at least one year of secondary education, were graduated from Johns Hopkins in May of 1977. At that time, three were 17 years old, one was 18, and another was barely 19 years of age (ibid.).

Accelerative Methods at the Elementary Level. The earliest reported program "permitting rapid advancement of the capable" occurred in Saint Louis's secondary schools in the 1890s (Hollingworth 1929, pp. 276–77). Related programs prior to 1920 also were operational in New Jersey, Massachusetts, Oregon, and New York. For the most part, however, identification of prospective accelerants depended upon teachers' judgments and class marks (ibid.). Following widespread intelligence testing in the 1920s, special programs (e.g., Terman classes) for intellectually superior pupils based on tested intelligence scores were begun in New York City schools. Through the effective combination of enriched curricula and moderate acceleration such programs generally permitted educational facilitation appropriate to intellectually able students' needs.

Lamson (1930) reported a follow-up of fifty-six very bright high school students who had participated in special accelerative-enrichment classes in a New York elementary school. The fifty-six gifted students' average Stanford-Binet IQ was reported to be 155 (range 137 to 188); 110 control students were matched for sex, grade, and school, but not for intellectual ability. Lamson reported, "The rate of achievement on the part of the gifted program was significantly superior to the achievement of the control group . . . in spite of the fact that their chronological age was, on the average, two years less than that of the control group" (ibid., p. 73). In addition, a related study (Engle 1935) reported successful double promotion for twenty-five students who were compared with fifty nonaccelerants for educational, vocational, and social adjustment. However, without controlling for mental age differences between groups in both the Lamson and the Engle studies, it is difficult to separate effects of acceleration from those due to intellectual ability.

Another early investigation (Elder 1927) reported downward shifts in grades for a group of twenty-two "bright" and "very bright" elementary school children who had skipped one grade. Elder assessed academic performance before and after acceleration for the experimental group and for a control group of 696 nonaccelerated agemates. Although he found a general decline in academic grades following acceleration, Elder reported a *greater* drop for those accelerants who had low grades prior to acceleration. According to Elder, "if one were to represent the standings before and after acceleration by two ogive curves drawn from the same origin and combined into a single diagram, the parts of the curve representing the higher percentiles would nearly coincide, while the parts representing the lower percentiles would be far apart" (p. 7). Thus, Elder underscored the importance of *not* accelerating elementary school students unless their academic performance demonstrated the intellectual ability necessary to meet the greater academic demands of a higher grade.

A considerable portion of the 1950s acceleration literature was concerned with underage versus overage grade placement (e.g., Baer 1958, Holmes and Finley 1957, Klausmeier 1958, Worcester 1956). Holmes and Finley (1957) reported individual differences in combined achievement in six areas (reading vocabulary, spelling, mechanics of grammar, reading comprehension, arithmetic reasoning, and fundamentals of arithmetic) as having contributed 25 percent of the variance in grade placement deviations within any one class for pupils in grades five through eight. "Grade placement deviation" (p. 455) here refers to differences between a pupil's actual grade placement and that grade to which he or she would have been assigned according to chronological age. Related investigations have indicated careful attention to results following either grade placement deviations based on birth date alone (e.g., Baer 1958) or deviations following specific educational interventions such as early admission to school based on mental and physical tests (e.g., Hobson 1948, 1963; Worcester 1956). These studies will be reviewed in the next section.

Elwell (1958) reported successful accelerative methods for intellectually able fourth and seventh graders; however, he noted some curricular adjustments were necessary for fourth and seventh graders in arithmetic and for seventh graders in geography and history. Nonetheless, little social maladjustment was cited for children who had been accelerated in groups. A related investigation

(Morgan 1959) presented a five-year follow-up of a combined sex sample of twenty-three very bright youths who had a reported mean Stanford-Binet IQ of 149. Twelve students were accelerated one year on the average; the remaining eleven comprised the comparison group. According to Morgan's report, "The accelerated [group] equaled the nonaccelerates in school achievement, surpassed them in academic distinction and social leadership, and tended to have better emotional adjustment" (1959, p. 653). Therefore, grade-skipping at the elementary level had a decidedly beneficial result for a bright though small sample of accelerants.

A series of important investigations on acceleration at the elementary level was conducted during the early 1960s in the Wisconsin public schools (see Klausmeier 1963; Klausmeier, Goodwin, and Teckla 1968; Klausmeier and Ripple 1962; Ripple 1961). Klausmeier and his colleagues were interested in the effects of acceleration on intellectually able old-in-grade second graders. Fifty-two students who were above the median chronological age of all second graders and who had Kuhlman-Anderson IQs of at least 115 were "ordered in pairs, matched by sex, and then randomly assigned, one from each pair to the accelerated group, the other to the control group of nonaccelerates" (Klausmeier and Ripple, 1962, p. 93). The twenty-six older accelerants then attended a five-week summer session prior to their entrance into fourth grade. Six control groups were reported: "Two groups of 26 nonaccelerated 3rd graders of SLA [superior learning abilities], 1 above and 1 below median CA; 2 groups of 26 nonaccelerated 4th graders of SLA, 1 above and 1 below median CA; and 2 groups of 26 nonaccelerated 4th graders of average learning ability, 1 above and 1 below median CA" (ibid.). This design permitted evaluation of the effects of acceleration while experimentally controlling chronological age and mental ability.

Evaluations of subjects' academic and socioemotional adjustment were reported after one year (Klausmeier and Ripple 1962, Ripple 1961), two years (Klausmeier 1963), and six years (Klausmeier, Goodwin, and Teckla 1968). After two years, no unfavorable socioemotional, academic, or physical correlates of acceleration were found. Klausmeier and co-workers (1968) followed up twenty-two of the initial twenty-three accelerants after six years; in addition, data were pooled from fourteen children accelerated from grades three to five. Four control groups yielded base-rate data permitting evaluation of the effects of chronological age and mental ability.

Results from this Wisconsin research series may be summarized in three points. First, on fourteen of fifteen cognitive tests, neither accelerated group performed significantly differently from a group of twenty-seven comparably bright students who averaged six months older. Second, no differences were reported between the two accelerated groups despite the fact that each had been accelerated at different points in elementary school. Third, the accelerants' participation in school activities and in athletics was comparable to that of older, bright nonaccelerants.

Overall accelerative methods at the elementary level, then, indicate positive academic performance and social adjustment to be no different, on the average, from that of comparably bright, though somewhat younger-aged students. The next section will set forth results concerning the earliest educational level at which acceleration has been reported, the age at which the educational lock step begins.

Early Admission to Elementary School

At approximately the time the United States entered the "space race" with the Soviet Union, American educators were advocating early entrance to elementary school as an accelerative method analogous to compensatory educational interventions for the disadvantaged (see Klausmeier 1958, McCandless 1957). It was noted previously that approximately three-quarters of elementary grade placement variance was attributable to factors other than achievement performance in six basic cognitive skills areas (Holmes and Finley 1957). Accordingly, most of the variation in elementary grade placement depended upon chronological not mental age at the time the child enrolled into school. Therefore, proponents of early admission advocated provision for the intellectually able, overage student to gain a year's time at the outset of schooling.

An example of how chronological age-grade grouping adversely affects the education of intellectually precocious youths recently has been reported (Stanley 1976d, pp. 5-6). Suppose an extremely bright child (e.g., of Stanford-Binet IQ 140) planned to enter kindergarten in a school system in which one must become 5 years old before 31 December in the year during which he/she desires to gain admission. The average student would be approximately 5 years, 2 months old and have an IQ of 100. At the same chronological age but with an IQ of 140, a child would have a mental age of 7 years, 3 months. This would place the bright child slightly *above* the average child entering *second* grade. According to Stanley, a child's date of birth either attenuates or aggravates the degree of one's academic "retardation," assuming school admission is based upon some fixed date before which a child must be a certain age in order to enter. If we follow Stanley's example further, then a child born on 31 December and aged 4 years, 8 months at entrance to kindergarten would have a mental age of 6 years, 6 months, while one born on 1 January of the same year would have a mental age *more than two and a half years higher than the average kindergarten pupil!* This discrepancy due to school admission based on chronological and not mental age prompted Stanley to note, "If you expect to have unusually bright children, arrange to have them born late in the year so that they will be somewhat less overqualified than if they are born during the winter" (ibid., p. 6).

The remainder of this section summarizes four studies; three report on early admission to school (Birch 1954, Hobson 1963, Worcester 1956), while the fourth compares underage and overage students' academic performance and social behavior (Baer 1958). Because the most recently published report is based upon the earliest sample of underage entrants, we will consider it first.

Hobson (1963) described a follow-up of underage pupils first admitted to

Brookline, Massachusetts, schools in 1932 (cf. Hobson 1948). His design called for evaluation of two objectives: comparison of the high school scholastic performance and extracurricular activities of students who were admitted to school early based on mental and physical tests with that of their high school classmates; and evaluation of the relative success of college admissions for the two groups. Two samples of underaged students were reported. Group A comprised 550 underaged pupils admitted by tests (ABT) who were compared with 3,891 Brookline public school classmates. Group B included 91 underaged and 274 regular-aged pupils, subjects initially described in the 1948 report.

Academic performance data were available for group A; both academic performance and extracurricular activities data were reported for group B. According to Hobson, group A boys and girls exceeded their older classmates in percentages graduating from high school with honors and by the margin who gained entrance to an honor society. Group B's scholastic performance, based on separate course marks received during four years of high school, was significantly better than that of the conventional-aged pupils during 1946 and 1947. Also, group B's average number of extracurricular activities exceeded that of regular students over the four-year high school period, but the underaged boys seldom achieved outstanding recognition in the so-called contact sports. Group B's college admissions data for the 1946–47 cohort were quite favorable. According to Hobson, "A significantly larger percentage of underaged boys and girls went on to post secondary education" (1963, p. 165). In addition, if only four-year accredited college data were included in the analysis, the test-screened males and females exceeded their regular-age classmates by 22.6 percent and 21.0 percent, respectively.

Hobson's (1963) results may be summarized in four points. First, scholastic performance continued and even increased throughout elementary and secondary education for underage students admitted early to school on the basis of mental and physical tests. Second, underage ABT pupils participated in extracurricular activities more often than conventional-age classmates, although their participation in contact sports was not as great. Third, ABT youths exceeded classmates in the number of honors and awards earned at high school graduation. Fourth, more ABT high school graduates sought and gained admission to accredited four-year colleges.

A second series of early entrance studies in urban and rural regions of Nebraska during the early 1950s was reported by Worcester (1956). Prior to 1955, and according to the law, a mental age of 5 years, 3 months was the criterion for admission to Nebraska public school kindergarten.[3] In addition, early admission was contingent upon an examiner's judgment of social and

---

[3]According to Worcester (1956), the mental age criterion for admission to kindergarten was changed from 5 years, 3 months to 5 years, 6 months in 1955. Apparently, it was thought that this increase in age required for school admission would bolster chances for a higher success rate with the early entrants compared to older, conventional entrants. From the point of view of acceleration proponents like Worcester, this turned out to be an unfortunate amendment to an otherwise judicious Nebraska law.

physical readiness. Two points concerning Worcester's review of the Nebraska programs are interesting in light of Hobson's Brookline, Massachusetts, findings. First, the amount of acceleration was relatively less for the Nebraska series. However, according to Worcester, given the improbability of midyear promotions within the Nebraska school systems, the underaged pupils actually gained one year compared with what that state's conventional age-grade grouping otherwise would have permitted. Second, IQs of the Massachusetts and Nebraska samples were comparable, although neither state's underaged population demonstrated unusual intellectual precocity. IQs averaged approximately 110 for the underaged who were an average of about 8 months younger than conventional admissions students.

Worcester reported findings that supported early school admission for 381 Lincoln pupils and for smaller samples of underaged students who attended rural Nebraska elementary schools.

> There were no statistical differences in physical development. In academic work, the younger did as well or better than their older classmates. Judged by their peers or by teachers' ratings, they are socially and emotionally as well or better adjusted. They have as good or better coordination. They are accepted by their peers. They like school. They do as well or better than those of the same age who were a year later in getting started in school. Indeed, no negative effects have been discerned. As compared with those who took the test and did not pass it, the younger ones had gained a year of school life without loss in social adjustment. (1956, p. 28)

On the basis of this evidence, Worcester concluded that chronologically younger aged pupils who were able to demonstrate academic readiness on mental tests should be admitted early to elementary school. Moreover, if we consider that the mean IQ for underaged students reportedly was 110, then by extrapolation, pupils of greater intellectual ability defined by higher mental age are better qualified for early admission to school.

A third investigation (Birch 1954) afforded a two-year evaluation of forty-three children admitted underage to the first grade in Pittsburgh schools. Based on principals' and teachers' judgments of educational and socioemotional adjustment, thirty students received completely positive evaluations. Only five of the forty-three students received any negative evaluations; yet Birch noted these evaluations were not totally characteristic of the five children. In addition, Birch pointed out that Pittsburgh schools advised early entrance for those with IQs of 135 and above. Therefore, these data not only are consistent with Hobson's and Worcester's findings but also denote the advantages of one year's acceleration for intellectually able 5-year-olds.

The fourth study reported a retrospective experimental design in which seventy-three children with birth dates in January and February were matched with seventy-three children whose birthdates were in November and December of the same year (Baer 1958). The young-in-grade pupils were matched with the old-in-grade students for IQ, sex, and in two-thirds of the cases, the school they had entered. Mean IQs for both groups were approximately 111, and equivalent IQ ranges from 100 to 130 were reported.

It is important to note that neither group in Baer's study was accelerated through early admission to school at ages younger than conventional. In other words, the design specified an eleven-year retrospective comparison between underage and overage groups of pupils. Given the fact that the groups had comparable mean IQs but differed in chronological age from 9 to 12 months, one reasonably might expect the old-in-grade pupils to have higher mental ages and, thus, to outperform the younger pupils. Baer's results indicated this indeed was the case: "During the elementary school years . . . overage students were marked significantly higher than the underage student, but the differences between overage and underage students tended to decrease as higher grade levels were reached" (1958, pp. 17–18).

Two interesting and important findings emerged from Baer's data. First, sex differences were greater than underage versus overage group differences on three of the personal trait ratings: dependability, attitude toward school regulations, and emotional stability. This implies that the underage pupils were no different from the overage students on important indices of personality quite related to socioemotional adjustment. Second, according to Baer, the young-in-grade pupils made *average* school progress, and "as a group, they made average marks in subjects, average scores on achievement tests, received average ratings by their teachers on personal traits, and did not mark significantly more problems on the problem inventory than did the overage students" (ibid., p. 19). If the young-in-grade students made average school progress but were surpassed in performance by the old-in-grade pupils, then the overage students must have made better than average academic progress. If that was the case, then it was quite likely the overage students were, indeed, quite ready for an accelerative intervention of perhaps one year, possibly at the time of admission to elementary school. Moreover, old-in-grade and *very* bright (e.g., IQ = 140) students most likely would excel (even these bright students mentioned by Baer) in achievement and would serve as even more appropriate candidates for *at least* one year's acceleration in school.

Thus, data from four investigations of early admission to either kindergarten or first grade and studies comparing overage with underage students unequivocally favor acceleration through early admission to school. Underage pupils who can demonstrate mental age performance comparable to mean performance of the grade they desire to enter should be permitted to enroll in that grade. Also, bright overage pupils are at a distinct disadvantage in that certainly they are competent to handle more appropriately difficult curricular materials but, nonetheless, they must remain in their "proper" chronological age grade.

SUMMARY

The relative merits of enrichment versus acceleration for gifted students no doubt will continue to be debated and researched in future years. At present, an objective evaluation of the empirical findings leads us to the following conclusions: (1)

Academic enrichment (whether it is "relevant" or "irrelevant") may be worthwhile for all students, and not specifically for the intellectually gifted. In this way, enrichment programs seem to be more open to accusations of "elitism" than acceleration is, since no "special" curricula need to be established for the accelerated student. (2) No studies have shown enrichment to provide superior results over accelerative methods. Enrichment at best may only defer boredom until a later time. (3) Much resistance to acceleration (or "grade-skipping") is based on preconceived notions and irrational grounds, rather than on an examination of the evidence. Most resistance stems from concerns about the socioemotional development of the accelerated student. When the facts are studied, however, we find that such adjustment problems generally are minimal and short-lived. (4) Accelerated students are shown to perform at least as well as, and often better than, "normal-aged" control students, on both academic and nonacademic measures.

It seems evident that, according to the findings of most of the studies reported here, acceleration appears to be the more feasible method for meeting the needs of gifted students. We would expect to find a diminishing adherence to the age-grade lock step as more educators, administrators, and parents become aware of the facts as opposed to the myths.

REFERENCES

Addicott, I. O. 1930. An experimental class for bright children. *Department of Elementary School Principals' Bulletin* 9: 287–93.

Adler, M. J., Pass, L. E., and Wright, E. N. 1963. A study of the effects of an accelerated programme in Toronto secondary schools. *Ontario Journal of Educational Research* 6: 1–22.

Albers, M. E., and Seagoe, M. V. 1947. Enrichment for superior students in algebra classes. *Journal of Educational Research* 40: 481–95.

Allison, J. M., and Bloom, B. S. 1950. The operation and evaluation of a college placement test program. *Journal of General Education* 4: 221–33.

Alltucker, M. M. 1924. Is the pedagogically accelerated student a misfit in senior high school? *School Review* 32: 193–202.

Anderson, H. A. 1954. Principles for selecting methods and materials to promote growth through reading. *Supplementary Educational Monographs* 81: 85–89.

Bachtold, L. M. 1974. Effects of learning achievement on verbal creativity of gifted students. *Psychology in the Schools* 11: 226–28.

———, and Werner, E. E. 1970. An evaluation of teaching creative skills to gifted students in grades 5 and 6. *Journal of Educational Research* 63: 253–56.

Baer, C. J. 1958. The school progress and adjustment of underage and overage students. *Journal of Educational Psychology* 49: 17–19.

Barbe, W. B. 1954. A follow-up study of graduates of special classes for gifted children. *Dissertation Abstracts* 14: 299.

———. 1955. Evaluation of special classes for gifted children. *Exceptional Children* 22: 60–62.

Bear, R. H. 1926. Factors in the achievement of college freshmen. *School and Society* 24: 370–72.

Berg, I. A., and Larsen, R. P. 1945. A comparative study of students entering college one or more semesters before graduation from high school. *Journal of Educational Research* 39: 33–41.

Birch, J. W. 1954. Early school admission for mentally advanced children. *Exceptional Children* 21: 84–87.

————, and Reynolds, M. C. 1963. The gifted. *Review of Educational Research* 33 (1): 83–98.

Blaudauf, R. J. 1959. A comparison of the extent of educational growth of mentally advanced pupils in the Cedar Rapids Experiment. *Journal of Educational Research* 52: 181–83.

Bloom, B. S., and Allison, J. M. 1949. Developing a college placement test program. *Journal of General Education* 3: 210–15.

————, and Ward, F. C. 1952. The Chicago Bachelor of Arts degree after ten years. *Journal of Higher Education* 23: 459–67.

Bonsall, M. R. 1955. Reactions of gifted high school pupils to elementary education. *California Journal of Educational Research* 6: 107–09.

Bowman, L. L. 1955. Educational opportunities for gifted children in California. *California Journal of Educational Research* 6: 195–99.

Braumbaugh, F. 1944. A school for gifted children. *Childhood Education* 20: 325–27.

Braunstein, F. L. 1968. The effect of an elementary school experience in a first grade learner program on academically talented children in Valley Stream, New York. *Dissertation Abstracts International* 28 (10-A): 3989–90.

Bridges, S. 1973. *Problems of the gifted child: IQ 150.* New York: Crane and Russak Company.

Briggs, L. L. 1947. Intensive classes for superior students. *Journal of Educational Psychology* 38: 207–15.

Brown, M. V. 1949. Teaching an intellectually gifted group. *Elementary School Journal* 49: 380–88.

Burks, B. S., Jensen, D. W., and Terman, L. M. 1930. The promise of youth. *Genetic Studies of Genius,* vol. III. Stanford, Calif.: Stanford University Press.

Chauncey, H. 1958. How tests help us identify the academically talented. *Journal of the National Educational Association* 47: 230–31.

————, and Hilton, T. L. 1965. Are aptitude tests valid for the highly able? *Science* 148: 1297–304.

College Entrance Examination Board. 1973. *College Advanced Placement Policies.* Princeton, N.J.: College Board.

————. 1974. *Sophomore Standing through Advanced Placement.* (Supplement). Princeton, N.J.: College Board.

Cook, W. W. 1948. Individual differences and curriculum practice. *Journal of Educational Psychology* 39: 141–48.

Cox, C. M. 1926. The early mental traits of three hundred geniuses. *Genetic Studies of Genius,* vol. II. Stanford, Calif.: Stanford University Press.

Crockenberg, S. B. 1972. Creativity tests: A boon or boondoggle for education? *Review of Educational Research* 42: 27–45.

Cutts, N. E., and Moseley, N. 1953a. Bright children and the curriculum. *Educational Administration and Supervision* 39: 168–73.

————. 1953b. Providing for the bright child in a heterogeneous group. *Educational Administration and Supervision* 39: 225–30.

Danielson, C. L. 1929. A study of the effect of a definite course of reading in general literature upon achievement in content subjects with children of superior mental ability. *Journal of Educational Psychology* 20: 610–21.

Dransfield, J. E. 1933. Administration of enrichment to superior children in the typical classroom. Teachers. New York: Teachers College of Columbia University. College Contributions to Education, No. 558.

Dunn, B. J. 1972. The El Monte Project for high risk talent retrieval. *Gifted Child Quarterly* 16: 235–39.

Dwyer, P. S. 1939. Correlation between age at entrance and success in college. *Journal of Educational Psychology* 30: 251–64.

Edelston, H. 1950. Educational failure in high intelligence quotient: A clinical study. *Journal of Genetic Psychology* 77: 85–116.

Elder, H. E. 1927. A study of rapid acceleration in the elementary school. *Journal of Educational Research* 15: 5–9.

Elwell, C. 1958. Acceleration of the gifted. *Gifted Child Quarterly* 2: 21–23.

Engle, T. L. 1935. Achievement of pupils who have had double promotions in elementary school. *Elementary School Journal* 36: 185–89.

Enzmann, A. M. 1963. A comparison of academic achievement of gifted students enrolled in regular and separate curricula. *Gifted Child Quarterly* 7(4): 176–79.

Ewing, T. N., and Gilbert, W. M. 1967. Controlled study of the effects of counseling on the scholastic achievements of students of superior ability. *Journal of Counseling Psychology* 14: 235–39.

Feldman, D. H., and Bratton, J. C. 1972. Relativity and giftedness: Implications for equality of educational opportunity. *Exceptional Children* 38: 491–92.

Fine, H. G. 1953. The work group program for gifted children in a Detroit elementary school. *Dissertation Abstracts* 13: 1062.

Flesher, M. A. 1946. An intensive study of seventy-six women who obtained their undergraduate degrees in three years or less. *Journal of Educational Research* 39: 602–12.

————, and Pressey, S. L. 1955. War-time accelerates ten years after. *Journal of Educational Psychology* 46: 228–38.

Fliegler, L. A., and Bish, C. E. 1959. The gifted and talented. *Review of Educational Research* 29: 408–50.

Fox, L. H. 1974. A mathematics program for fostering precocious achievement. In J. C. Stanley, D. P. Keating, and L. H. Fox (eds.), *Mathematical talent: Discovery, description, and development.* Baltimore, Md.: The Johns Hopkins University Press, pp. 101–25.

Frierson, E. L. 1969. The gifted. *Review of Educational Research* 39: 25–27.

Fund for the Advancement of Education of the Ford Foundation. 1953. *Bridging the gap between school and college.* New York: Research Division of the Fund.

————. 1957. *They went to college early.* New York: Research Division of the Fund.

Gallagher, J. J., Greenman, M., Kernes, M., and King, A. 1960. Individual classroom adjustments for gifted children in elementary schools. *Exceptional Children* 26: 409–22.

————, and Rogge, W. 1966. The gifted. *Review of Educational Research* 36: 37–55.

George, W. C. 1976. Accelerating mathematical instruction for the mathematically talented. *Gifted Child Quarterly* 20: 246–61.

————, and Denham, S. A. 1976. Curriculum experimentation for the mathematically talented. In D. P. Keating (ed.), *Intellectual talent: Research and development.* Baltimore, Md.: The Johns Hopkins University Press, pp. 103–31.

Getzels, J. W., and Jackson, P. W. 1962. *Creativity and intelligence.* New York: Wiley.

Gilfoy, L. M. 1958. Educating the most able high school students at Indianapolis. *Education* 79: 25–27.

Glennon, V. J. 1957. Arithmetic for the gifted child. *Elementary School Journal* 58: 91–96.

Goddard, H. H. 1928. *School training of gifted children.* Yonkers-on-Hudson, N.Y.: World Book.

_____. 1933. The gifted child. *Journal of Educational Sociology* 6: 354–61.

Gould, A. 1939. Education for gifted pupils in the secondary schools of Los Angeles. *Journal of Educational Sociology* 13: 103–11.

Gowan, J. C. 1961. *An annotated bibliography on the academically talented.* Washington, D.C.: National Educational Association of the United States.

_____. 1971. The relationship between creativity and giftedness. *Gifted Child Quarterly* 15: 239–43.

Gray, H. A. 1930. Some factors in the undergraduate careers of young college students. Teachers College Contributions to Education, No. 437. New York: Teachers College, Columbia University.

Gross, F. P., and Sabatino, D. A. 1965. Role of the school psychologist in evaluating an experimental program for gifted students. *Journal of School Psychology* 3: 56–61.

Hall, G. V. 1958. Programs for the benefit of able students. *Education* 79: 28–33.

Handy, M. L., and Lindstrom, A. L. 1944. Special education for gifted children. *Journal of Exceptional Children* 10: 103–07, 126.

Hanson, V. J. 1968. The enrichment program for high ability students in the Sweetwater Union high school district. *Dissertation Abstracts International* 29 (2-A): 405–06.

Hausdorff, H., and Farr, S. D. 1965. The effects of grading practices on the marks of gifted sixth-grade children. *Journal of Educational Research* 59: 169–72.

Havighurst, R. J., Stivers, E., and De Haan, R. F. 1955. A survey of education of gifted children. *Supplementary Educational Monographs* 83: 1–114.

Hayes, M. 1954. Promoting guidance and stimulation in personal reading. *Supplementary Educational Monographs* 81: 178–82.

Herr, W. A. 1937. Junior high school accelerants and their peers in senior high school: The social factors. *School Review* 45: 287–99.

Hildreth, G. 1943. Stanford-Binet retests of gifted children. *Journal of Educational Research* 37: 297–302.

_____. 1952. *Educating gifted children at Hunter College Elementary School.* New York: Harper & Row.

Hobson, J. R. 1948. Mental age as a workable criterion for school admission. *Elementary School Journal* 48: 312–21.

_____. 1963. High school performance of underage pupils initially admitted to kindergarten on the basis of physical and psychological examinations. *Educational and Psychological Measurement* 23(1): 159–70.

Hollingworth, L. S. 1929. *Gifted children: Their nature and nurture.* New York: Macmillan.

————. 1931. Special gifts and special deficiencies. In C. Murchison (ed.), *A handbook of child psychology.* Worcester, Mass.: Clark University Press.

————. 1932. The child of very superior intelligence as a special problem in social adjustment. *Proceedings of the First International Congress on Mental Hygiene* 2: 47–60.

————. 1936. The Terman classes at Public School 500. *Journal of Educational Sociology* 13: 90–102.

————. 1939. Problems of the relationship between elementary and secondary schools in the case of highly intelligent pupils. *Journal of Educational Sociology* 13: 90–102.

————. 1942. *Children above 180 IQ, Stanford-Binet: Origin and Development.* Yonkers-on-Hudson, N.Y.: World Book.

Holmes, H. W. 1913. Youth and the dean: The relations between academic discipline, scholarship, and age of entrance to college. *Harvard Graduate Magazine* 21: 599–610.

Holmes, J. A., and Finley, C. J. 1957. Under and overage grade placements and school achievement. *Journal of Educational Psychology* 48: 447–56.

Houghton, M., and Douglas, H. A. 1935. Age and grade classifications as factors of achievement in high school economics. *School Review* 43: 766–70.

Husband, R. W. 1923. Studies in student personnel at Dartmouth. *Journal of Personnel Research* 2: 70–79.

Isaacs, A. F. 1971. Giftedness, the Greeks, and common sense judgment. *Gifted Child Quarterly* 15: 64, 68.

————. 1973. Giftedness and careers. *Gifted Child Quarterly* 17: 57–59.

Jensen, D. W. 1927. The gifted child. *Journal of Educational Research* 15: 126–33, 198–206.

Jones, A. L. 1916. College standing of freshmen of various ages. *School and Society* 3: 717–20.

Keating, D. P. (ed.). 1976. *Intellectual talent: Research and development.* Baltimore, Md.: The Johns Hopkins University Press.

Keating, D. P., and Stanley, J. C. 1972. Extreme measures for the exceptionally gifted in mathematics and science. *Educational Researcher* 1: 3–7.

Kett, J. 1974. History of age grouping in America. In Coleman, J. S. et al. (eds.), *Youth: Transition to adulthood,* a report to the panel of youth of the President's Science Advisory Committee. Chicago: University of Chicago Press.

Keys, N. 1938. The underage student in high school and college. *University of California Publications in Education* 7: 145–271.

Klausmeier, H. J. 1958. Critical questions related to the education of the gifted. *Education* 79: 39–44.

————. 1963. Effects of accelerating bright older elementary pupils: A follow-up. *Journal of Educational Psychology* 54(3): 165–71.

————, Goodwin, W. L., and Teckla, R. 1968. Effects of accelerating bright older elementary pupils: A second follow-up. *Journal of Educational Psychology* 59: 53–58.

————, and Ripple, R. E. 1962. Effects of accelerating bright older pupils from second to fourth grade. *Journal of Educational Psychology* 53: 93–100.

Kogan, N. 1955. Studies of college students. *Journal of Counseling Psychology* 2: 129–36.

Lamson, E. E. 1930. *A study of young gifted children in senior high school.* New York: Teachers College of Columbia University.

Laycock, F. 1964. Acceleration for the gifted? A brief note on the use of evidence. *Perceptual and Motor Skills* 19: 1006.

Lazar, A. L., Gensley, J., and Gowan, J. C. 1972. Developing positive attitudes toward curriculum planning for young gifted children. *Gifted Child Quarterly* 16: 27-31.

Learned, W. S., and Wood, B. D. 1938. *The student and his knowledge.* New York: Carnegie Foundation for the Advancement of Teaching.

Lesse, J. 1957. What the gifted child needs is inspirational teaching. *New York State Education* 44: 615-17.

Lloyd-Jones, E. McD. 1929. *Student personnel work at Northwestern University.* New York: Harper and Brothers.

Lorge, I., and Hollingworth, L. S. 1936. Adult status of highly intelligent children. *Journal of Genetic Psychology* 49: 215-26.

MacDonald, B., Gammie, A., and Nisbet, J. 1964. The careers of a gifted group. *Educational Researcher* 6: 216-19.

McCandless, B. R. 1957. Should a bright child start to school before he's five? *Education* 77: 370-75.

McWilliams, E. M., and Birch, J. W. 1957. Counseling gifted children. *Vocational Guidance Quarterly* 5: 91-94.

Martinson, R. A. 1960. The California study of programs for gifted pupils. *Exceptional Children* 26: 339-43.

————, Hermanson, D., and Banks, G. 1972. An independent study-seminar program for the gifted. *Exceptional Children* 38: 421-26.

Mauger, P. A., and Kolmodin, C. A. 1975. Long-term predictive validity of the Scholastic Aptitude Test. *Journal of Educational Psychology* 67: 847-51.

Meeker, M. 1968. Differential syndromes of giftedness and curriculum planning: A 4-year follow-up. *Journal of Special Education* 2(2): 185-96.

Meister, M., and Odell, H. A. 1951. What provisions for the education of gifted students? *NASSP* (National Association of Secondary School Principals) *Bulletin* 35: 30-46.

Miles, C. C. 1946. Gifted Children. In Carmichael, L. (ed.). *Manual of child psychology.* New York: Wiley.

Montour, K. M. 1976. Three precocious boys: What happened to them? *Gifted Child Quarterly* 20: 173-79.

————. 1977. William James Sidis, the broken twig. *American Psychologist* 32(4): 265-79.

————. 1978. The highly precocious: How well did they succeed? In J. C. Stanley, W. C. George, and C. H. Solano (eds.), *Educational programs and intellectual prodigies.* Baltimore, Md.: Study of Mathematically Precocious Youth, Department of Psychology, The Johns Hopkins University, pp. 47-61.

Moore, M. W. 1933. Study of young high school graduates. Teachers College Contributions to Education, No. 583. New York: Teachers College of Columbia University.

Morgan, A. B. 1957. Critical factors in the academic acceleration of gifted children: Hypotheses based on clinical data. *Psychological Reports* 3: 71-77.

_____. 1959. Critical factors in the academic acceleration of gifted children: A follow-up study. *Psychological Reports* 5: 649–53.

Mosso, A. M. 1944. An experiment with and for pupils of superior ability. *School Review* 52: 26–32.

_____. 1945. A seminar for superior high-school seniors. *School Review* 53: 464–70.

Nelson, E. A., and Carlson, E. G. 1945. Special education for gifted children: Evaluation at the end of three years. *Journal of Exceptional Children* 12: 6–13, 24.

Nevin, D. 1977. Young prodigies take off under special program. *Smithsonian* 8(7): 76–81, 160.

Newland, T. E. 1941. The education of exceptional children: The mentally gifted. *Review of Educational Research* 11: 277–87.

_____. 1953. The gifted. *Review of Educational Research* 23: 417–31.

_____. 1976. *The gifted in socioeducational perspective.* Englewood Cliffs, N.J.: Prentice-Hall.

Odell, C. W. 1933. The effect of early entrance upon college success. *Journal of Educational Research* 26: 510–12.

Oden, M. H. 1968. The fulfillment of promise: 40-year follow-up of the Terman gifted group. *Genetic Psychology Monographs* 77: 3–93.

Oliver, A. I. 1954. The gifted pupil: A challenge to educators. *Education* 74: 312–22.

Osburn, W. J., and Rohan, B. J. 1931. *Enriching the curriculum for gifted children: A book of guidance for educational administrators and teachers.* New York: Macmillan.

Parker, C. 1956. A measured experiment with mentally advanced children. *American School Board Journal* 133: 23–24.

Payne, A. F. 1930. An experiment in human engineering at the College of the City of New York. *School and Society* 32: 292–94.

Phillips, P. C. 1934. What age college entrance? *Amherst Graduates' Quarterly* 24: 12–21.

Pittenger, B. F. 1917. Efficiency of college students as conditioned by age at entrance and size of high school. *16th Yearbook of the National Society for the Study of Education:* 9–112.

Plowman, P. D. 1969. Programming for the gifted child. *Exceptional Children* 35: 547–51.

Powell, H. R. 1954. Specific patterns of classroom organization. *Supplementary Educational Monographs* 81: 162–65.

Pregler, H. 1954. The Colfax Plan. *Exceptional Children* 20: 198–201, 222.

Pressey, S. L. 1944a. Acceleration the hard way. *Journal of Educational Research* 37: 561–70.

_____. 1944b. Educational acceleration and post-war scientific leadership. *Psychological Bulletin* 41: 681–88.

_____. 1944c. A neglected crucial psycho-educational problem. *Journal of Psychology* 18: 217–34.

_____. 1949. *Educational acceleration: Appraisal and basic problems.* Bureau of Educational Research Monographs, No. 31. Columbus, Ohio: The Ohio State University Press.

_____. 1955. Acceleration: Basic principles and recent research. *Proceedings of the 1954 Conference on Testing Problems, Educational Testing Service:* 107–12.

————. 1962. Age and the doctorate: Then and now. *Journal of Higher Education* 33: 153–60.

————. 1967. "Fordling" accelerates ten years after. *Journal of Counseling Psychology* 14: 73–80.

Regensberg, J. 1926. Emotional handicaps to intellectual achievement in supernormal children. *Mental Hygiene* 10: 480–94.

————. 1931. Studies of emotional success and failure in supernormal children. *Archives of Psychology* 129: 1–150.

Remmers, H. H. 1930. Distinguished students: What they are and why. *Bulletin of Purdue University* 31(2).

Rippin, M. 1969. Teaching: Round table. *Journal of emotional Education* 9: 33–39.

Ripple, R. E. 1961. A controlled experiment in acceleration from the second to the fourth grade. *Gifted Child Quarterly* 5: 119–20.

Rowe, E. R. 1967. Creative writing and the gifted child. *Exceptional Children* 34: 279–82.

Ryder, V. 1972. A docent program in science for gifted elementary pupils. *Exceptional Children* 38: 629–31.

Sarbaugh, M. E. 1934. The young college student. *University of Buffalo Studies* 9: 58–73.

Saslaw, M. S. 1961. Gifted young scientists' laboratory research program. *Gifted Child Quarterly* 5: 3–4, 6.

Sato, I. S. 1974. The culturally different child: The dawning of his day. *Exceptional Children* 40: 527–76.

Sears, R. R. 1977. Sources of life satisfaction of the Terman gifted men. *American Psychologist* 32: 119–28.

Seegers, J. C. 1949. Teaching bright children. *Elementary School Journal* 49: 511–15.

Shearer, E. M., and Fannin, L. 1949. Reading for the bright child. *Library Journal* 74: 1289–91.

Shouksmith, G., and Taylor, J. W. 1964. The effect of counseling on the achievement of highly able pupils. *British Journal of Educational Psychology* 34(1): 51–57.

Shouse, R. D. 1937. Acceleration of high school students by groups. *Educational Administration and Supervision* 23: 51–62.

Shufele, M. 1953. *The gifted child in the regular classroom.* New York: Teachers College Bureau of Publications, Columbia University.

Silverman, Y., and Jones, V. 1932. A study of early entrance to college. *Journal of Educational Psychology* 23: 58–72.

Solano, C. H. 1976. Precocity and adult failure: Shattering the myth. Manuscript available from the Study of Mathematically Precocious Youth, Department of Psychology, The Johns Hopkins University, Baltimore, Md. 21218.

————, and George, W. C. 1976. College courses and educational facilitation for the gifted. *Gifted Child Quarterly* 20(3): 274–85.

Stanley, J. C. 1973. Accelerating the educational progress of intellectually gifted youths. *Educational Psychologist* 10: 133–46.

————. 1976a. Use of tests to discover talent. In D. P. Keating (ed.), *Intellectual talent: Research and development.* Baltimore, Md.: The Johns Hopkins University Press, pp. 3–22.

————. 1976b. Special fast-mathematics courses taught by college professors to fourth-through twelfth-graders. In D. P. Keating (ed.), *Intellectual talent: Research and development*. Baltimore, Md.: The Johns Hopkins University Press, pp. 132–59.

————. 1976c. Test better finder of great math talent than teachers. *American Psychologist* 31: 313–14.

————. 1976d. Brilliant youth: Improving the quality and speed of their education. Speech presented at the annual meeting of the American Psychological Association, Washington, D.C., 3 Sept.

————. 1976e. Identifying and nurturing the intellectually gifted. *Phi Delta Kappan* 58: 234–37.

————. 1976f. Concern for intellectually talented youths: How it originated and fluctuated. *Journal of Clinical Child Psychology* 5: 38–42.

————. 1977. Rationale of the Study of Mathematically Precocious Youth (SMPY) during its first five years of promoting educational acceleration. in J. C. Stanley, W. C. George, and C. H. Solano (eds.), *The gifted and the creative: A fifty-year perspective*. Baltimore, Md.: The Johns Hopkins University Press, pp. 75–112.

————. 1978a. Educational non-acceleration: An international tragedy. *G/C/T* 1(3): 2–6, 54–57, 60–63.

————. 1978b. The predictive value of the SAT for brilliant seventh- and eighth-graders. *The College Board Review* 106: 31–37.

————. 1979. The study and facilitation of talent for mathematics. In A. Harry Passow (ed.), *The gifted and the talented: Their education and development*. The 78th Yearbook of the National Society for the Study of Education.

————, and George, W. C. 1978. Now we are six: The ever-expanding SMPY. *G/C/T* 1(1): 9–11, 43–44, 50–51.

————, George, W. C., and Solano, C. H. (eds.). 1977. *The gifted and the creative: A fifty-year perspective*. Baltimore, Md.: The Johns Hopkins University Press.

————, George, W. C., and Solano, C. H. (eds.). 1978. *Educational programs and intellectual prodigies*. Baltimore, Md.: Study of Mathematically Precocious Youth, Department of Psychology, The Johns Hopkins University.

————, Keating, D. P., and Fox, L. H. (eds.). 1974. *Mathematical talent: Discovery, description, and development*. Baltimore, Md.: The Johns Hopkins University Press.

Strabel, E. 1936a. The accelerated high school graduate. *University of Buffalo Studies* 13: 79–99.

————. 1936b. A comparison of the various atypically aged groups. *University of Buffalo Studies* 13: 113–23.

Sumption, M. R. 1941. *Three hundred gifted children: A follow-up study of the results of special education of gifted children*. Yonkers-on-Hudson, N.Y.: World Book.

Taylor, K. W. 1943. Creative intelligence: Are we giving it a chance? *Understanding the Child* 12: 14–16.

Terman, L. M. 1916. *The measurement of intelligence*. Boston: Houghton-Mifflin.

————. 1925. Mental and physical traits of a thousand gifted children. *Genetic Studies of Genius*, vol. I. Stanford, Calif.: Stanford University Press.

————. 1931. The gifted child. In C. Murchison (ed.), *Handbook of child psychology*. Worcester, Mass.: Clark University Press.

————. 1954. The discovery and encouragement of exceptional talent. *American Psychologist* 9: 221–30.

_____, and Oden, M. H. 1947. The gifted child grows up: Twenty-five years' follow-up of a superior group. *Genetic Studies of Genius,* vol. IV. Stanford, Calif.: Stanford University Press.

_____, and Oden, M. H. 1959. The gifted group at midlife. *Genetic Studies of Genius,* vol. V. Stanford, Calif.: Stanford University Press.

Thom, D. A., and Newell, N. 1945. Hazards of the high IQ. *Mental Hygiene* 29: 61–77.

Thorndike, E. L. 1941. Gifted children in small cities. *Teachers College Record* 42: 420–27.

Time. 1977. Smorgasbord for an IQ of 150. 109(23, 6 June): 64.

Toomin, M. K., and Toomin, H. 1973. Biofeedback: Fact and fantasy. Does it hold implication for gifted education? *Gifted Child Quarterly* 17: 48–55.

Torrance, E. P. 1962. *Guiding creative talent.* Englewood Cliffs, N.J.: Prentice-Hall.

_____. 1970. Broadening concepts of giftedness in the '70's. *Gifted Child Quarterly* 14: 199–208.

_____, and Myers, R. E. 1962. Teaching gifted elementary pupils research concepts and skills. *Gifted Child Quarterly* 6: 1–6.

United States Office of Education. 1972. *Education of the gifted and talented: Report to the Congress.* Washington, D.C.: U.S. Government Printing Office.

Unzicker, S. P. 1932. A study of acceleration in the junior high school. *School Review* 40: 346–56.

Walsh, J. 1977. Harold Brown and defense: From scientist to secretary. *Science* 195: 463–66.

Ward, F. C. (ed.). 1950. *The idea and practice of general education.* Chicago: University of Chicago Press.

Weinstein, B., Mitchell, P., Schwartzstein, M., and Hirschhorn, B. 1966. The adjustment of children in a suburban community who were accelerated in elementary school. *Journal of School Psychology* 5: 60–63.

Wells, F. L. 1949. Adjustment problems at upper extremes of test "intelligence": Cases 19–28. *Journal of Genetic Psychology* 74: 61–84.

_____. 1950. Psychometric patterns in adjustment at upper extremes of test "intelligence": Cases 39–56. *Journal of Genetic Psychology* 76: 3–37.

West, J. 1958. Teaching the talented. *Education* 78: 434–38.

Whinnery, S. M. 1926. Psychological test rating and college entrance age. *School and Society* 24: 370–72.

Wilkins, W. L. 1936. High school achievement of accelerated pupils. *School Review* 44: 268–74.

Williams, W. W. 1958. Program for superior students. *Education* 78: 492–95.

Wilson, F. T. 1949. A survey of educational provisions for young gifted children in the United States and of studies and problems related thereto. *Journal of Genetic Psychology* 75: 3–19.

Wilson, J. A. 1959. Some results of an enrichment program for gifted ninth graders. *Journal of Educational Research* 53: 157–60.

Wilson, S. H., Greer, J. F., and Johnson, R. M. 1973. Synectics: A creative problem-solving technique for the gifted. *Gifted Child Quarterly* 17: 260–67.

Witty, P. 1940. A genetic study of fifty gifted children. *Yearbook of the National Society for the Study of Education* 39: 401–09.

_____. 1954. Guidance of the gifted. *Personnel Guidance Journal* 33: 136–39.

_____. 1956. Education for the talented and for leadership. *Teachers College Record* 57: 295–300.

Woods, E. L. 1944. The mentally gifted. *Review of Educational Research* 14: 224–30.
Woolf, L. 1957. The selection of accelerated course students at the Baltimore Polytechnic Institute. *Journal of Educational Research* 51: 11–15.
Worcester, D. A. 1956. *The education of children of above average mentality.* Lincoln, Neb.: University of Nebraska Press.
Zorbaugh, H. 1937. Is instability inherent in giftedness and talent? *Proceedings of the Third Conference on the Education of Exceptional Children.*

II
Enrichment: Highlights of the Literature

3

WHAT PROVISIONS FOR THE EDUCATION OF GIFTED STUDENTS?

Morris Meister and Harold A. Odell

PART 1: MORRIS MEISTER

The democratic right to attend high school has come to mean for most youth, the right to study the same subjects, in the same way, at the same rate, for the same length of time and subject to what are believed to be the same standards. The trouble is that half of our youth cannot stand the process, and drop out before graduation. The pity is that half of the dropouts could have completed the course, such as it is. Now, we must not be indifferent to the needs which all youth share in common; but it is not inherent in democracy that it emphasize a leveling process. Our schools must become safe for differences.

How Many in the High Schools Are Gifted?

Although there is no general agreement on the answer to this question, it is essential to deal with it realistically. Let us, then, accept the rough line of demarcation proposed by the Educational Policies Commission; namely that 10 percent of the six million boys and girls in American high schools have IQs better than 120 and that, therefore, 600,000 of them are either "moderately" or "highly" gifted. Twenty-five years from now, a very large proportion of this group will be running the country; its business, its politics, its law, its professions, its arts, its science. Even if we disagree violently with using the intelligence quotient as a criterion, and even if the 600,000 include some who should not be there or exclude some who should be there, a major fraction of them is certainly destined for leadership.

This paper includes excerpts from chapter 10, written by Dr. Meister, of P. Witty (ed.), *The gifted child*. D. C. Heath & Co.

Reprinted with permission of editor, *NASSP Bulletin*. Published 1951 in *NASSP* (National Association of Secondary School Principals) *Bulletin* 35: 30–46.

How Large Are the High Schools which They Attend?

Of the 600,000 gifted students, as here defined, 200,000 live in cities with populations of 100,000 and over. Such communities can afford to maintain perhaps four or five different high school structures, each accommodating at least 500 students. Another 100,000 of the gifted boys and girls live in areas where consolidation of resources are possible; so that again, several high schools of reasonable size can be organized. In other words, about half of the gifted children attend high schools of 500 or more students and live in areas where several high schools are reasonably available. The remaining half, or 300,000 gifted boys and girls, live in such small communities where the high school population numbers less than 500, or if it is larger, only one school is reasonably available in the region.

These rough estimates are of prime importance. Cost of instruction, variety of teacher talent, flexibility of program, and many other factors which determine provisions for individual needs, all depend upon the size of school unit. It is safe to say that even with twice the amount of money now in sight for high school support, no school unit of less than 500 students can offer the enriched and flexible program required by the varying interests and abilities of its students, not to mention the special enrichments called for to meet the needs of the fifty moderately and highly gifted boys and girls in every such school.

From a practical point of view, therefore, there is little to be gained for the larger school from a consideration of what is best to do for the gifted in the very small school. Such schools are equally handicapped in caring for the entire range of abilities, and represent a problem so different in degree as to constitute a problem different in kind. Two tracks of study, research and teacher training must therefore be launched. While the findings in each of the tracks will have bearing on the other, each must proceed independently and in its own frame of reference. The important fact to note is that each of the tracks concerns itself and will continue to concern itself for the next twenty years or more with half of the 600,000 gifted high school boys and girls in America.

What Opportunities for the Gifted in the Larger School?

At the high school level variability in achievement probably reaches its maximum. The teacher meets about 150 or more students each day. It often takes a month before he can call each of them by name. Associating different sets of abilities and interests with these names is another time-consuming task. Yet, in the class assembled at random, we expect the teacher to organize smaller groups for learning purposes. There may be need for as many as four or five such groups. Not only interest and ability, but also subject status is important. Reading comprehension also plays a part. Assignments must be varied. As many as five or six committees must be kept going. Students are transferred in or out. Such groupings may be continued for a long time; others for only a day or two. Different texts, tests, and supplementary materials must be procured, assembled, and otherwise made available to each of the groups. He must meet parents and become familiar with home conditions. Truly, the teacher of a heterogeneous class must be Superman himself!

If society could afford a teacher for each student, the problem of caring for individual needs would be largely solved. Since that is impossible, we must perforce develop procedures for dealing with groups, large groups most of the time, small groups some of the time, and with individuals occasionally. Since the larger school makes grouping more feasible, the development of procedures for varying groups becomes more attainable.

Some Devices Proposed and Tried

During the past twelve years the New York City high schools have experimented with at least three grouping devices for dealing with gifted children. Each of the devices has its devotees and its critics. The first is the organization of so-called Honor Classes in the various subject areas. Thus, Honor Classes in English, history, mathematics, language, and science are formed at each grade level. The basis for admission is usually a high grade in the previous semester's work in the particular subject in question. Occasionally the IQ is combined with grades. Since work is departmentalized, any given boy or girl may be doing Honors work in English but attend a so-called normal class in other subjects. Some ticklish administrative problems frequently arise and even the very large schools find it necessary to abolish some Honors Classes on occasion. No thoroughgoing study has ever been made of the outcomes from this plan; yet many teachers and students like the arrangement. It does provide opportunity for enriching the curriculum and for raising standards of achievement in keeping with student ability.

A second device, somewhat less used because it is feasible only in a very large school, is to organize an Honors School within the school. This tends to select the college-bound students. A portion of the faculty is usually selected to deal with these students. All the classes are then in the Honors category. The special staff of teachers find opportunity to confer at regular intervals, so as to coordinate their efforts. The degree of homogeneity attainable by this device is not nearly as great as in the case of special Honors Classes. Administrative problems are less severe, if the school is large enough; but parent and teacher objection is greater. There is also frequent complaint from students when compelled to meet standards higher than those applied to their fellows in the more normal segment of the school. Though much criticized, those schools which have Honor Schools praise them highly on the ground that they provide opportunities for the gifted they would never have had otherwise. While no thoroughgoing studies on Honors Schools have been published, they have been discussed in detail, with pros and cons in the references cited below.[1]

Opportunities for the Gifted in the Specialized High School

A third device for reducing the magnitude of differences in instructional groups is to organize an entire school, its curriculum, faculty, equipment, and procedures, around a *purpose* that is meaningful and attractive to the students. The latter apply for admission; they need not enroll if the announced purpose does not appeal to them. Further, all who apply are not admitted. The school is permitted to develop such standards of admission, as are in keeping with the school's purpose and which will make it more likely that the student will profit from the school's offering. Early identification on the part of an individual of a strong interest or aptitude produces a "halo effect." It often services as motivation for learnings in related fields and stimulates generalized achievements. Furthermore, in the case of those "purposeful schools" which are based on areas of learning requiring reading comprehension, possession of fundamental skills and ability to reason, the school's very purpose tends to select automatically a group of high-level ability students.

So far as we know, the role of *purpose* has never been thoroughly explored as a means of providing opportunities for the gifted. The specialized high school is attempting to do this for large groups of moderately and highly gifted boys and girls who, early in life, have identified for themselves a serious life interest and aptitude.

The Specialized High Schools in New York City

The specialized high school is a school above the eighth grade, designed throughout to meet the needs, interests, abilities, and terminal aims of a particular segment of the adolescent population. The opposite of the specialized high school is the general or neighborhood high school, designed to educate all the children of the neighborhood with only such adjustments to individual needs as can be provided under one roof.

1. Student Selection on the Basis of Interest, Ability, and Terminal Aims Creates Both a Favorable Learning Situation and a Democratically Desirable Social Environment.   Educators agree that the optimum learning situation is one in which the tasks set the learner are within the range of his ability but difficult enough to require considerable effort. If the task exceeds the capacity of the learner, not only does he fail to learn anything by it, but, if the situation is repeated often enough, he may also develop a sense of frustration.

[1]Bulletins of *High Points,* New York City Schools, December 1930, November 1940, and May 1940.

A heterogeneous student body is sometimes urged on the ground of democracy. This argument is specious. It is not true that individuals in a democracy live and work in groups as heterogeneous as the generality of the population. The home, the family, and the circle of friends which surrounds it are all fairly homogeneous groups. Even at work, one's associates are not as heterogeneous as the generality of the population. The goal to be striven for is a well-articulated society and not a perfectly diffused one. It is not always true that bringing widely divergent groups together in a school is the best method of teaching them to understand each other, or of teaching them the way to make such contacts pleasant and mutually helpful.

A completely homogeneous student body is neither possible, nor is it ever an end which is sought directly by a specialized high school. The specialized high school does seek to avoid the unworkable ranges now commonly found in the general high school.

2. The Specialized High School Provides Many Students with a Purpose, Which, for Them, the General High School Lacks.   Purpose is the motive power of the learning process. Students can accomplish tasks quite beyond the degree of competence they usually display if they have a strong purpose which is their own. The many recent youth studies have shown clearly that the purpose which dominated the general high school never became the abiding purpose of many of the students.

The upper segment of high school students finds in the appropriate special school a realization of purpose which they cannot find in the general high school. They can do the required work in much less time than it takes the other students. When this extra time is not wasted, it is rarely employed at levels which bring the maximum return. In a specialized high school this extra time is used to better advantage.

3. The Specialized High School Is Consistent with the Ideal of a Well-rounded Education.   The specialized high school does *not* encourage narrow specialization, nor an education devoid of the aesthetic and cultural content. And there is nothing in the specialized school which makes this necessary. On the basis of any definition of culture, the specialized high school is in a more favorable position to create an environment conducive to cultural growth. The fact is that students in science high schools, for example, study more English, more social studies, more mathematics and as much foreign language, music, and art by comparison with the students in general high schools.

A well-rounded program does not necessarily produce well-rounded students. A broad education is the product of broad interests. And interests do not operate in single compartments; they reach out and include a number of related fields. If, on the other hand, the student lacks a real interest, the entire school machinery will be able to do little more than to bring him to the point of passing an examination.

The interest pattern of the very intelligent is broad and it extends to things not directly connected with the individual. For such an individual a real and lively interest in world problems, in literature, in art, in music comes naturally.

4. The Specialized High School Makes a Better Integration of the Curriculum Possible.   The human mind, like the human body, tends to function as an organism rather than as a mechanism. Yet, the high school curriculum, with its many "subjects" in airtight compartments, suggests a mechanistic approach. For the students the curriculum is the sum of a number of constants and variables. Little provision is made for weaving the subjects into an organic, integrated whole. This is not to say that all parts of all subjects can or should be fused. It does imply that there are many ideas which belong together and that they should be brought together in the learning process.

To do this with any effectiveness at all for the adolescent, one must utilize the binding power of his central purpose. Such a purpose exists for students in a specialized high school. We can more readily bring ideas together that belong together. While "subjects" and their syllabi look the same when written down on paper for both types of school, the teaching and the learning which results are totally different. One need only to visit a classroom in English or social studies or physics in a specialized high school to be impressed by the extent and the quality of curriculum integration.

How Many Specialized High Schools in New York City?

The publicly supported secondary schools in New York City number about eighty, exclusive of the junior high schools. About twenty of them might be termed "specialized" in the sense that their philosophies, organizations, curricula, and equipment center about a "purpose." Not all of them set up specific tests for admission; yet all of them are, in effect, selective; their "purposes" are well communicated and well understood by teachers, parents, and students. At least four of them center about "purposes" which tend to select high-level ability students. These are Brooklyn Technical High School, High School of Music and Art, High School of Science, and Stuyvesant High School. Only the High Schools of Music and Art and of Science are coeducational.

What Kind of Children Are They?

Here is a brief and generalized profile: While he (or she) wants to go to college and make "science" his career, he is not too specific in this interest. He is a year younger than the average high school student of the same grade; but he knows his fundamentals in arithmetic and spelling. He reads voraciously all kinds of books and periodicals. He is alert to current issues and is capable of profound loyalties and support to causes. He gripes about too much homework but puts a considerable amount of time on daily study, spending much spare time in his home "lab" and with other hobbies. Because he is eager and vocal, he is sometimes difficult to control in class. He is hard on the teacher and can spot at once the one who "doesn't know his stuff." He has achieved an early sophistication in the importance of marks and is prone to become an "eager beaver," wise to the ways of short cuts to high grades. His mental and physical health is splendid. In our school he welcomed the advent of girls with wild acclaim—the alumni mourning this event as "too little and too late." Though young, he is proficient in athletics, participating in baseball, soccer, swimming, basketball, tennis, handball, and track. He may work after school and during the summer. He is a great joiner of clubs. His IQ is exactly at the median for the school and it is about 130. He gives his teachers the greatest possible lift, spiritually and professionally; he leaves them limp as rags at the end of the day.

About 2 percent of his classmates are maladjusted in one way or another; some of them run away from home, or cheat, or cause other disciplinary infractions. About 5 percent of his classmates are hit hard by adolescence in about the junior years, and go to pieces scholastically. The parents come from every economic level and are engaged in many types of work and professional activities; but are all keenly interested in the school and the progress of their children.

The Faculty

In the early years of the school's history, the principal was able to select ten young, well-trained, and competent heads of departments. They have been towers of strength in developing the school's philosophy and practice. Among the remaining ninety members of the staff, many able and superior teachers volunteered to transfer to the school from other schools. Due to an annual turnover of about 10 percent in personnel, the staff as a whole has changed considerably over the years. New personnel are obtained from civil service lists of licensed teachers, and are, by and large, well-equipped. It may be pointed out that in twelve years, more than thirty of the staff have won promotions as heads of departments or school principals. Nevertheless not all of the present faculty are ideally suited for the task of guiding gifted children. In this connection we wish to endorse the point of view of the NEA Policies Commission as to the qualities especially needed in a teacher of gifted children.

Some Student and Alumni Achievements

Practically all of the students are admitted to college. The record is perhaps best summarized in the results of the class of June, 1950, which numbered 391 boys and girls. They received 875 admissions from 125 different colleges and were awarded 175 scholarships worth about $200,000.

Space hardly permits a description of the thousands of brilliant achievements to the credit of these gifted students. One 16-year-old was elected Fellow of the Royal Microscopic Society of London for his work on microscopes. Another discovered a new species of fruit fly and was acknowledged the discoverer by a world-famous entomologist. A third student sent a sample of a new variety of mold of neurospora to Dr. Doge of the New York Botanical Gardens, who named it H.S.S., the initials of the school. Another boy made a discovery in protozoology which was independently made by a professor at Brown University and published. One alumnus, as a junior at Harvard, was assigned to Dr. Oppenheimer's staff at Los Alamos and assisted at the trial of the first atom bomb. The alumni now numbers about 300 doctors and dentists, about 1,500 engineers, about 200 research men, about 500 laboratory technicians, and about 1,000 school and college teachers of science. Fifteen percent of the alumni have gravitated to business, journalism, nonscience teaching, and other nonscience professions. One has become a well-known concert pianist; another an outstanding artist.

Community Reactions

Dr. Vannevar Bush, formerly Director of the Office of Science Research and Development, had this to say about the school five years ago:

> Convinced as I am that there has never been a time when cultivation of science talent is so important to the welfare of our nation and the world, I welcome the opportunity to speak a word for the kind of program which the Bronx High School of Science has been carrying on during the past seven years. This is a very positive contribution toward replenishing of our sadly depleted stock of scientifically trained intelligence. The breadth of the program of the Bronx High School of Science—in its inclusion of ample study of the humanities—is not only a safeguard against the hazard of narrow specialization but also the best guarantee that its graduates will have the depth of understanding necessary for the full utilization of scientific skill in their later careers.

This praise in high places is couched in terms especially meaningful for these times.

An internationally known writer, whose son attended the school and was killed in the recent war, memorializes his son's name in a biography in which he speaks high words of praise for the school. In addition, he offers a prize of several hundred dollars at each commencement to some graduate.

A parent whose son died while in attendance at the school has established a foundation which is currently paying all expenses of twelve graduates through college and professional school, and supplies the school liberally with current needs not otherwise obtainable. Recently the foundation established a Music Lounge in the Library, with thousands of dollars of recordings and a sound system which enables students to listen to records through earphones.

A leading department store merchant in the community, whose son found security at Science after being unhappy in a private school, is seeking to express his appreciation in a contribution, *without strings,* which is measured in thousands of dollars.

These material gifts symbolize the spirit of good will that has permeated the community regarding the work of the school.

Some Unsolved Problems

Like any other venture into uncharted seas, the sailing has not all been smooth. The general question of the specialized school as a moot educational problem is encountered here in intensified form.

Some contend that the secondary school is too early in a student's career for him to engage in any type of specialization. They point to the student whose interest in science wanes, but who is unable to make the easy adjustment in course that a large, diversified school makes possible. Of course, the school attempts to avoid criticism on this score, by careful explanation of its purpose and by screening of its entrants.

Another criticism concerns itself with the issue of democracy. Much has been said on this question and surely the pros and cons of this issue have by now been thoroughly set forth; but they have never been subjected to rigorous objective test. To those who deal with boys and girls in specialized schools day by day, this criticism brings only smiles. They would challenge the critics, invite them into the school to observe the children at work and at play. In all that they do, they exemplify a free society in pursuit of democratic ideals in democratic fashion. Modesty rather than snobbishness is the quality that predominates. There are leaders and there are intelligent followers. The "purpose" around which the school centers cannot and does not eliminate individual differences. Democracy cannot mean that it is more important for a student to reach the teacher's minimum than to reach his own maximum.

Another criticism that has been raised arises from the undisputed fact that the entrance testing procedure tends to select students of superior intelligence. This results in a concentration of such students in one school, and may attenuate the honor rolls of others. While the answers to such questions as these lie in the general province of educational values, it must be said that students with clearly defined talents and interests ought not to be neglected. It has never been proved that the less able need the presence of the gifted in order to achieve their maximum.

Some members of the faculty feel that some of our students work under too severe tensions and at too great speed, with insufficient recreation. Others feel that the school's curriculum as organized at present does not allow pupils enough time to avail themselves of the full and varied offerings of such departments as art and music. These matters have been the subject of long faculty discussions, and some modifications have resulted and others are under consideration.

Among other unsolved problems is the problem of teacher recruitment.

There is great unwillingness on the part of school authorities to give special consideration to the teacher needs of specialized schools. The teaching load is still too heavy. Administrative and organizational regulations are too sharply applied in view of the special needs of gifted children. One of the most annoying, sometimes frustrating problems is the attitude of some superintendents and principals toward the importance of special provisions for the gifted. Whenever a crisis of one kind or another occurs, the authority is likely to say: "Well, the bright kids will come out all right; they'll take care of themselves." The fact is that they do not.

A Final Word

I realize that in discussing opportunities for gifted high school students I have focused attention entirely upon only half of the 600,000 gifted students in America—the half that happen to live in populated areas. Yet, an attack upon half of the problem is certainly worth while. Again, we stress that the other half of the problem is so different in kind that it warrants an entirely new approach by those who must deal with the situation day by day.

The High School of Science is now in its thirteenth year. In that time it has been accumulating convincing evidence that science talented youth need a specialized type of secondary-school education—specialized, however, only in the sense of giving science a special part to play in educating such youth for a free society. It seems vital to the welfare of the country that we conserve this special human resource for the needs of a scientific age. No great nation can now afford to neglect its science talent. Not only is national security at stake, but the security of civilization itself.

PART 2: HAROLD A. ODELL

At the outset, it should be noted that the wording of the title of this discussion commits us to the premise that special provision should be made for the group of students identified as gifted. This point of view implies that such provision will provide a more sound educational program for this group. This writer wants to go on record as saying: there is (1) the need of school administrators for a recognition of this problem, and (2) the need for special curricular provision for the education of our superior boys and girls. It should be conceded that this will not be a definite discussion of this subject; but instead, some problems will be posed and some alternatives suggested.

There has been considerable research in the diagnosis and selection of gifted children and some experimentation in the organization of ability groups as a technique for educating the intellectually gifted. Little can be found in educational literature relative to the curriculum of special classes for bright children in high school. How shall the curriculum be organized for such a class? What shall it include? How will teaching methods be affected under this plan? How can results be evaluated? These and many other questions have not been conclusively answered.

In adult life, we have an obligation to our gifted contemporaries and these leaders in turn have a debt to society. In the days of the "Jacksonian Democracy" we were taught the rather fallacious doctrine that all men are equal. We still seem to idealize the average man and tend to underestimate the worth of the exceptional man. (This point of view does not include our professional athletes or Hollywood personalities.) A scientific or artistic genius may be somewhat revered, but we usually regard such people as "different." The popular concept of tolerance toward the gifted is not enough. All schools are responsible for the discovery and the education of outstanding human talent in a society of self-government where good leaders are indispensable.

Superintendent Campbell of the New York City schools succinctly stated a long time ago that: "Education is something more than the process of guiding youth out of the realm of incompetence. . . . The school that fails to offer opportunity for the child of unusual gifts is as fully neglectful as the school that offers nothing to the child of limited endowment. The school must be as zealous to do for the genius as for the dullard."

Most laymen and professional educators will agree that, in order to perpetuate democracy, one of the prime requirements is to provide for an equality of opportunity for all boys and girls of public school age. They would also concede that schools should provide conditions that will permit *all* pupils to develop to the fullest extent. This is one of the fundamental concepts of the American public schools (Cohen and Coryell 1935).

Another fundamental principle of education is the law of individual differences. This concept of psychology has led most school administrators to attempt the adjustment and adaptation of their educational programs to meet these individual differences.

With the recent trend to raise the compulsory school age, the adoption of child labor legislation, and the economic depression, the secondary-school population has changed in the character of its members as well as in the character of its enrollment. A good many pupils of average or below average mental ability, who have less interest in academic learning, are now attending school. This segment of the school population in a good many areas would be employed in industry or agriculture, if it had the choice to make.

The increased range of the mental capacity of our pupils has resulted in contributing to a condition where we do not actually provide equalization of educational opportunity for our bright children. Some would go as far as to say that the schools are undemocratic because they are not providing opportunities for the superior pupils to develop their maximum abilities. Democracy, in order to endure, must develop leaders that have the training, the vision, the courage, and the ability to furnish enlightened leadership. One place to stress leadership training is during adolescent growth. All the people can't become leaders, but people can be trained for leadership. Our gifted children constitute the schools' greatest political asset.

One factor that influenced the policies of the school administrators toward the problem of the atypical child was the emergence and refining of the science of education. The use of tests and measurements, statistics, and the research in the psychology of learning all contributed to the recognition of the problem.

Galton in 1865 (Hollingworth 1935) made probably the first scientific observation that the outstanding contributions to society were made by people of superior ability. Cattell (ibid.) observed in his investigation of 1,000 American men of science living between 1910 and 1915, who were the most outstanding in the opinion of their contemporaries, that (1) the majority of the fathers of these men came from the learned professions, (2) that laborers' children were not among them, and (3) that scientists tend to grow up in the city.

These and other investigations seem to indicate that intellectual capacity is inherited. Psychologists and sociologists do not all agree that great achievement can be attributed entirely to the native qualities of the individual or to the environmental conditions. It should be apparent, however, that a democracy, in its own interest, should require that each person contribute to its society all that inheritance and training can permit him. The public schools have an inescapable responsibility in contributing to the maintenance of democracy. The high school should make provision for the gifted for these main reasons: (1) such provision will in itself discharge this responsibility by providing for the development of *all* the pupils to the full extent of their potentialities; and (2) it will furnish a training ground for the future leaders of our democracy. If an adequate educational program is to be provided, it must be adapted to meet the individual needs of *all* the pupils.

We have long admitted the need for special provision for the slow learner and the mentally defective. We have gone to great expense in considering the welfare of the mentally and physically deficient in the public schools, and in private and public institutions today such financing is inadequate. Our sympathies are aroused immediately when the needs of this segment of our school population are known. We are justly sentimental in our desire to help those who are unable properly to help themselves.

Although we do not intend to play one against the other, the large group of mentally handicapped (Goodwin 1941) has diverted our attentions from a more important group of the "educationally neglected"—the gifted. Schools and teachers have, by habit or inclination, assumed that the superior child will learn without special attention. In the typical school room of a heterogeneous group, the teacher of average ability devotes most of his time to the average or slow learner. The superior pupil either forms habits of neglect or inattention that lead to boredom and laziness or, upon his own initiative, he will vary his class activities to suit his interests. Occasionally, a child of superior intelligence becomes a disciplinary problem, but usually he causes no disturbance. Working at a fraction of his capacities, he shows little interest in drill but still manages to meet the minimum scholastic standards required of the class. By permitting a range of 80 IQ to 150 IQ in the same class, we are actually promoting mediocrity.

There is general agreement that schools are failing adequately to educate the superior child. But there is no agreement on the *best* provision for the solution of this problem.

Of 1,430 young adults who scored in the top 1 percent on an intelligence test twenty years before, only 12 failed to complete high school, but 121 stopped their education with high school graduation. More than one-fourth of the group were employed in occupations requiring no more than average intelligence. Terman (Terman and Oden 1947) established that "practically all the gifted subjects were potentially college material and probably one third left school with less—often much less than they should have had." Tests administered to fifteen million men in the military services in World War II revealed that many gifted men had not been discovered. The sinews of war demanded that the armed forces utilize the talents of these men.

A recent study (Goetsch) revealed that 90 percent of the superior students who come from the upper economic class were attending college. Less than 20 percent of the superior student from the lower economic brackets attended college. World problems of vital importance are leaving their impact. Education is challenged to develop leadership. Special education for the gifted is not only warranted, but the very continuance of democracy demands it.

Two main problems emerge in a consideration of this problem: I. Identifying the Gifted, and II. Special Provisions for the Gifted.

I. Identifying the Gifted

Verbal ability is frequently overemphasized in our attempts to identify the superior students. The world needs talents of many types—scientific, artistic, and social—and much progress has been made in measuring talent as compared to the casual, informal observations used formerly, but very few studies have been made of the subsequent education of people with scientific or artistic gifts. The discovery of the gifted is not easy. It involves serious problems in the personality development of young people. It would be well for a school to define the gifted before it begins the task of discovering students with these characteristics.

In order to identify the gifted, the following criteria could be considered:

1. *Teacher Judgment*—Classroom teachers, guidance counselors, homeroom teachers, athletic coaches, and activities sponsors should all be consulted. They should be asked to differentiate between actual achievement and the capacity to achieve. Special aptitudes should be identified and recorded in such activities as writing, acting, and music. Studies have shown that boys

and girls with marked mental ability are not always talented in other activities than intellectual, but other investigations indicate that geniuses in music, art, and science are usually characterized by a high degree of intellectual ability. Teachers must also be aware that chronological age is of paramount importance in identifying the gifted.

2. *Scholastic Record*—This should show evidence of a continuity of achievement in relation to the personality traits of the student. Even though school marks are not infallible, if enough evidence is available from a variety of teachers, it becomes a reliable index of the scholastic ability of the student.

3. *Standardized Tests*—Intelligence and achievement tests should be administered. Professor Terman's policy of a "cutting" score of 140 IQ to identify the intelligent gifted has found common usage, or about the top 1 percent of the total population. In selected communities or schools, this ratio would increase. If the evidence selected from the above criteria is properly appraised, a basis will have been established for the identification of the superior students.

II. Special Provisions for the Gifted

The education of the gifted must be different from the education of other students in quantity, kind, and the demands for the use of insight. Ideally every school and teacher should have a systematic organization and procedure for the education of superior students, based on a local study and local needs.

Acceleration.   St. Louis pioneered in the acceleration of bright pupils by promoting them at short intervals (National Society of the Study of Education). In 1868, Dr. W. T. Harris reported to the annual convention of the National Education Association that the plan had the advantages of stimulating the superior children to work up to their capacity. It is common practice, especially in the elementary school, to permit bright pupils to "skip" one grade, on the assumption that it would be uneconomical for them to spend the next year with their own class.

This method has the advantage of challenging the more able student, and it permits him to avoid frustration and growth of bad work habits. It is the easiest administrative procedure to utilize. Time and expense will be saved for these students. They will become productive at an earlier age. This technique has the disadvantage of involving the danger of possible social maladjustment of the youngster unless the bright student has matured in direct ratio to his intellectual capacity, and, even with acceleration, the younger, brighter child will learn faster than his older classmates. Acceleration should not be resorted to unless a systematic evaluation has been made of the individual student concerned.

Enrichment.   Superintendent Shearer in 1896 devised a plan in Elizabeth, New Jersey, for the division of each of the eight grades into sections according to ability. Essentials were covered by each section in proportion to the ability of the class. The concentric plan at Santa Barbara, which divides each grade into an A, B, and C group is somewhat similar. Minimum essentials are covered by all the groups, but the B group does more work than the C section, and the A group goes a faster pace and covers more than Section B. This plan seems to provide more for enrichment of the course of study than for the acceleration of the good students. The students may advance from one section to the next, however, which has the advantage of flexibility.

By his very nature, the gifted child has an enriched life in his experiences, insights, and appreciations. But the child cannot grow to his potential with self-direction only. He needs a *planned* enrichment. The enrichment of subject matter and other educational experiences seem to have the advantage of adapting the material and teaching to the individual as enrichment does in acceleration, without the accompanying possible danger of social maladjustment involved in "skipping." It also follows the ideal of adapting school work to every individual student and not for a group of students. One study (Sumption 1941) revealed that better all-around results were obtained where a program of enrichment was followed in comparison to a general school program. There is no available evidence of cases where there was too much enrichment. There is no apparent dichotomy between enrichment and acceleration. As a matter of fact, they complement each other.

Enrichment in the area of literature and writing is almost boundless when motivated by superior teaching. It provides opportunities for more specialized study as well as for opening up new, unexplored areas. In the activities program, gifted students have an ideal climate in which to develop—student government, music, a wide variety of clubs and athletics.

Ability Grouping. One of the plans developed relatively recently, to compensate for the weakness and ineffectiveness of the regimentation of the grades system, was the development of homogeneous ability grouping. According to Billett, only one article appeared on this subject before 1910 (Billett). There were out five cities that provided for special classes or schools for gifted pupils before 1911 (U.S. Bureau of Education). Although there has been a substantial increase n this technique, there has not been complete acceptance of such grouping.

One of the first references to ability grouping is found in the Annual Report of San Francisco in 1873 (Annual Report 1873). This report stated that pupils in high school, "Shall be arranged in divisions according to proficiency." In 1908, Cleveland grouped some pupils according to a "proficiency, scholarship, ability, industry, health, capacity during the preceding term, successive examinations of he previous year, and marks received in examinations for admission" (Annual Report 1908). By 1917, the Cleveland schools had begun a limited use of standardized tests in grouping pupils for rapid progress (ibid.). But it was not ntil 1921, with the aid of improved intelligence tests, that Cleveland began its well-known Major Work Groups. The Cleveland superintendent reported in 1938 that "the school program that best meets the needs of the child is the one that gives consideration to, and is based on, the child's ability to do school work successfully'' (ibid.).

Ability grouping had its inception in the high schools, but in recent years this classification has found greater popularity in the elementary schools. In 1935, out of a total school enrollment of 5,941,605 for the cities in the United States with a population of 100,000 or over, only 2,293 pupils were classified in a special class for the gifted. One thousand two hundred and forty-one of these were in the Cleveland schools, and 273 in the Boston schools (Foster and Martens 1938). In its Honors Schools and Classes, New York City has made rapid and significant studies in solving this problem.

Optimum learning in school is closely related to intellectual ability; therefore, as in acceleration, group learning can be accomplished more efficiently by grouping students on the criterion of ability than by chronological age. It is desirable to use the IQ, the scholastic record, teacher judgment, and chronological age as criteria for ability grouping. By this policy all children are promoted by natural growth and at the same time as are their classmates. In a ninth-grade English class of 300 pupils, ten sections might be organized from one to ten in decreasing ability. Accompanied by the characteristic of pupil ability, provision could be made of the variations in courses of study for college preparatory work, business education, and general education. The number of sections in the English college preparatory course would be determined by the number of students enrolled in that curriculum. The average and the slow learners would, by that plan, have their class work adapted to their abilities and needs. These pupils would not be as likely to get discouraged in competing with the bright pupils in a heterogeneous class. This facility of variation could be applied to common learnings in high school or college.

Because of the higher achievement standards required, ability grouping has the advantage of challenging the more able students to a greater degree than does a heterogeneous class. The course of study for such a gifted group should actually provide the enrichment argued for by the advocates of enrichment. Enrichment and individualization of instruction in a heterogeneous class is difficult if not impossible for the average teacher. Ability grouping, say its proponents, would facilitate the differentiation of instruction required for the best educational results. Bright students would have less opportunity for the rapid growth of their ego in a class where it is not as possible for them to be superior to their fellows. Superior teachers, with skill and imagination that will inspire boys and girls, are essential for producing the best results in a class of superior students. Most subject teachers say that teaching a bright class is much easier than a normal class.

Advocates of acceleration maintain that ability grouping is undemocratic because it offers different and better opportunities to a selected few and that it results in the development of a stigma for the lower ability groups. Other opponents of ability grouping contend that in the adult world one has to live with all types of people and that ability grouping provides for an artificial conditioning for adult life. This argument may be countered by stating that if ability grouping is followed, homeroom groups, athletic teams, social affairs, and other school activities should be composed of all students of all levels of intelligence. It is generally agreed that ability grouping would be uneconomical, and probably unwise, in small high schools.

Elective Courses.   Schools that provide effective guidance services will be able to tailor individual students' schedules to the varying needs and abilities of each student. Rightly or wrongly, gifted boys and girls will usually elect a sequence of the traditional college preparatory subjects. Those with musical, artistic, or mechanical talents will be interested in choosing courses that will promote the utilization of these talents. Good counseling will be essential in a school program that makes provision for a wide choice of electives. Such a program has the advantage of enabling the student to be better qualified to choose an area of specialization in college while, at the same time providing opportunities for necessary general education.

No one of the four educational devices discussed above will be adequate to meet all the educational needs of the gifted. Every superior student needs enrichment. All need programs of elective courses. Able school administrators should consider acceleration in individual cases and some school principals will record success with ability grouping. In medium and large high schools, a combination of several of these special provisions could be applied; in fact, many high schools have incorporated all of these special techniques in their programs.

At the risk of seeming inconsistent, one should point out that some people do object to making any special provision for superior students. People who object to any recognition of gifted youngsters argue that it is incongruous in a democracy to promote the formation of an aristocracy of the intellectually elite. In passing, we might note that the same group also opposes any deferment for military service of superior boys. They seem to confuse the issue with an appeal to the emotions—believing that universal military service is a moral question, as opposed to selective service. It would seem to us that the important criterion on this question is what is best for the preservation of our country and of our way of life. Some would go as far as to say that bright boys can contribute more to their country by continuing in their training than by being soldiers.

Fundamentally, the same issue exists in our public schools. Should the schools, dedicated to the teaching of a democracy and good citizenship, make special provision for gifted boys and girls? Should teachers apply or reject what we have learned about the law of individual differences? There are many things at stake inherent in this question among which are: (1) What is best for the bright boy or girl? (2) How does this relate to society?

High school administrators have been frequently criticized as reactionary and unwilling to adopt changes in educational practice. There are many reasons why some high school principals find it undesirable or impossible to try out many "new" educational techniques—some of these reasons are justifiable, but it should be possible for responsible educational authorities, such as state boards of education, professional associations, or field service adjuncts of teachers' colleges, to promote and encourage pilot studies in the area of the gifted child. Without sacrificing educational standards, schools should be laboratories for such experiments. High school principals should not resort to the old shibboleth that college admission requirements prohibit such experimentations. This argument has assumed the role of rationalization with many school administrators.

When our high school principals agree that they have a special responsibility to our gifted children and are willing to translate this belief into some experimentation in educational practice to help carry out this responsibility—then we will begin to record the evidence we need to support the conviction that, as a precious resource, our gifted boys and girls deserve special consideration.

REFERENCES

Annual report of the board of education, Cleveland. 1908, p. 49.

Annual report of the superintendent of schools, San Francisco. 1873. p. 151.

Billett, R. O. *Provisions for individual differences and promotion.* Washington, D.C.: U.S. Government Printing Office, p. 18.

Cohen, H. L., and Coryell, N. G. 1935. *Educating superior students.* American Book Company. (See foreword 1 by H. G. Campbell).

Foster, E. M., and Martens, E. H. 1938. *Bienniel survey of education in the United States, 1934–35,* vol. II, bull. 2, 1937. Washington, D.C.: U.S. Government Printing Office, pp. 29–30.

Goetsch, H. Parental income and college opportunities. Teachers College Contributions to Education, No. 795. New York: Teachers College of Columbia University.

Goodwin, W. 1941. One in twenty spend some time in a mental hospital. *Progressive Education* (May): 251.

Hollingworth, L. S. 1929. *Gifted children: Their nature and nurture.* New York: Macmillan, chapter 1.

National Society of the Study of Education. *23rd yearbook,* p. 8.

Sumption, M. R. 1941. *Three hundred gifted children: A follow-up study of the results of special education of gifted children.* Yonkers-on-Hudson, N.Y.: World Book.

Terman, L. M. and Oden, M. H. 1947. The gifted child grows up: Twenty-five years' follow-up of a superior group. *Genetic Studies of Genius,* vol. IV. Stanford, Calif.: Stanford University Press.

U.S. Bureau of Education. 1911. *Bulletin 14.*

4

THE ENRICHMENT TRIAD MODEL: A GUIDE FOR DEVELOPING DEFENSIBLE PROGRAMS FOR THE GIFTED

Joseph S. Renzulli

This chapter will describe and attempt to show the relationships that exist among the three different types of enrichment that are presented in figure 4.1. The first two types, General Exploratory Activities and Group Training Activities, are considered to be appropriate for all learners; however, they are also important in the overall enrichment of gifted and talented students for at least two reasons. First, they deal with strategies for expanding student interests and developing the thinking and feeling processes and for this reason they are viewed as necessary ingredients in any enrichment program. Second, and perhaps more importantly, these two types of enrichment represent logical input and support systems for Type III Enrichment which is considered to be the only type that is appropriate mainly for gifted students. Type III Enrichment, entitled Individual and Small Group Investigations of Real Problems, is the major focus of this model and the proportions suggested in figure 4.1 are intended to imply that approximately one-half of the time that gifted students spend in enrichment activities should be devoted to these types of experiences. Because of the importance of Type III Enrichment in the present model, it will be dealt with in two different ways. In this section, Type III experiences will be described and a rationale will be developed to support the assertion that investigations of real problems should be the mainstay of programs for the gifted and talented. In the final section of the book, specific suggestions will be offered in an effort to provide some practical guidance for implementing Type III experiences. Although some practical suggestions regarding Types I and II are discussed in the present chapter, these two types of enrichment have received a great deal of attention in contemporary educational literature and therefore will be discussed here only as they interrelate with Type III.

Reprinted with permission of publisher, Creative Learning Press. Originally published 1977 as chapter 3 (pp. 13–17) in *The enrichment triad model: A guide for developing defensible programs for the gifted and talented*. Wethersfield, Conn., Creative Learning Press.

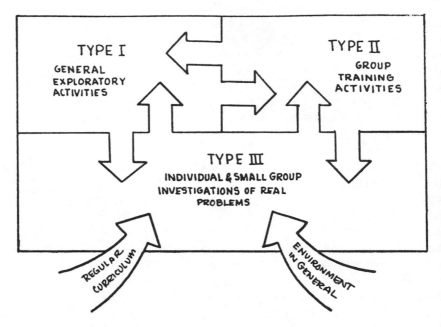

Fig. 4.1.   The enrichment triad model

Before getting into a description of the three types of enrichment, however, I would like to point out a few assumptions underlying the model. The first assumption relates to the way in which I will define the entire concept of enrichment. By *enrichment* I simply mean experiences or activities that are above and beyond the so-called regular curriculum. Since I am defining enrichment in relation to aspects of the regular school experience, I would like to discuss briefly a few concerns about the regular curriculum and how it relates to the concept of enrichment.

A great deal of our energy in gifted education has been expended on citing the ills and woes of the so-called regular curriculum, and there is indeed much justification for such criticism. But because we live in a "credentialing" society, one in which youngsters must pass SAT exams and possess certain basic skills to climb educational and career ladders, I will make two simple observations about the regular curriculum. First, there are indeed certain basic competencies that all students should master in order to adapt effectively to the culture in which they are growing; and second, the mastery of these competencies should be made as streamlined, exciting, and relevant as possible. This is true for all students, and especially for those youngsters who can master basic competencies in a highly efficient and rapid manner. I am certain that you will agree that gifted programs would be in serious trouble if high potential students fell behind on basic skills or if they failed to get into college because of poor scores on admission examinations.[1] But rather than attacking the regular curriculum, I have simply learned to live with it and hope that it will improve through evolution (and perhaps through some influence from the types of experiences that are being advocated in gifted education). We may not agree with the hurdles that students must jump in a credentialing society, but we should not be naïve enough to pretend that these hurdles do not exist.

The word *enrichment* is, of course, an important concept in general education and the concept certainly is not the exclusive "property" of persons interested in the gifted and talented. In a certain sense it is impossible to disagree with persons in general education who are fond of expounding irrefutable truisms such as "all circular experiences should be enriching for all students," and "there is no such thing anymore as the regular curriculum; we individualize and enrich the curriculum for all of our students." But these statements are more nearly idealistic rhetoric than reality; and even in schools which make much fanfare about that magic word, *individualization,* it is a reality that most youngsters spend the majority of their time covering a common body of prescribed material at each grade level. They may cover the material at different rates of speed, but there are very few youngsters who don't jump through essentially the same set of hoops.

It is, however, precisely because the regular curriculum (even in its most excellent manifestations) fails to meet the needs of all students that we require special provisions for some youngsters, and in the case of the gifted and talented, these special provisions almost always take the form of some type of curricular enrichment. In its simplest form, enrichment may be merely a matter of introducing gifted students to advanced courses early. This practice, sometimes referred to as vertical enrichment or acceleration, usually consists of allowing students to enroll in courses to which they would not ordinarily have access until later years. Although this approach lacks imagination so far as curricular reconstruction is concerned, it may very well be appropriate in subjects such as mathematics, physics, and computer science that are highly structured and sequential in concept complexity. Placing a youngster in an advanced course may indeed take care of his or her need to be challenged and to interact with equally advanced peers and a more specialized instructor; however, such placement may respect only one dimension of the learner—his or her advanced ability. I am not against acceleration or advanced placement courses, but the word *course* automatically implies a certain amount of structure and uniformity; and my experience has been that when youngsters have simply been enrolled in advanced courses without any concern for two other important dimensions of the learner, then everyone ends up marching to the tune of the same drummer, albeit at a faster beat.

This leads me to the second assumption underlying this enrichment model.

[1]Witness the recent congressional concern about the continuous drop in SAT scores and critical articles in news magazines about incompetency in basic skill areas. See, for example, "Why Johnny Can't Write," *Newsweek,* 8 December, 1975.

The learner has two other dimensions that must be respected in an enrichment situation, and even an advanced course may fail to take account of (1) the student's specific content interests and (2) his or her preferred style(s) of learning.[2] An almost universal finding in the evaluation work that I have done in numerous programs for the gifted has been that the greatest source of student satisfaction almost always resulted from the students' freedom to pursue topics of their own choosing in a manner with which they themselves felt most comfortable. Thus, the second underlying assumption is that enrichment activities (with the possible exception of some Type II activities) must show complete respect for the learner's interests and learning styles, and that the point of entry for all enrichment must be an honest and sincere desire on the part of the student to pursue a particular topic or activity of his or her own choosing. Piaget has pointed out many times that all learning should emanate from the spontaneous interests and activities of students. Although there may be some disagreement with this statement so far as certain basic or required skills are concerned, I believe that student interests should be the cornerstone of all enrichment activities. This approach almost guarantees a highly motivated learner, but it also means that we must offer students many options, and we must take the time and develop the skills for assisting students in the identification of their true interests.

The third and final assumption underlying the model has to do with when and where enrichment opportunities are offered. Since the model deals with basic aspects of learning, I have no predetermined notions about the physical circumstances under which enrichment experiences should take place. It could be in the regular classroom as an extension of the regular curriculum or it might be in a special resource room or independent study carrel in the library. It might take place in the community (indeed, Socrates did it in the market place in Athens), in a college classroom or laboratory, or even through a correspondence course in which the student never comes face-to-face with his or her instructor. It might involve one child or many children, and it does not necessarily require that only gifted children be involved in certain group projects which hold enrichment opportunities. The unique feature is, however, that if a particular student has a superior potential for performance in a particular area of sincere interest, then he or she must be allowed the opportunity to pursue topics therein to unlimited levels of inquiry.

---

[2]An instrument that is currently available to assist teachers in the identification of learning style preferences is called the Learning Styles Inventory. This instrument is filled out by students and provides scores for nine learning style dimensions including lecture, discussion, simulation, and independent study. For further information about the Learning Styles Inventory, write to Linda H. Smith, University of Connecticut, Box U-64, Storrs, Conn. 06268.

5

CAREER EDUCATION
FOR GIFTED PREADOLESCENTS

Lynn H. Fox

There has been some recent interest among educators and parents in increasing the emphasis on career education in the general school curriculum. Many believe that the learning of basic skills will be more meaningful to students if they have some understanding of the need for these skills and knowledge for their later adult roles. Intellectually gifted students are as likely as less academically oriented students to need career education programs and counseling.

Although definitions of *career education* vary, it is generally agreed that there should be three stages or phases in career education programs. The first stage is the development of awareness of the world of work during the elementary school years. The second stage is career exploration in the early secondary school years. The third stage is career preparation during the later secondary school years until full-time entry into the labor force (Hoyt and Hebeler 1974).

In the development of the first stage of career education programs (career awareness) it is important that the special needs of intellectually gifted children be considered. Most children, even the gifted, have few opportunities to learn about the world of work, especially professional careers that are not highly visible to the public. Some gifted students, particularly females and blacks, limit their career options in scientific and technical fields by self-selecting themselves out of mathematics and science courses in the high school years (Sells 1976). The importance of female role models for gifted girls has been demonstrated elsewhere (Fox 1976a, 1976b). Thus, for intellectually gifted students it would seem important to include exposure to mathematical and scientific career areas and role models in an elementary school career awareness program.

A series of discussions among Mr. Raymond Trimmer, director of education for the Maryland Academy of Sciences, Dr. Gwendolyn Cooke, gifted child coordinator for Baltimore City Public Schools, and this author, project coordinator of the Intellectually Gifted Child Study Group (IGCSG) at The Johns

Reprinted with permission of editor, *Gifted Child Quarterly*. (Originally published 1976 in *Gifted Child Quarterly* 20(3): 262–73.

Hopkins University, led to the development of a model for a career awareness program for elementary school students of high intellectual ability.[1] Several unique aspects of this model evolved from these discussions. First, it focused on the career awareness needs of students who at an early age demonstrate superior academic potential. Second, it is designed for students at the pre- and early adolescent age when they may be presumed to be somewhat naïve about careers, open to and enthusiastic about new experiences and learning, and yet entering into a level of cognitive development that enables them to deal with abstract ideas. Third, this program stresses the teaching of broad job-related skills rather than knowledge about specific occupations per se. Fourth, the program brings college professors and college students into the elementary school to serve as appropriate role models for gifted students.

In the fall of 1974, a design for a pilot program was developed. The program itself began in the spring of 1975. Because computer science and statistical skills are becoming important for careers in a variety of fields at several levels, yet are typically excluded from the core of elementary or secondary school curricula, applied mathematics was chosen as the focus for the pilot program. Four course topics were chosen: computer science, probability, statistics, and geometric drawing.

DESIGN OF THE PROGRAM

The format for the program was a series of four mini-courses in applied mathematics developed and taught by three college and university mathematicians from The Johns Hopkins University, Towson State College, and Essex Community College, and a professional staff member of the Maryland Academy of Sciences. The classes met one day a week for one or two hours from February through June of 1975. The majority of the classes were held at the GATE (Gifted And Talented Education project) school, which was then housed at the George Kelson Elementary School in downtown Baltimore. Two classes of twelve students each met separately for three of the courses and together for one of them.

Selection of Students

Twelve sixth-grade students, six boys and six girls, at the GATE school were selected by Dr. Cooke and her staff for the program on the basis of testing for admission to the GATE school,[2] and teacher or staff recommendations. Twelve

---

[1]The Intellectually Gifted Child Study Group was established by a grant from the Spencer Foundation of Chicago. Funding for the project was provided by the Spencer Foundation of Chicago and the John W. Graham Fund.

[2]For admission to GATE, students are selected for general intelligence on the basis of subtest scores on WISC, Raven's Progressive Matrices, and other measures, including teacher, parent, and

fourth and fifth graders (six boys and six girls) from a public elementary school in Baltimore who in September of 1974 had been identified by IGCSG as being mathematically gifted were also invited.[3] Three of the boys were fourth graders and the remainder were fifth graders.

All in all, twelve boys and twelve girls from the two schools were selected. The group was racially mixed. One boy was Oriental, and four boys and five girls were black. The majority of the children came from middle-class families.

Description of the Courses

A computer terminal typed out a picture of Snoopy; students constructed or tested dice of different shapes for "fairness"; newspaper articles on population statistics and unemployment were analyzed; and students' drawings of honeycombs were compared with the real thing. These activities and more were part of the four mini-courses in mathematics. Brief descriptions of the four mini-courses are given below:

Geometric Drawing—taught by Dr. Martin Levin of Essex Community College. Five weekly two-hour classes on geometric drawing were held. The imaginative, artistic, and creative applications of mathematics were considered. Students were actively involved in geometric constructions and drawings. Students compared their own geometric drawings to patterns found in art and nature.

Statistics—taught by Dr. Susan Horn of The Johns Hopkins University. Three one-hour classes introduced some basic concepts in statistics. Students learned about the use of statistical tests to analyze observed outcomes of events and to predict future events. Students also gained experience with interpreting statistical graphs and information of the type reported in newspaper articles on the population and economy.

Probability—taught by Dr. Phyllis Chinn of Towson State College. Six one-hour classes were held to introduce the concepts of probability of observed events. Students constructed dice of different shapes and number of sides and tested dice and coins for "fairness" and for decision making in varying situations.

Computer Science—taught by Stephen Karon of the Maryland Academy of

---

peer nominations. Recommendations by teachers and nominations by psychologists on the basis of the WISC subtest scores were used to select the students for the career project. Later testing on the numerical subtest of the Academic Promise Test showed that these students were very heterogeneous with respect to mathematical aptitude. Some seemed very gifted overall, whereas others were clearly more verbally than quantitatively gifted. All students seemed to enjoy the program and expressed a strong interest in continuing the following year. Subsequent groups will be chosen on the basis of mathematical aptitude.

[3]These students were selected in the fall of 1974 on the basis of scores on the numerical subtest of the Academic Promise Test.

Table 5.1. Summary of responses to pre- and post-questionnaires, by sex, for the Career Education and Mathematics Skills Project

		Boys %	Girls %	Chi-square significance level
Mathematics is favorite subject	Pre Post	92 83	67 92	Pre- to post-changes were not significant for either sex.
Interest in mathematical or scientific career	Pre Post	42 92	33 75	Pre- to post-change for boys was p<.01, for girls was p<.05.
Liked mathematics more after the courses		92	75	N.S.
Like school more after the courses		59	67	N.S.
Courses liked a lot Computer Probability Statistics Geometry		100 58 42 25	83 18 73 42	N.S. p<.05 N.S. N.S.

Sciences. This was a five-week series of two-hour classes on fundamentals of computers. Students learned about the binary number system and worked with a computer terminal and an audio-oscillator. Students constructed a mini-computer game out of beads and match boxes. The course was similar to the program used at the Maryland Academy of Sciences for older students.

EVALUATION

The evaluation centered around two questions. First, did the students who participated in the special career education program show any immediate change in attitude toward mathematics and mathematical careers? Second, did the students become more knowledgeable about mathematics and mathematical careers? Questionnaires were given to the students before and after the program, over a period of about five months. Parents were also asked to evaluate the program's impact upon their children.

Students' Attitudes

A questionnaire was administered to the students at the beginning and end of the program. The students were asked about their interest in mathematics and careers. On the second questionnaire the students were asked how well they had liked each of the four courses. The responses to the questionnaires are summarized in table 5.1.

On the first questionnaire, 92 percent of the boys and 67 percent of the girls said mathematics was their favorite subject. At the end of the program, mathematics was reported as the favorite subject for 83 percent of the boys and 92 percent of the girls. These changes were not statistically significant.

On the first questionnaire, 42 percent of the boys and 33 percent of the girls expressed strong interests in careers in science or mathematics. At the end of the program 92 percent of the boys and 75 percent of the girls expressed strong interest in such a career. These differences were significant.

On the second questionnaire, 92 percent of the boys and 75 percent of the girls reported liking mathematics more after being in the program. Fifty-nine percent of the boys and 67 percent of the girls reported liking school more, too. The sex differences were not significant.

Of the four courses, the computer course was the most popular. It was liked a lot by 92 percent of the students. Significantly more boys than girls liked the probability course.

On the basis of the questionnaires, it appeared that the program was effective in increasing interest in scientific careers and liking for mathematics, for both girls and boys.

Students' Knowledge

A second part of the pre- and post-questionnaire assessed students' knowledge of careers and selected topics in mathematics before and after the program. The pre- and post-questionnaire responses were typed and then put into random order, with all identification as to name or sex of student or school omitted. The questionnaires were then sent to two outside readers to rate the answers to each question. The raters did not know that they were rating more than one response for a given child or the nature of the intervention program in which the children had participated. Discrepancies between the judgments of the two original raters were resolved by a third rater.

On this questionnaire, students were asked to describe six occupations. Three of these (mathematician, statistician, and computer programmer) were directly related to the four mini-courses, and three of these (sociologist, botanist, and choreographer) served as controls. The pre- and post-questionnaire responses were rated as clearly wrong or not known; unclear or circular; or correct. The numbers of correct responses on the pre- and post-questionnaires are shown, by sex, in table 5.2. The percent change is also shown.

On the pre-questionnaire, only a third or fewer of the students could give a correct description of any of the six occupations. On the post-questionnaire, the students were more likely to give a correct response to all six occupations. The occupation for which there was the most change was statistician. On the pre-questionnaire, only three of the twenty-four students (13 percent) could describe that job, but on the post-questionnaire, nineteen of the twenty-four students (79

Table 5.2. Number and percentage of students correctly describing the occupations on the pre- and post-questionnaires for the Career Education and Mathematics Skills Project

Occupations	Pre #	Pre %	Post #	Post %	Percentage gain	Chi-square significance level
Math-related						
Statistician	3	13	19	79	533	p < .01
Mathematician	4	17	12	50	200	N.S.
Computer programmer	8	33	9	38	13	N.S.
Non-math-related						
Sociologist	5	21	10	41	100	N.S.
Choreographer	4	17	8	33	100	N.S.
Botanist	9	38	16	67	78	N.S.

percent) could give a sophisticated description of the occupation statistician. This change was statistically significant.

The next greatest improvement was on the description of mathematician. This difference was not significant. The descriptions of computer programmer showed little improvement because both pre- and post-descriptions tended to be too circular to evaluate. For example: computer programmers program computers to solve problems.

The questionnaire also asked the student to define arithmetic and mathematics, and to answer several mathematical questions related to the mini-courses. The number of students correctly answering these questions is shown in table 5.3. Although no attempt had been made to teach the answers to many of the questions directly, more students accurately answered the post-questionnaire than the pre-questionnaire, with the exception of defining a fraction, which was answered correctly by all but one student on both questionnaires. On the pre-questionnaire, four of the seven questions were answered correctly by at least half the students. On the post-questionnaire all seven questions were answered correctly by 75 percent or more of the students.

The five questions which showed significant change after the program were: what is arithmetic?, what is mathematics?, the question on probability and fair dice, the question on how artists use geometry, and the question on memory and the computer. These results indicate that the students did learn some of the content of the mini-courses. The teachers of statistics and probability expressed amazement at the insights shown by some of the students.

Parents' Evaluations

Parents of the twenty-four students were sent a questionnaire to help evaluate the program. A summary of their responses is shown in table 5.4. Parents of two girls did not respond. All of the parents who responded felt the program should

Table 5.3. Number and percentage of students correctly answering the mathematics question on the pre- and post-questionnaires for the Career Education and Mathematics Skills Project

Question	Pre #	Pre %	Post #	Post %	Percentage gain	Chi-square significance level
What is arithmetic?	16	67	22	92	38	$p < .05$
What is mathematics?	1	4	18	75	1,700	$p < .001$
What is a fraction?	23	96	23	96	0	N.S.
Proportion question[a]	16	67	20	83	25	N.S.
Probability question[b]	4	17	19	80	375	$p < .001$
How might an artist use geometry?	12	50	19	80	58	$p < .05$
What is memory in a computer?	9	38	21	88	133	$p < .001$

[a]If 600 people in a city of 7,200 living people all get sick with the flu, what *proportion* of the population has the flu? What changes in these numbers will make this proportion larger?
[b]What is the difference between fair and unfair dice?

be continued. Ninety-five percent felt the program had been *very* interesting for their child and that the child had learned *a lot* about mathematics in the program. Only 38 percent, however, felt the program had helped their child learn *a lot* about careers, although 55 percent said their child showed increased interest in career and educational plans.

Sixty-eight percent of the parents felt the program had increased their child's feelings of self-confidence *a lot*. Sixty-eight percent of the parents felt that the program had increased their child's liking for school, and 91 percent felt the program had increased their child's liking for mathematics. Eighty-two percent of the parents said their children talked more about the program than they typically talked about school. Thus, from the parents' perspectives, the program would seem to have been highly effective.

DISCUSSION

The evaluation of this pilot project suggests that the model is a good one. Students clearly enjoyed the experiences and asked for them to be continued the following year. Other students at the GATE school asked to be allowed to participate in the future. Parents also approved of the program. The measures of change in attitude and knowledge indicated that, even on a very short-term basis, the program accomplished some of its objectives. It is unlikely that this program will have long-range effects in the coming years unless the students, particularly the girls, have continued positive experiences in mathematics and science. Enrichment such as career education may be important, but it is not sufficient for the development of mathematical talent.

The major drawback of the model is that it involves a great deal of time on the part of the professionals, yet they reach only a small group of gifted students. It is

Table 5.4. Responses of parents to a questionnaire for evaluating the Career Eduation and Mathematics Skills Project

	Percentage of parents		
	Parents of Boys	Parents of Girls	Total
Thought the program was *very* interesting to the child	100	90	95
Thought the child learned *a lot* about mathematics	92	100	95
Thought the child learned *a lot* about careers	45	30	38
Child talked to parent about the special program after every class	67	70	68
Child talked about program more than he/she usually talks about school activities	92	70	82
Child showed increased interest in career and educational plans	50	60	55
Program increased child's feelings of self-confidence *a lot*	83	40	68
Program increased child's interest in math *a lot*	92	90	91
Program increased child's liking for school *a lot*	67	70	68
Believe program should be continued	100	100	100

far easier to get professionals to speak on a one-time basis to a large group of students than it is to have a professional take time to develop a curriculum and actually teach several classes. Many professionals are willing to do so for the equivalent of the salary they would receive for teaching a college course on a part-time basis. Although this cost is minute relative to the huge amounts of money spent on special programs for the disadvantaged and retarded, it is a fact that few schools or school systems are willing to spend the money for this type of program.

One possible solution is to develop and field test the curriculum for the courses in much the manner reported here and then have the college professors and professionals teach the programs to classroom teachers who in turn can reach many children. The units taught by the classroom teacher could be enhanced by visits to the classroom by the professionals or field trips for the students to see the professionals. This would make the program more cost effective. Whether or not it would be as interesting for the students is not known. IGCSG hopes to test this approach in the near future. Mr. Robert Johnson, Director of Education for the Baltimore Zoo, is currently helping with the first stage of this model. In the meantime, students in the initial program and one new group of students are continuing to enjoy a temporary extension of the original model from funding provided by the Maryland State Department of Education.

Another alternative would be to have very able sixth and seventh graders enroll for credit in computer science, elementary applied statistics, or related subjects at a local college. As Solano and George [(1976)] show in their article in this issue, unusually able students as young as 10 to 12 years old can readily succeed in such courses.

REFERENCES

Fox, L. H. 1976a. Sex differences in mathematical precocity: Bridging the gap. In D. P. Keating (ed.), *Intellectual talent: Research and development*. Baltimore, Md.: The Johns Hopkins University Press, pp. 183–214.

————. 1976b. Women and the career relevance of mathematics and science. *School Science and Mathematics* 76: 347–53.

Hoyt, K. B., and Hebeler, J. R. 1974. *Career education for gifted and talented students*. Salt Lake City, Utah: Olympus Publishing Company.

Sells, L. W. 1976. The Mathematics filter and the education of women and minorities. In L. H. Fox, L. E. Brody, and D. H. Tobin (eds.), *Women and the mathematical Mystique*. In press.

[Solano, C. H., and George, W. C. 1976. College courses for the gifted. *Gifted Child Quarterly* 20(3): 274–85.]

6

ENRICHMENT

Dean A. Worcester

Enrichment as a way of giving better educational opportunities to the mentally advanced child implies providing experiences for which the average or below-average child lacks either the time, the interest, or the ability to understand. Clearly, these experiences, if they are to be enriching, will be such as to widen and deepen the child's understanding.

GENERAL ASPECTS

To be enriching in the best sense, the added work should be integrated with the general curriculum activities. Too frequently, enrichment has been assumed to result from casual museum trips, a foreign language taken for a semester or two in the early grades and then dropped, turning on television for some national or political event, answering the telephone for the principal, helping the teacher with her records, helping the less gifted student with his work, making unsystematic collections of almost any kind of material, and the like. Frequently, the parents supply enrichment through such things as music lessons, typing lessons, and travel.

The line between enrichment and busywork is sometimes a thin one. The activities listed above may be enriching if they are carried on in a way that develops meaningful relationships in the developing child. Enrichment requires of the teacher much ingenuity and understanding. It is not enough just to say, "Go find something to do." Necessary is the same discerning guidance needed in the teaching of any subject.

Enrichment without acceleration is favored, at least verbally, by most administrators and most teachers. It is in keeping with the tradition that it is good for a child just to live a certain number of years in a school situation. It is a plan by which he will not leave home "too early." While he is still a child he has an

Reprinted with permission of University of Nebraska Press. Originally published 1956 as chapter 3 (pp. 39–50) of *The education of children of* above average *mentality*. Lincoln, Neb.: University of Nebraska Press.

opportunity to enjoy a wide range of new experiences. He has his childhood. There is truth in all of these points, but in each case only partial truth. To try to keep a bright child thinking like a baby is as unsuccessful as to continue to dress him in baby clothes. Where enrichment is real and adapted to the child, it is highly valuable. But what is enriching for one may be boring for another. Sometimes all of the group are "required" to experience the same enrichment. To hold to any one method exclusively is merely to move from one lock step to another.

Enrichment may be provided in any class anywhere. There is no school so small, no community so isolated, that opportunities do not exist. An understanding of the number system, and of other number systems, is not affected by geographical location. Sandhill country abounds in flora and fauna which may be *systematically* collected and classified. The imagination and the inquiring mind of the gifted child need only slight suggestions, encouragement, and sympathetic cooperation to find valuable outlets of expression. But for enrichment the teacher herself must be alert and imaginative. She must want to learn with the child and be happy when his understanding goes beyond hers. She must give generously of her time.

Enrichment is really very rarely encountered except in special classes in which that is a definite aim. In a segregated (or selected) class in which there is little or no acceleration, such as is found in the Cleveland Major Work classes or in those of Hunter College, we find genuine enrichment.

The Modesto Plan

At the senior high school level, an excellent provision for enrichment is the Independent Study plan as used at Modesto, California (1954). Here, a group of gifted high school seniors who are preparing for college are assigned a daily two-hour period with a special instructor. A program is mapped out in terms of the interests of the individual student. Each, in addition to the regular required work of his course, goes faster, further, and deeper, or engages in the study of new fields. It is an avowedly "hard work" program and only those whose parents and who themselves agree to it are accepted. The reports of this program are enthusiastic.

When Should Enrichment Be Given?

Quite clearly, enrichment should be available to the bright child throughout his learning experience. The kindergarten child may already be eager to get new meanings of words; the fifth grader wants to explore methods of using nuclear power; the high school student is studying the possibilities of international cooperation.

When determining the kind of enrichment, and the time for it, it is well to consider the degree of insight which is likely to occur. This writer observed a third and fourth grade class discussing the opening of the United Nations which they had witnessed on television. The teacher led the children to comment on the purposes of the United Nations. The observer had the definite feeling that their comments were largely in terms of words rather than understandings, and he could not help wondering if accelerating in tool subjects and enrichment in terms of insight into the United Nations' affairs at a later time in the educational venture might not in the long run have been more profitable.

The secondary school with its wide range of courses and its long list of "activities" offers many possibilities for enrichment. Not only may a person take subjects other than those in his course of study, but numerous other avenues of interest are at hand.

In the college or university the chance for enrichment is, of course, almost unlimited, *provided* that a hidebound university administration does not refuse permission to register for extra hours. Even then, many a student has circumvented the rules by spending many joyous hours in the library or the laboratory—with great profit, though no credit.

Enrichment should be provided for all children who can profit from it whatever type of program they are in. The accelerated child should have enrichment. Indeed, if it *be* enrichment, acceleration in the sense of becoming more and more separated from the average group is inevitable, whether or not it is recognized by name, and whether or not the individual meets classes in another school building.

Values of Enrichment

The value of enrichment is so obvious that little needs to be said about it. If it is truly enriching, it has to be of value. In small schools where there may be only one gifted child at a particular educational level, or in schools with limited facilities but good teachers, or in schools where there is prejudice against acceleration, enrichment is particularly needed.

At the senior high school-freshman college level, much of the present overlapping could be obviated by planned enrichment. The study of the Ford Foundation for the Advancement of Education has shown that instead of taking the same courses in these two years, with little added value, students may well be provided with other content areas of study through cooperation of the high school and the college.

Evaluation of Enrichment

There have been few attempts really to evaluate enrichment programs. Such programs appear to be good prima facie. Those who have been enrolled usually say that they liked the experience. One thoroughgoing attempt at a follow-up study of an enrichment program is Barbe's (1953) study of graduates of Major Work classes in Cleveland. The Cleveland program began in 1920 and has grown steadily with special classes for the gifted in both elementary and high schools. Children whose IQs are 125 or more are eligible for these classes. They are completely segregated. There is no acceleration. The aim is to cover more material and to cover it in a more thorough and meaningful manner.

It is clear that the graduates of these Major Work classes have been successful. College education was emphasized in the classes and a very large proportion of the students went to college (90 percent of the men and 63 percent of the women). Of those who went to college 67 percent were in the upper quarter of their class. As a group, they are engaged in higher-level occupations than the average. They are well adjusted socially and emotionally. More than 50 percent of those who went to college were members of social fraternities. Most of them are married and the divorce rate has been low. The results are very similar to those obtained from other studies of gifted children—especially the study of Terman and Oden. Since most of the children in these other investigations did not have the opportunity for educational experiences given to the Cleveland children, it cannot be asserted that the latter's success was due directly to the Major Work program. On the other hand, many of the Cleveland children lived in less favorable circumstances than most of those in the Terman-Oden study.

Barbe (1955) also secured from a large number of those who had been graduated from the Major Work program their own evaluation of it. About half of them approved the program with enthusiasm and 37 percent or more approved with hesitancy. Only 7.9 percent disapproved.

It may be specially noted that 61 percent of the males and 74 percent of the females believed that the classes had aided them in making good adjustment. The aspect of the program liked best was the opportunity to express individuality in an atmosphere free from regimentation. Least liked was the lack of social contact with other pupils.

It appears, then, that in the minds of those who have been in it the program is successful. Certainly it did not interfere with their progress (except that it delayed it), and in many respects it aided it.

Disadvantages of Enrichment

1. As has been pointed out above, the term *enrichment* may cover activities which are only busywork or, rarely we hope, enriching only to the teacher who gets some of her work done for her.

2. When enrichment is accomplished in a special class in which enrichment is the only planned difference from other classes, the school may become blind to how different these children are from the others, and the children may become restive—desiring the opportunity to move on to experiences for which they feel their competence.

3. After all, enrichment is an individual matter; a program based on enrich-

ment as its primary purpose is in danger of becoming *merely a program*—a set of activities which are supposed to be equally attractive and profitable to all. This denies the uniqueness of genius.

SELECTED CLASSES

Classes designed for gifted or mentally advanced children have been variously named. The more common general titles have been *segregated,* sometimes *partially segregated* or *special.* This writer prefers the word *selected,* as proposed by Hildreth (1952). In particular school systems specific names are commonly used—such as Cleveland's Major Work classes.

Whether or not children who are advanced mentally should be placed in separate classes has been a matter of much debate.

Several years ago selected classes, under plans for homogeneous grouping, were fairly common. Many of these were discontinued for various reasons. Sometimes they were attacked as being undemocratic. Some people were influenced by researches purporting to show that gains over those obtained in heterogeneous groups did not justify them. (Some of these researches forgot that the reason for a selected class is to give the opportunity to do different things in different ways. Clearly, then, the measure of success could not be the same for these as for nonselected groups.) The present trend is toward more of these classes.

Where the school is so large that there is more than one class of a given grade in the same building, it is relatively easy to put the brighter ones together unobtrusively. In the secondary school, divisions can be made among those who show differences in competence in particular subjects. There is no implication of a superiority-inferiority difference in the fact that one student is studying algebra and another general mathematics, or that one is doing more advanced mathematics than another. Some people just like mathematics.

There are several matters to be kept in mind relating to selected classes:

1. Size of school. These classes are feasible only in those school systems whose enrollment is large enough to justify a special room and a special teacher. While such a class may combine more than one grade level—although in large systems this might not be necessary—perhaps twelve pupils of approximately the same educational level will be the minimum requirement. There are those who will think this minimum too low. However, when one thinks of the willingness to provide special instruction for the physically handicapped and the mentally retarded in classes of this size, and when he then thinks of the stupendous contributions which society may expect from the finest training of its finest minds, he becomes eager to see what can be done when a teacher really has time to devote to the needs of a few outstanding pupils. Possibly the maximum size of such a class may be as high as twenty, but it must be remembered that time for attention to individual pupils is of first importance.

2. Are selected classes democratic? A democratic society selects individuals for all kinds of special purposes. In school we select for the band, the school paper, the football team. So long as the selection is based upon ability and no one is excluded because of race, social or economic status, or other factors not related to ability, there can be no basis to the charge that selected classes are undemocratic.

3. Do the classes produce snobs? It is sometimes feared that these classes will result in their members' thinking too highly of themselves. Much careful observation has been given to children in selected classes with the almost 100 percent conclusion that such fears are groundless. Children are working together in groups and on individual projects. In group activities they find others who are their equals or superiors. They learn to respect the knowledge which each possesses concerning his own project. They mingle outside of their class with others in the school.

It is much more likely that an attitude of superiority will develop if the gifted child is in a mixed class. Here he is almost always right—he knows the answers and the others know that he does. He may constantly compare himself with those who do not have the answers. He is frequently resented by the others.

An exceedingly common practice, and one far more likely to produce snobs than a selected class, is to have those in a single classroom divided into fast learners, slow learners, and, perhaps, a middle group. No situation could be devised which is better adapted to making the bright child feel superior and the slower one believe he is "dumb."

4. Special subjects. When upper grades are reached there may be selected classes in special subjects. For example, a group interested in mathematics, science, or literature may be formed which will not only cover the regular work in the subject but roam far afield in it. This is one of the best ways of encouraging talent. Where there are not enough children for a class, laboratory or library facilities or special correspondence courses may be made available to an individual.

Partially Segregated Classes

Some schools organize what are usually called partially segregated classes. The children of high ability are kept together for certain portions of their work, the remainder being done with the general group. In the Colfax School in Pittsburgh the children of high mentality meet together for their academic work but are undifferentiated from other pupils for social activities, music, and the like. The Modesto plan, described above, also takes the gifted high school pupils from their classmates for only a portion of the time.

This type of class is almost always employed as an enrichment procedure. It usually *assumes* that the gifted children are like, or ought to be like, others in all except "intellectual" matters. The assumption is of doubtful validity. However, when a well-organized program of work is provided, children in these classes do profit substantially, and the lack of social contact with other children, mentioned by those who had been in the Major Work program at Cleveland, is lessened.

Values of Selected Classes

Selected classes give opportunity for rapid progress, enrichment, or both. A flexible program adapted to the needs of the particular group is possible. The class moves at its own pace, neither waiting for nor neglecting the one who learns a bit more slowly,

ACCELERATION AND ENRICHMENT COMPARED

It is unfortunate that we have no good studies which reliably compare the merits of various methods of caring for the needs of the gifted. Apparently *any* scheme which tries to do something for them yields value. Studies of enrichment show those who have experienced it to be successful beyond the average in almost every measurable respect. Studies of acceleration also show successful results in every way. Whether or not one group would have been more successful if it had had the other's experience, we do not know. We do know that the accelerated students have saved time.

REFERENCES

Barbe, W. R. 1953. A follow-up study of the graduates of special classes for gifted children. *University Microfilm,* August.
————. 1955. Evaluation of special classes for gifted children. *Exceptional Children* 22.
Hildreth, G. 1952. *Educating gifted children.* New York: Harper and Brothers.
Modesto Public Schools. 1954. Modesto (Calif.) program for gifted students.

III

Acceleration:
Highlights of the Literature

7

THE PROBLEM OF SCHOOL ACCELERATION

Lewis M. Terman and Melita H. Oden

There has been much controversy regarding the extent to which children of high IQ should be allowed to become accelerated in school. At one extreme is the opinion that the gifted child should be given a grade placement corresponding to his mental age; at the other extreme are those who would base promotions on the calendar without regard to mental ability. Neither of these extreme views has many advocates, though the latter is perhaps more commonly held than the former. The fact remains, however, that many educators believe considerable acceleration is desirable, whereas many others are opposed to it.

An alternative is to provide special classes with an enriched curriculum for the gifted. Such classes have been established in many cities during the last two decades and have thoroughly demonstrated their value. In view of the fact that at present special classes are available to only a small minority of gifted children, we are usually faced by the choice between acceleration and nonacceleration in grading systems designed primarily for the average child. Attempts are often made to enrich the program for especially bright children in the ordinary classroom, and such programs at their best can be very helpful. Unfortunately, the so-called enrichment often amounts to little more than a quantitative increase of work on the usual level. This may keep the gifted child out of mischief, but it is hardly educational. Since only a very few of our California subjects had enjoyed any special educational opportunities in the elementary or secondary schools—beyond the opportunity to skip an occasional grade or half-grade—this chapter will be devoted to an examination of the evidence which bears on the advantages and disadvantages of acceleration.

The most common arguments in favor of acceleration are that it improves the child's motivation, prevents him from developing habits of dawdling, allows earlier completion of professional training, and makes earlier marriage possible. The total cost of the child's education would be somewhat reduced, but this is hardly a major consideration. On the other side it is argued that grade-skipping

Reprinted with permission of director, Stanford University Press. Originally published 1947 as chapter 20 (pp. 264–81) of The gifted child grows up. *Genetic Studies of Genius,* vol. IV. Stanford, Calif.: Stanford University Press. Copyright renewed 1975.

aggravates the child's problem of social adjustment, promotes bookishness and one-sided development, is dangerous to physical or mental health, and leaves gaps in the child's academic knowledge and skills. Although our data do not afford an accurate measure of all these alleged effects, they do furnish evidence of considerable value with respect to some of them.

As an index of degree of acceleration, we have used the age at high school graduation and have divided our subjects into three groups: (1) those who graduated below the age of 15 years 6 months; (2) those graduating between 15 years 6 months and 16 years 6 months; and (3) those graduating at or above the age of 16 years 6 months. The distribution of ages for the three groups at high school graduation is shown in table 7.1. If age 18 plus or minus 6 months is considered the normal age for completing high school, those in group I are accelerated from 2 to 4 years, those in group II from 1 to 2 years, and those in group III from 0 to 1 year. Only 6.8 percent of men and less than 2 percent of women graduated above the upper limit of normal age as above defined; that is, above 18 years 6 months. The mean ages at completing high school were as follows for groups I, II, and III, respectively: 14.9, 16.0, and 17.3 years.

When in the following passages the groups are referred to as "accelerates" and "nonaccelerates," the former includes groups I and II—i.e., those graduating from high school before the age of 16 years 6 months (average 15.9)—and the latter term includes all graduating at 16 years 6 months or over (average 17.4).

Our data regarding the above groups will be presented under six heads: (1) intelligence, (2) educational history, (3) vocational history and avocational interests, (4) social adjustment, (5) marital status, and (6) physical and mental health.

ACCELERATION AS RELATED TO INTELLIGENCE

The data here include the childhood IQs of those qualifying for the gifted group on the Stanford-Binet test, 1940 scores on a group intelligence test (the Concept Mastery), and 1940 self-ratings on the extent to which early mental superiority had been maintained. The information is summarized in table 7.2. In this and the following tables, the Ns for which data are available *both* on acceleration and on the item in question are given in parentheses. Means and percentages are given to the nearest first decimal.

The reader is reminded that not all the items in the case-history record were available for every subject. In the first place, there are thirty-seven men and thirty-eight women not included in any of the acceleration groups because their education had been irregular, because they had not completed high school, or because the exact age at completion could not be obtained from our records. Furthermore, the Stanford-Binet had been given only to those subjects who were 13 years or younger when located. These numbered 1,030 cases.[1] The Concept

---

[1]Of the original 1,070 Binet-tested subjects, 40 were deceased by 1940.

Table 7.1. Grouping by age at high school graduation

	Men		Women	
	N	Percentage	N	Percentage
Group I:				
13-6 to 13-11	..	..	1	0.2
14-0 to 14-5	6	0.8	3	0.5
14-6 to 14-11	10	1.3	7	1.1
15-0 to 15-5	20	2.5	15	2.5
Total, group I	36	4.6	26	4.3
Group II:				
15-6 to 15-11	71	9.0	61	10.1
16-0 to 16-5	110	14.0	90	14.8
Total, group II	181	23.0	151	24.9
Group III:				
16-6 to 16-11	170	21.7	184	30.3
17-0 to 17-5	192	24.5	136	22.4
17-6 to 17-11	95	12.1	69	11.4
18-0 to 18-5	58	7.4	30	4.9
18-6 and above	53	6.8	11	1.8
Total, group III	568	72.5	430	70.8
Total, all groups	785		607	
Mean ages (years)				
Group I	14.93		14.90	
Group II	16.00		16.00	
Group III	17.43		17.22	
Groups I and II	15.87		15.89	
Groups I, II, and III	16.99		16.78	

Mastery test of 1940 required supervision for its administration and so was given only at group meetings or during a personal interview with subjects; those living at too great a distance for personal contacts were not given this test. There were in all 954 Concept Mastery tests given, without regard to whether the subjects had originally qualified for the gifted study on a Binet or a group test. The subjective report on maintenance of mental superiority was available for 1,252 subjects who responded to this item on the General Information Blank of 1940. Thus the populations in parts 1, 2, and 3 of table 7.2, though overlapping, are not identical.

The table shows a significant relationship between the degree of acceleration and childhood IQ. Although the IQ difference between the accelerates (groups I and II) and the nonaccelerates (group III) is not great in the absolute sense, being only 6.4 points for men and 3.9 points for women, it is statistically reliable. The respective critical ratios are 5.6 and 3.5. Even so, the correlation between acceleration and IQ is very low, for among the nonaccelerates are fifty men and thirty-nine women in the IQ range 160 to 190. In the schools these subjects attended, IQs played little part in grade placement.

Table 7.2. Acceleration versus intelligence

	Acceleration groups			
	I	II	I + II	III
1. Childhood IQ (Binet)				
Mean for men	161.1	155.1	156.1	149.7
	(27)	(130)	(157)	(365)
		CR: I + II vs. III = 5.6		
Mean for women	155.3	152.8	153.1	149.2
	(20)	(125)	(145)	(300)
		CR: I + II vs. III = 3.5		
2. Concept Mastery point score (1940)				
Mean for men	118.9	102.7	105.1	96.1
	(18)	(108)	(126)	(387)
	CR: I vs. III = 3.4; CR: I + II vs. III = 2.8			
Mean for women	105.2	93.6	95.1	93.7
	(15)	(96)	(111)	(303)
		CR: I vs. III = 1.9		
3. Subjective report on present mental superiority: now "less marked"				
Men	43.3%	35.0%	36.5%	31.0%
	(30)	(140)	(170)	(455)
		CR: I vs. III = 1.3		
Women	54.5%	41.7%	43.8%	46.8%
	(22)	(115)	(137)	(342)
		CR: I vs. II = 1.1		

The 1940 Concept Mastery scores show much the same trends as the childhood IQs. Again the differences are more marked for men. For both sexes, group I rates well above group III, the critical ratio being 3.4 for men and 1.9 for women. However, when the total accelerates (groups I and II) are compared with group III, the difference, though still in favor of the accelerates, is not striking. For men it is fairly reliable, with a critical ratio of 2.8, but in the case of women the average score is as high for group III as for group II.

The subjective reports in the table on the extent to which early mental superiority had been maintained are contradicted by the test scores. The latter indicate that the highly accelerated have maintained their ability as well as the nonaccelerates, whereas the subjective reports indicate a greater tendency among the accelerates for mental superiority to become less marked. One must accept the evidence of the test scores. The reports are probably influenced by the natural tendency of an accelerated child to become more conscious of his or her early superiority than does the equally bright child who is not accelerated.

ACCELERATION AS RELATED TO EDUCATIONAL HISTORY

Table 7.3 presents data on the relationship of acceleration to the proportion graduating from college, the proportion completing one or more years of

Table 7.3. Acceleration versus educational history

	Acceleration groups			
	I	II	I + II	III
1. Graduated from college				
Men	86.1%	76.0%	77.7%	68.8%
	(31)	(136)	(167)	(373)
		CR: I vs. III = 2.8; I + II vs. III = 2.6		
Women	79.1%	71.6%	72.7%	66.3%
	(19)	(106)	(125)	(272)
		CR: I vs. III = 1.5; I + II vs. III = 1.5		
2. Mean age at college graduation (years)				
Men	19.9	21.1	20.9	22.1
	(29)	(131)	(160)	(354)
Women	19.8	20.6	20.5	21.6
	(19)	(105)	(124)	(261)
3. Average college grade of B or better				
Men	75.8%	77.1%	76.8%	71.5%
	(33)	(144)	(177)	(390)
		CR: I + II vs. III = 1.3		
Women	78.9%	86.9%	85.8%	77.4%
	(19)	(115)	(134)	(297)
		CR: I + II vs. III = 2.2		
4. One or more graduation honors				
Men	40.0%	41.9%	42.2%	39.0%
	(30)	(136)	(166)	(346)
Women	47.4%	33.7%	35.8%	30.9%
	(19)	(104)	(123)	(265)
5. One or more years of graduate work				
Men	58.3%	54.8%	55.3%	43.4%
	(21)	(98)	(119)	(235)
		CR: I + II vs. III = 3.0		
Women	58.3%	41.9%	44.2%	34.4%
	(14)	(62)	(76)	(141)
		CR: I + II vs. III = 2.2		
6. Earning 15 or more recommending units in high school				
Men	93.9%	87.0%	88.1%	82.4%
	(31)	(140)	(171)	(417)
		CR: I + II vs. III = 1.8		
Women	95.2%	92.6%	92.9%	93.2%
	(21)	(135)	(156)	(381)
7. Mean achievement test quotient (1922)				
Men	155.5	150.8	151.5	144.7
	(16)	(94)	(110)	(278)
		CR: I + II vs. III = 4.9		
Women	154.2	145.6	146.5	139.6
	(12)	(102)	(114)	(211)
		CR: I + II vs. III = 5.3		

graduate work, age at college graduation, average grade in college, the winning of graduation honors, and the high school scholastic record. At the end of the table are the mean achievement quotients for those given the Stanford Achievement Test battery in 1922, though here the Ns are relatively small because this test was given only to members of the Main Experimental Group enrolled in the second school grade or above.

Table 7.3 shows that the greater the degree of acceleration, the greater is the likelihood of graduation from college and of remaining for one or more years of graduate work. In the case of men both trends are statistically significant. However, the relationship may not be entirely one of cause and effect, since the accelerates had also a little advantage in IQ.

A slightly larger proportion of accelerates than nonaccelerates made an average grade of B or better in college, and the accelerates did a trifle better in winning graduation honors, despite the fact that for men the mean age of graduation was 2.5 years younger in group I than in group III, and for women 2.3 years younger.

Turning to the high school record we find in the case of men a fairly definite trend toward better scholastic achievement by the accelerates. There is no such relationship between high school achievement and acceleration in the case of women.

The last section of the table shows that the accelerates greatly excelled nonaccelerates in achievement as measured by a three-hour battery of objective tests given in 1922 when the subjects were in the elementary grades. The difference is highly reliable, the critical ratio being 4.9 for men and 5.3 for women. In the main, however, promotions were only very loosely correlated with the amount of curriculum material the child had mastered. Probably the question of promotion or nonpromotion was usually decided on the whims of individual classroom teachers or school principals.

ACCELERATION AS RELATED
TO VOCATIONAL HISTORY AND AVOCATIONAL INTERESTS

Table 7.4 gives for men the occupational classification by census groups, and the proportion of each acceleration group in the A and C classifications for vocational success. These groups include, respectively, the most and least successful 20 percent of men.

The table shows that among men the accelerates more often than nonaccelerates are in the professional and higher business occupations, and less often in occupational groups III to VI. The data do not tell to what extent acceleration in itself has caused subjects to choose a profession who would not otherwise have done so, but we know of individual cases who believe that acceleration was a factor in such choice. Especially in such professions as medicine, law, or university teaching, an early entrance into graduate study is a real advantage to the

Table 7.4. Acceleration versus occupational classification and vocational success (men)

	Acceleration Groups			
	I Percentage	II Percentage	I + II Percentage	III Percentage
1. Census occupational grouping of men				
Census group I	51.5	51.2	51.3	44.4
		CR: I + II vs. III = 1.6		
Census group II	36.4	28.3	29.7	24.2
		CR: I vs. III = 1.4		
Census groups III to VI	12.1	20.5	19.0	31.4
		CR: I + II vs. III = 3.6		
2. In class A for vocational success				
(A, B, C grouping)	42.2	22.2	25.6	19.4
		CR: I vs. III = 2.6		
N for percentages	33	166	199	509

gifted student. Part 2 of the table gives additional evidence on the greater vocational success of men who were accelerated. Of the most highly accelerated men, 42.2 percent are in the A group for vocational success as compared with 19.4 percent of the nonaccelerates. In the case of women there was no significant relation between acceleration and occupational status.

Finally, we have compared the acceleration groups with respect to their avocational interests and their interest in twelve specific fields. One question in the 1940 General Information Blank asked the subjects to indicate their avocational interests. Another item in the same blank called for ratings of amount of interest in travel, outdoor sports, religion, mechanics, social life, literature, music, art, science, politics, domestic arts, and pets. The results of these inquiries showed no significant difference between accelerates and nonaccelerates in the frequency with which any given avocational activity was mentioned, in the number of avocational activities engaged in, or in the average rating of interest in the twelve specific fields named. The figures for accelerates and nonaccelerates were almost identical with respect to these variables. The conclusion is that even marked school acceleration has little if any effect upon either the kind or the number of avocational activities, and that it has no narrowing effect upon such interests as are represented in the twelve fields mentioned.

ACCELERATION AS RELATED TO SOCIAL ADJUSTMENT

The data on social adjustment given in table 7.5 include the following items: (1) a social adjustment rating based on information from parents and teachers in 1922; (2) a rating on social adjustment by field workers in 1928; (3) another rating on social adjustment in 1928 based on reports from parents; (4) preferred age of companions as reported by the subjects when in high school; (5) and (6) extracurricular activities of the subjects in high school and college; (7) 1940 scores on a

Table 7.5. Acceleration versus social adjustment

	Acceleration groups			
	I	II	I + II	III
1. Social adjustment (1922): parent-teacher rating "satisfactory"				
Men	88.2%	88.0%	88.1%	90.4%
	(34)	(167)	(201)	(518)
Women	95.7%	95.8%	95.8%	95.1%
	(23)	(142)	(165)	(388)
2. Social adjustment (1928): rated as "satisfactory" by field workers				
Men	70.0%	76.7%	75.7%	82.8%
	(20)	(95)	(115)	(268)
		CR: I vs. III = 1.5		
Women	100.0%	81.7%	83.3%	85.9%
	(8)	(88)	(96)	(235)
3. Social adjustment (1928): rated as "satisfactory" by parents				
Men	81.5%	96.2%	93.7%	92.1%
	(27)	(132)	(159)	(356)
		CR: I vs. II = 1.9		
Women	90.5%	92.2%	92.0%	97.4%
	(21)	(128)	(149)	(303)
4. Preferred older companions in high school years				
Men	71.4%	64.5%	65.7%	49.7%
	(28)	(138)	(166)	(364)
		CR: I vs. III = 2.4; I + II vs. III = 3.5		
Women	77.3%	72.3%	73.0%	50.5%
	(22)	(130)	(152)	(313)
		CR: I vs. III = 2.9; I + II vs. III = 4.9		
5. Extracurricular activities in high school: "several" to "outstanding"				
Men	32.4%	54.7%	50.8%	57.5%
	(34)	(159)	(193)	(497)
		CR: I vs. III = 3.0; I + II vs. III = 1.6		
Women	65.0%	59.3%	60.0%	62.3%
	(20)	(135)	(155)	(363)
6. Extracurricular activities in college: "several" to "outstanding"				
Men	33.3%	32.3%	32.5%	37.6%
	(30)	(130)	(160)	(343)
Women	22.2%	41.1%	38.2%	39.2%
	(18)	(102)	(120)	(257)
		CR: I vs. II + III = 1.7		
7. Mean score on test of aptitude for marital adjustment (1940)				
Men	84.18	86.72	86.29	86.28
	(31)	(153)	(184)	(499)
Women	69.09	78.87	77.27	77.67
	(24)	(124)	(148)	(375)
		CR: I vs. III = 2.2		

Table 7.5. Continued

	I	II	I + II	III
		Acceleration groups		
8. Proportion mentioning only disadvantages of acceleration				
Men	76.7%	58.8%	62.1%	61.0%
	(30)	(136)	(166)	(195)
		CR: I vs. II + III = 2.0		
Women	52.2%	63.3%	61.4%	59.1%
	(23)	(109)	(132)	(159)
		CR: I vs. II + III = 0.8		

test of aptitude for marital adjustment; (8) opinions of the subjects themselves on the advantages and disadvantages of any acceleration they had experienced.

The social adjustment rating of 1922 was a composite based on twelve items in the School Information Blank and six items in the Home Information Blank. The information called for related to such matters as the following: amount of play with other children, sex of playmates, relationships with other children (companionship sought or avoided, teased, considered queer or different), unusual or abnormal sex interests or behavior. The information thus supplied was evaluated as indicating "satisfactory adjustment," "some difficulty in adjustment," or "serious maladjustment." Table 7.5 shows that for each sex the proportion rated in 1922 as "satisfactory" was almost exactly the same for all the acceleration groups.

The field workers' adjustment ratings of 1928 were for men slightly less favorable to the accelerates than to the nonaccelerates, but for women there was no consistent trend. The 1928 ratings based on information from parents indicated a slight tendency to less-satisfactory adjustment among the most highly accelerated, but for neither sex was this trend statistically significant.

Part 4 of the table shows a marked relationship between degree of acceleration and preference expressed during adolescent years for older companions, the trend being about the same for boys and girls. The reader will have to judge the significance of this fact for social adjustment. Our opinion is that at the high school age a preference for older companions is a favorable rather than an unfavorable sign.

The ratings on extracurricular activities in high school showed no relationship to acceleration in the case of women. The one significant relationship in the case of men was in the smaller proportion of high ratings among those graduating from high school before the age of 15 years 6 months. This sex difference may reflect the difference between boys and girls in the age of reaching physical maturation. The high school girl who is greatly accelerated is usually more mature physically than the high school boy equally accelerated. In college, however, the participation in extracurricular activities by men was about the same for all the acceleration groups. The highly accelerated women made a poor showing on extracurricular activities in college, but the N of eighteen here is too small to warrant any generalization.

The mean scores on the 1940 test of aptitude for marital adjustment were, in the case of men, about the same for all the acceleration groups. In the case of women the mean for the highly accelerated was somewhat lower than for the other groups, but the difference was not entirely reliable (CR = 2.2).

In the last section of the table we have summarized the opinions expressed by the subjects regarding the advantages and disadvantages of acceleration they had experienced. In the General Information Blank the statement was worded as follows: "Were you greatly accelerated in school? If so to what extent do you consider this was an advantage or disadvantage?" It turned out that there were subjects in all the groups who did not regard themselves as having been accelerated; in fact there were sixty-four men and fifty-three women graduated from high school before 17 who said they were not accelerated. Eight of these were under 16 at high school graduation. On the other hand, there were a number of nonaccelerates (according to our definition) who considered themselves accelerated. Ninety-two men and sixty women who finished high school at 17 years or over felt that they had been "greatly accelerated" in school. We have omitted those who did not consider themselves accelerated from our computation of the percentages given in part 8 of table 7.5. The responses were classified into three categories: those which mentioned advantages only, those mentioning disadvantages only, and those mentioning neither or both; but we have included in the table only the percentages alleging disadvantages. The figures for group II and group III did not differ appreciably for either sex. Among the highly accelerated (group I) there was a marked sex difference, a larger proportion of men than of women stressing its disadvantages. This is probably another reflection of the fact that boys are retarded in their physical and social maturation as compared with girls.

Our conclusion from the evidence of table 7.5 is that the influence of school acceleration in causing social maladjustment has been greatly exaggerated. There is no doubt that maladjustment does result in individual cases, but our data indicate that in a majority of subjects the maladjustment consists of a temporary feeling of inferiority which is later overcome. The important thing is to consider each child as a special case.

ACCELERATION AS RELATED TO MARITAL STATUS

Table 7.6 gives the data on four items relating to marriage: the proportion who have married, mean age at marriage (first marriage if more than one), proportion separated or divorced, and mean score on a test of marital happiness.

The differences in the marriage rate are not statistically reliable. For men, the highest incidence was among the most accelerated, whereas women in this group had the lowest marriage rate. Separations and divorces occurred less often among the highly accelerated.

Table 7.6. Acceleration versus marital status

	Acceleration groups			
	I	II	I + II	III.
1. Are or have been married				
Men	72.7%	68.2%	68.9%	70.5%
	(36)	(179)	(215)	(559)
Women	60.0%	74.0%	72.0%	71.5%
	(25)	(150)	(175)	(425)
		CR: I vs. II = 1.3		
2. Mean age at marriage				
Men	24.8	25.5	25.4	26.1
	(26)	(115)	(141)	(358)
		CR: I vs. III = 2.1; I + II vs. III = 2.1		
Women	22.8	23.5	23.4	24.1
	(15)	(108)	(123)	(290)
		CR: I vs. II = 2.1; I + II vs. III = 1.8		
3. Separated or divorced (percentage of number married)				
Men	(1 case)	10.7%	9.5%	11.9%
	(26)	(122)	(148)	(394)
Women	(1 case)	12.6%	11.9%	12.8%
	(15)	(111)	(126)	(304)
4. Mean score on test of marital happiness				
Men	56.6	62.8	61.7	58.8
	(18)	(82)	(100)	(274)
Women	64.7	63.6	63.8	62.0
	(13)	(68)	(81)	(213)

The mean age at marriage was appreciably lower for the accelerated group. For each sex, group I was 1.3 years and group II was 0.6 of a year below the mean of group III. This trend is significant from the point of view of eugenics.

The test of marital happiness showed no reliable differences in mean score between accelerates and nonaccelerates. Among the women, both accelerated groups averaged a trifle higher than the nonaccelerates. On the whole, the data suggest that marital adjustment is not appreciably correlated with degree of acceleration.

ACCELERATION AS RELATED TO PHYSICAL AND MENTAL HEALTH

Our information on this topic includes the following items: (1) a health rating based on information secured from medical examinations and from several questions in the Home Information Blank and the School Information Blank of 1922 (our ratings of these data being in terms of "very good," "good," "fair," "poor," and "very poor"); (2) a rating on nervous tendencies based upon the responses to several questions in the Home Information Blank and the School Information Blank of 1922; (3) a 1928 health rating made by parents; (4) a 1928 rating on information furnished by parents regarding nervous tendencies; (5) age of puberty as reported by the parents, based upon first menstruation of girls and on voice change in the case of boys; (6) a self-rating on health made by the subjects in 1940 on a five-point scale from "very good" to "very poor"; (7) a rating by us on all-round adjustment in 1940 based upon field workers' conferences with subjects, reports by parents or other relatives, and information which came to us through letters or conferences.

The outstanding facts given in table 7.7 can be briefly summarized. The proportion whose health was rated "good" or "very good" on the 1922 evidence was highest in group I, but for neither sex was the difference reliable. It is possible that good health was regarded by some of the teachers as a necessary condition for granting extra promotions. The rating on nervous tendencies based on 1922 evidence was best for the most accelerated, as was also the 1928 health rating by parents. In the case of men the same was true of parents' rating on nervous tendencies in 1928, but on this rating women did not show any consistent trend.

The mean age of puberty of group III was for men 0.6 of a year later than for group I; for group II it was 0.3 of a year later than for group I. The trend for women was the same as that for men, the figures corresponding to those just given being 0.4 of a year and 0.3 of a year. The differences for both sexes between the accelerates (groups I and II) and nonaccelerates (group III) in the age at puberty are fairly reliable, the critical ratio being 2.4 for men and 2.5 for women.

The 1940 self-ratings on health by men averaged almost exactly the same for all three groups; in the case of women, the self-ratings were highest for group I (CR = 1.5).

Ratings on the all-round adjustment of men in 1940 were lower for group I than for the other groups, but the difference is not reliable. In the case of women, the percentages rated "satisfactory" were almost identical in the three groups.

The data reviewed give no support to the fairly widespread opinion that rapid promotion in school is likely to be detrimental to physical or mental health, though one must bear in mind the possibility that physical health and good general adjustment may sometimes have been regarded by teachers as necessary conditions for extra promotion.

Section 5 of the table suggests that children most accelerated in school were on the average also accelerated in physical maturation as indicated by the age of puberty. The relationship verges on reliability. Here again it is possible that teachers are sometimes influenced by the child's apparent physical maturity in permitting rapid advancement.

CONCLUSIONS

The controversy on the advantages and disadvantages of acceleration hinges on the relative weight that should be given to intellectual and social values in the

Table 7.7. Acceleration versus physical and mental health

	Acceleration groups			
	I	II	I + II	III
1. Health rating (1922) "good" to "very good"				
Men	78.1%	75.5%	75.9%	74.3%
	(25)	(117)	(142)	(359)
Women	90.9%	83.2%	84.3%	83.1%
	(20)	(114)	(134)	(304)
		CR: I vs. III = 1.2		
2. Rating on nervous tendencies (1922) "satisfactory"				
Men	96.9%	84.2%	86.3%	82.6%
	(31)	(139)	(170)	(409)
	CR: I vs. III = 4.1; I + II vs. III = 1.2			
Women	95.7%	93.6%	93.9%	90.1%
	(22)	(131)	(153)	(345)
		CR: I vs. III = 1.2		
3. Parents' rating on health (1928) "good"				
Men	100.0%	89.2%	91.1%	84.3%
	(33)	(140)	(173)	(398)
		CR: I + II vs. III = 2.5		
Women	100.0%	89.6%	91.1%	86.8%
	(24)	(120)	(144)	(302)
		CR: I + II vs. III = 1.5		
4. Parents' rating on nervous tendencies (1928) "satisfactory"				
Men	96.9%	89.8%	91.0%	87.4%
	(31)	(131)	(162)	(368)
	CR: I vs. III = 2.7; I + II vs. III = 1.3			
Women	85.7%	91.5%	90.7%	88.2%
	(18)	(119)	(137)	(292)
5. Mean age at puberty				
Men	14.2 yrs.	14.5 yrs.	14.5 yrs.	14.8 yrs.
	(21)	(100)	(121)	(358)
		CR: I + II vs. III = 2.4		
Women	12.7 yrs.	12.8 yrs.	12.8 yrs.	13.1 yrs.
	(25)	(142)	(167)	(414)
		CR: I + II vs. III = 2.5		
6. Self-rating on health (1940) "good" to "very good"				
Men	90.6%	89.9%	90.0%	91.2%
	(32)	(158)	(190)	(497)
Women	92.0%	82.8%	84.3%	83.3%
	(25)	(134)	(159)	(389)
		CR: I vs. III = 1.5		
7. Composite of 1940 data on all-round mental adjustment "satisfactory"				
Men	74.3%	83.2%	81.7%	79.5%
	(35)	(167)	(202)	(537)
		CR: I vs. II = 1.1		
Women	79.2%	83.6%	83.0%	82.0%
	(24)	(147)	(171)	(411)

educative process. If the child's intellectual welfare were the sole criterion, then promotion ought to be based primarily on mental age, since it is this factor that chiefly determines the intellectual difficulty of the school tasks one is able to master. The child who starts to school at the age of 6.5 years with a mental age of 10 years, can be brought to fourth-grade achievement before the end of his first school year. We know this as fact because it has happened over and over among the subjects of this group. Others in the group equally capable of making such progress—and this includes half or more of the subjects—have been caught in the lock step and held to school work two or three full grades below the level on which they could have functioned successfully.

Fortunately, this forced retardation does not slow up school achievement as much as one might expect. The gifted child may get bored, but, promoted or not, he manages somehow to achieve far more rapidly than his classmates. In a majority of school subjects the achievement quotient almost keeps pace with the intelligence quotient; or, stated in another way, the child's achievement in the school subjects closely parallels his or her mental age, although this is somewhat less true in such drill subjects as spelling and arithmetical computations than in the "thought" subjects. It is a fact of extraordinary significance that among our 10-year-olds there was almost no correlation between achievement test scores and the number of years and months they had attended school. Heilman's notable study (1928) shows that this is also largely true of the general school population at age 10. Achievement tests administered by Learned and Wood (1938) in forty-nine colleges and numerous high schools show that even at the upper educational levels there is only a mild correlation between achievement attained in a given subject and the months or years of formal study devoted to it. Incredible as it may seem, they discovered high school seniors who knew more science than some university seniors who had majored in science and were about to begin their careers as high school teachers of that subject.

Although children can and often do achieve remarkably in spite of being denied the special promotions they have earned, a considerable proportion of those in our gifted group languished in idleness throughout the grades and high school and failed to develop the ambition or habits of work necessary to make them successful in college. The question is, how much risk of social maladjustment one can afford to take in order to keep the gifted child at school tasks difficult enough to command his attention and respect. The data here reviewed indicate that the risk of maladjustment is less than is commonly believed. Our case histories indicate that the disadvantages of acceleration so frequently mentioned by our subjects (see table 7.5) are usually temporary. Moreover, the handicaps of social immaturity among the accelerated would not be so great if a larger proportion of the gifted were promoted rapidly, since in that case the underage child would not feel so conspicuous.

Sometimes, however, the choice between acceleration and nonacceleration is unavoidably a choice between evils, each of which needs to be weighed against the background of the individual child's personality. No universal rule can be laid down governing the amount of acceleration that is desirable. Some gifted children are less injured by acceleration of three or four years than are others by one or two years. Important factors are the child's social experience and his or her natural aptitude for social adjustment. So far as physique is concerned, perfect health is probably less crucial than physical maturity or even mere size. The oversized, physically mature, and socially experienced child of 12 may be at less disadvantage in high school than the undersized, immature, and socially inexperienced child of 14.

It is our opinion that children of 135 IQ or higher should be promoted sufficiently to permit college entrance by the age of 17 at latest, and that a majority in this group would be better off to enter at 16. Acceleration to this extent is especially desirable for those who plan to complete two or more years of graduate study in preparation for a professional career.

For a carefully controlled study of acceleration at the college level the reader is referred to the excellent monograph by Keys (1938) whose findings support the conclusions of this chapter at almost every point. Keys's study is particularly valuable because of his use of a control technique that enabled him to compare accelerates in college with a group of nonaccelerates who were equally intelligent. Several recent studies by Pressey and his associates (1946) present equally striking evidence on the advantages of acceleration for bright students.

REFERENCES

Heilman, J. D. 1928. The relative influence upon educational achievement of some hereditary and environmental factors. *Yearbook of the National Society for the Study of Education* 27(2): 35–65.

Keys, N. 1938. The underage student in high school and college. *University of California Publications in Education* 7: 145–272.

Learned, W. S., and Wood, B. D. 1938. *The student and his knowledge.* New York: Carnegie Foundation.

Pressey, S. L. 1946. Age of college graduation and success in adult life. *Journal of Applied Psychology* 30: 226–33.

8

OUTCOMES AND CONCOMITANTS OF ACCELERATION IN COLLEGE

Sidney L. Pressey

At the beginning of the war, in four undergraduate colleges of Ohio State University, only 7 percent of men and 3 percent of women were finishing a four-year program in less than the conventional time of three years nine months, but the number gradually increased until, in the school year 1944–45, 49 percent of the men and 29 percent of the women finished in a shorter time—37 percent of the men and 17 percent of the women in three years or less. The question now concerns the effects of such shortened overall time for completing an undergraduate program and, more generally, the relation of length of time, from entrance to graduation, to college career. It should be understood that, throughout the following discussion, acceleration is in this connection given a somewhat special meaning: an accelerated student is one who has taken less than the conventional time of three years nine months to complete an undergraduate program. A regular student is one who has proceeded at the conventional pace; usually he entered in September and graduated the fourth June thereafter, but this leeway was allowed, that he might complete his degree at the end of the summer quarter or in exactly four calendar years. If a student entered in other than that autumn quarter, a comparable length of time was considered regular. Retarded individuals were students who took longer than the regular time. Students who had not taken all their undergraduate work at Ohio State University were excluded, but those who had transferred from one college to another within the university were included.

Reprinted with permission of administrative manager from College of Education, Ohio State University. Originally published 1949 as chapter 6 (pp. 75–91) of *Educational acceleration: Appraisals and basic problems*. Bureau of Educational Research Monographs, No. 31, The Ohio State University, Columbus, Ohio.

Table 8.1. Age at entrance of accelerated, regular, and retarded students—percentages in each group entering at each age

Student groups	Age of entrance							Number	Median age
	16	17	18	19	20	21	Over 21		
Men									
Accelerated	4*	33	40	10	4	3	6	397	18.3
Regular	3	28	42	12	6	4	5	540	18.4
Retarded	2	20	40	18	8	5	7	524	18.7
Women									
Accelerated	5*	40	45	5	1	1	3	419	18.1
Regular	4*	40	47	6	2	1	1	1,106	18.1
Retarded	5	35	42	10	3	1	4	355	18.2

*A few 15-year-olds (less than 1 percent) were included.

GENERAL RELATIONSHIP OF TIME IN COLLEGE TO SUCCESS THERE

For a first overview of the situation, all those accelerated for the school years 1941–42 through 1945–46 were combined in a total of 816 accelerated students, the regular students in a second total of 1,646 individuals, and the retarded students in a final group of 879. The first issue relates to the nature of these three groups.

Age and Abilities

Table 8.1 shows that, in general, those students who moved through their under-graduate programs at faster than the conventional pace entered college a little younger, and those who took longer entered older. However, both medians and distributions of entrance ages of accelerated and regular women are practically identical. And the slightly greater proportion of accelerated men under 18 can be accounted for by entrance during the war, immediately upon high school gradua-tion rather than in September. Only very rarely does a student move through the twelve precollege grades at faster than the lock step rate, entering at 6 or a little bit before and completing high school at 17 or 18.

Table 8.2 shows that, somewhat as a result of earlier entrance but primarily of speedier progress in college, the accelerated students graduated at a distinctly younger age than the regular; and the retarded were even older. Three percent of the accelerated graduated at 19 or younger. About a third of the retarded men and an eighth of the women graduated at 25 or older. Though many accelerated students graduated young, more of Terman's gifted group graduated even younger; and the youngest of them did best.

Another aspect of the issue is the abilities of these three groups. Table 8.3

Table 8.2. Percentages of the Ohio State groups and of the Terman gifted group graduating at each age*

Student groups	Age at graduation							Median age
	19	20	21	22	23	24	Over 24	
Men								
Accelerated	3†	19	47	16	5	3	7	21.6
Regular		6	35	37	9	6	7	22.2
Retarded			4	24	24	17	31	23.9
Women								
Accelerated	3†	29	52	9	3	1	3	21.9
Regular		7	54	32	4	2	1	21.8
Retarded		1	8	43	24	8	16	22.9
Terman group‡								
Gifted men	7†	26	29	20	10	5	2	21.6
Gifted women	10†	35	36	13	3	2	2	21.1

*The numbers in each group are given in column 9 of table 8.1.
†Of the accelerates, less than 0.5 percent of each sex graduated under 19, and of the Terman cases only 1 percent of each sex.
‡Terman, L. M., and Oden, M. H. *The gifted child grows up*, p. 164. There were 519 men and 386 women in the groups here considered.

shows, as would be expected, that the accelerated students scored highest on the test of general ability given at entrance, and the retarded students lowest. However, the differences were not great; the medians of the accelerated were only 10 and 7 percentiles higher than the medians of the regulars. Furthermore, about 30 percent of the regulars and a quarter of the retarded students scored in the upper tenth and presumably had sufficient ability to accelerate. It may also be noted that a few students below the median in ability, as tested, nevertheless were able to graduate in less than the conventional time.

Relation of Overall Time Taken for a College Program to Accomplishment

The conventional first issue is, of course, that concerning the scholarship of these three groups. Table 8.4 shows that the accelerated students had the highest scholarship, regular next, and retarded lowest, as shown both by median point-hour ratios and by numbers with superior scholarship. Thus 37 percent of the accelerated men and 46 percent of the accelerated women had records of *B* or above for their entire undergraduate program, as compared with 21 and 27 percent for the regular, and 11 and 18 percent for the retarded. Moreover, there is no evidence that shortened programs tended to pull students down near the danger point as regards graduation. Rather, the proportion of students just getting by the minimum requirement for graduation (1.8) is lowest for the accelerated group for the men (5 percent as compared with 16 percent for the regular and 28 percent for the retarded). In short, acceleration appears not to affect scholar-

Table 8.3. Percentages of accelerated, regular, and retarded students having the indicated percentiles on the Test of General Ability given at entrance*

Student groups	O.S.P.E. percentiles							
	Under 40	40	50	60	70	80	90	Median
Men								
Accelerated	6	7	7	10	11	17	42	85.6
Regular	13	7	9	13	14	16	28	75.1
Retarded	16	7	10	14	17	14	22	71.9
Women								
Accelerated	3	3	7	9	13	18	47	87.1
Regular	8	7	9	10	16	19	31	80.1
Retarded	9	8	9	17	16	12	29	74.6

*The numbers in each group are given in column 9 of table 8.1.

ship adversely—if anything, the reverse would appear to be true. However, there is still the possibility that the effort of acceleration caused too great a concentration on courses and marks, and loss of larger values in college life.

Here, as in the study of underage students reported earlier, records of participation in student activities were used as a rough indication of the student's adjustment to campus life and presumed beneficial participation. Table 8.5 summarizes the pertinent data from the student yearbooks. It shows in the first column of figures the percentage in each group listed as participating in some way in activities; the next three columns show the percentages in one or two, three or four, and five or more activities, the median number being given in the sixth column of the table; the "held office" column shows the percentages listed in the yearbook as officer (president, secretary, chairman of a committee) in some group. Almost all of the figures for the percentages participating in activities in five or more, and holding office, and for the median number of activities are slightly higher for the regular than for the accelerated students.

However, it should be remembered that activities are in a large part organized on a three-quarter four-year basis, so that a student who does not move at the conventional pace and in the regular quarters (autumn, winter, spring) is at a disadvantage. Most undergraduate student-organized activities are dormant during the summer. The student who begins with one class but graduates with another is less likely to become an active member of a group or to remain with it until he attains office. Such advantaging of the lock step student surely is not inevitable,[1] and might be modified if an institution set itself to do so. The figures given would suggest that even under these handicaps most accelerated students

---

[1] Students from Antioch College have reported to the writer that, between the first year and close to the time for graduation, there is little if any classification of students as sophomore, junior, or otherwise—rather, all are simply students together. The constant coming and going involved in the Antioch plan presumably is in large part responsible for this situation. However, the extreme emphasis on the class in the conventional small college appears both unfortunate and unnecessary.

Table 8.4. Percentages in each group having the designated final cumulative point-hour ratio*

Student groups	Point-hour ratio					
	Under 2.2	2.2	2.6	3.0	3.4 up	Median
Men						
Accelerated	5	25	33	23	14	2.85
Regular	16	33	30	13	8	2.61
Retarded	28	38	23	7	4	2.40
Women						
Accelerated	5	20	29	28	18	2.93
Regular	8	33	32	18	9	2.70
Retarded	23	35	24	14	4	2.51

*The numbers in each group are given in column 9 of table 8.1.

led a reasonably normal campus life; presumably more favorable conditions and a better guidance might have made outcomes still better. However, a third of the retarded students were not listed as participating in any activity during college; in median and in number holding office, they are the lowest group. Here, as in scholarship, the retarded students, not the accelerated, present the most serious problems.

A natural question arises concerning the use of various means for acceleration. Table 8.6, dealing with this topic, shows that, as would be expected, four-quarter attendance was most common, but heavy loads and credit by examination also helped some of the accelerated students to the extent that 6 percent completed the usual twelve quarters in ten (2 percent in nine quarters) and 37 percent of the women reduced time in residence by at least one quarter. Some retarded students were in irregularly, some took light loads because of employment or poor health or poor work; hence their summer attendance and more quarters in residence.

In short, it would appear that completing an undergraduate program in less than the conventional time from entrance to graduation had not adversely affected scholarship or seriously interfered with extracurricular activities. Rather, those students who took longer than the usual time presented problems in both respects. However, the figures given included all accelerated and retarded stubents, whether acceleration or retardation was only one quarter or was much more marked; and material was unanalyzed as regards various factors. The next step was to attempt some analysis, and with cases deviating substantially from the usual time taken for their college program.

Outcomes of Acceleration and Retardation of One School Year or More

To investigate more adequately possible effects of acceleration as separate from other factors, it seemed best to consider only women students, since they were not subject to the draft and other special circumstances of the war years, and to consider only those who had accelerated to a substantial degree—enough so that

Table 8.5. Participation in student activities of accelerated, regular, and retarded students— percentages of each group participating and number of activities engaged in

	Participation	Number of activities			Median	Held office	Total cases
		1–2	3–4	Over 4			
Men							
Accelerated	82	45	20	17	2.2	21	397
Regular	80	41	21	18	2.3	26	540
Retarded	60	40	12	8	1.4	9	524
Women							
Accelerated	82	33	22	27	2.9	19	419
Regular	89	29	27	33	3.8	31	1,106
Retarded	66	32	19	15	1.8	15	355

essentially a year was gained and that any unfortunate effects of acceleration would be likely to show. It was found that a total of 104 women for the years 1941 through 1945 in the four colleges studied, had completed a four-year program in three calendar years or less. These were paired with other women who had taken the regular time of three years nine months, or four years, to complete their college work, but who were of the same age and substantially the same ability at entrance, entered in the same college year, took the same types of program, and lived in Columbus or not, according as did the paired case. The median age at entrance of both accelerated and paired individuals was 18.2 (this being the same median age as that for all women entering over these years) and median percentile on the entrance test was 90 for the accelerated and 91 for the regular students. Both groups were thus superior; as indicated earlier in this chapter, the median for all regular women was 80. Similarly, eighty-two women who graduated one school year or more later than the conventional time were paired with comparable regular students. The median ages at entrance of these last two groups were 18.0 and 17.9, and median abilities for both 75.

An elementary question relates to age at graduation of these groups. Median age of the accelerated was 20.9, and of their pairs 21.8; for the retarded and their pairs, 23.8 and 21.7. The important concern is what these groups, which spent such different total times in getting a college education, accomplished in college. Table 8.7 compares their academic records, first, for the initial three quarters, as an indication of academic competence at the beginning of the college career before acceleration or retardation presumably had really begun or at least had had time very much to affect them; next, for the last three quarters, when any unfortunate results should show most; and finally, for the entire undergraduate program.

At the beginning, the accelerated group, though equated with the control group as to ability, was somewhat superior in scholarship, presumably as a result of better preparation, study habits, or greater interest. By the last three quarters, this superiority had decreased slightly so far as the median point-hour ratio is concerned, although the accelerated students show an increased percentage of very superior students and no marginal cases (below *C* or a point-hour ratio below 2). For the entire program, the superiority of the accelerated students is

Table 8.6. Percentages of each group that used three means by which acceleration could be obtained

Means of acceleration	Men			Women		
	Accelerated	Regular	Retarded	Accelerated	Regular	Retarded
Attended two or more summers	47	16	26	59	15	41
Average course load of 18						
hours or over	17	7	4	10	2	2
Credit of more than 10 hours						
by examination	9	3	2	13	5	5
Twelve quarters' work:						
Taken in 11 quarters	20	5	3	30	2	3
Taken in 10 quarters or less	6	1	1	7		
Over 15 quarters			15			22

clear, and also that of both groups, over the general run of students. Those taking five years or more throughout show poorer records than their controls. In short, it would appear that for those students completing an undergraduate program in three years or less, acceleration did not adversely affect scholarship; that longer periods of time tend to be associated with less satisfactory college work; and that, in general (taking all these results together), the longer the overall time taken for an undergraduate program, the poorer the academic record.

The next issue was, again, participation in activities. Table 8.8 indicates that, although the amount of participation and number of officerships were slightly less for the accelerated than for the regular students, the number participating was nevertheless the same in each group; and all differences were slight in view of handicaps which the three-quarter four-year organization of most activities puts upon individuals accelerating. Moreover, some accelerated students, by using the means of acceleration mentioned in table 8.9, finished in only eight quarters' residence and two years' total time.[2] The retarded students are the nonparticipating group.

A series of checks on after-graduation careers is planned. Table 8.10 shows the first. Since the accelerated and regular groups were both from the same graduating class, the accelerated group is almost a year younger. Comparison of accomplishment upon reaching the same age would seem fairer. But as it stands, the comparison shows many more of the accelerated group obtaining further schooling, almost as many having had jobs, almost as many married—more as of the same age—as indicated in the note following the table.

RESULTS OF GUIDED ACCELERATION

The preceding data deal with graduates; and most of the accelerates had, so far as is known, shortened their college programs on their own initiative and without

[2]See footnote below table 8.9.

Table 8.7. Percentages of accelerated and retarded students paired with regular students making certain point-hour ratios in the first three and the last three quarters in residence

Students paired	Point-hour ratio			
	Over 3.5	Less than 2	Median	Difference
First three quarters				
104 Pairs:				
Accelerated	12	3	3.11	.28
Regular	8	6	2.83	
82 Pairs:				
Retarded		27	2.32	
Regular	5	20	2.48	.16
Last three quarters				
104 Pairs:				
Accelerated	25		3.26	.20
Regular	11	2	3.06	
82 Pairs:				
Retarded	5	7	2.80	
Regular	9		2.85	.05
Final cumulative*				
104 Pairs:				
Accelerated	11		3.10	.23
Regular	7	2	2.87	
82 Pairs:				
Retarded		9	2.51	
Regular	5	1	2.56	.05

*For a general basis of comparisons it may be mentioned that the median final cumulative point-hour ratio for the total of 1,461 women graduating from 1941–42 through 1944–45 was 2.71, with 4 percent having 3.6 or over and 3 percent below 2.

special faculty guidance or help. Presumably, careful initial selection might have eliminated some individuals who did not do well and included some others well able to accelerate who did not make the attempt. If acceleration is to be undertaken, careful guidance of the program from the beginning might be advantageous to both academic and other outcomes. Following a group through from the freshman year would be even more informative. The procedure used so far might not locate the casualties of acceleration: those who did come through in a shorter time might do reasonably well, but many others might attempt to accelerate but wear themselves out, or for some other reason either leave school or drop back to a regular rate. On the other hand, conceivably more students might finish a program, if they could see their way clear to doing so quickly. The following material deals with these issues.[3]

[3]The first data of this section are from the doctorate thesis of Kenneth M. Peterson. Men were originally included in his study, but they were eliminated in compiling this report because their academic careers were too dominated by the draft and other war influences to be satisfactory for use in this report. The material on accelerated students in home economics is from the master's thesis of Eileen Smith.

Table 8.8. Percentage of the pairs participating in activities

	Participated in activities			
	In one or more	In five or more	Median	Held office
104 Pairs:				
Accelerated	94	31	3.1	20
Regular	94	44	4.3	36
82 Pairs:				
Retarded	68	12	1.8	16
Regular	90	23	3.6	26

Cases and Methods in the College of Education

A total of 251 freshman women entered the College of Education of Ohio State University in the autumn quarter of 1942. It was decided to present the possibility of acceleration to those who seemed good risks for expedited progress. First selection was of individuals scoring at or above the 70th percentile on the entrance test of general ability; 124 individuals so scored. The adviser of each of these students was then asked whether acceleration was considered feasible; in all but 9 cases it was. The student health service was next asked to go over the list and note any students whose health records were such as to make a special program unwise; in a few instances a special physical examination was given. Only two students were eliminated because of poor health as thus determined. The rest were asked to attend a meeting early in the autumn quarter when the proposed program was presented; attendance was excellent and the few absentees were reached through their advisers. All these women were told that they had been selected on the basis of ability, health, and advisers' judgment as capable of acceleration. The means of acceleration stressed as possible for the next quarter was a class load of twenty or more hours; however, summer attendance and credit by examination were also mentioned as later possibilities. Students who thought they might like to accelerate in some way were asked to talk the matter over with their advisers and families. By the beginning of the winter quarter, when the program was to commence, a few students had transferred to another college or withdrawn from the university, but 109 remained of those selected as probably good risks for acceleration. Of these, 61 decided not to attempt rapid progress. The reason given by 33 was part-time employment or a crowded schedule because of laboratory or other special courses; 10 were anxious lest their marks suffer; the parents of 9 students objected, on the ground either that the program might be too taxing or graduation would occur too young; 4 desired the regular time and more activities; 3 felt that there was ''no need to hurry''; one wanted speech corrective help; and one gave no reason. The remaining 48 proceeded with the program, making their plans in consultation with Mr. Peterson, who was in immediate charge of the undertaking throughout. As assistant junior dean, he was readily available to these students at any time. Once a year, from 1942 through 1945, he had a special individual conference with each. His effort

Table 8.9. Percentage of the pairs using various means of acceleration

Means of acceleration*	104 pairs		82 pairs	
	Accelerated	Regular	Retarded	Regular
Attended 2 or more summers	84	18	53	16
Average course load of 18 hours or more	29	5	1	3
Credit for 15 or more hours by examination	19	7	6	6

*As a result of attending summer school and credit by examination, 3 percent of the accelerated students competed their programs in eight quarters of residence, 5 percent in nine, 12 percent in ten, and 43 percent in eleven. Total time from entrance to graduation for 2 percent was only two years; for one individual, two years three months; for 4, two years six months; 31 percent took two years nine months, and the remainder three calendar years.

throughout was to assure a sound all-round development for each student. In the beginning it had been hoped that various special means of facilitating the progress of these students might be used, such as rapid progress sections and relaxing of prerequisites and requirements. Special means were not found possible, however. Instead 89 percent accelerated, at least in part, by carrying heavy loads; 72 percent attended summer quarters; and 24 percent obtained credit by examination. The question now is as to outcomes with these students, using such methods, and under such guidance.

Results of Guided Acceleration

For appraisal of the program, the selected accelerated group just described was compared with three other groups. One consisted of the 61 superior students who were invited to accelerate but decided not to do so, a second was a small group of other students who accelerated although not so advised, and the third was the comparatively large group of other students who did not meet the criteria established for acceleration and did not attempt any speed-up. Table 8.11 summarizes the academic careers of these women. It also includes in the lower part of the table results for a small group of accelerated students in the entering class of 1943. Partly because acceleration was not so much urged, partly because there seemed to be less interest, the number accelerating at this time was distinctly smaller. And it will be noted that, throughout, the accelerated groups were small. Nevertheless, the consistency of the findings would seem to warrant a consideration of them.

The median age at entrance was substantially the same for all groups— between 18 years 1 month and 18 years 3 months. The table shows negligible differences on the test of general ability given at entrance between those of the superior group who accelerated and those who did not, and similar ones for the accelerated and nonaccelerated among the remainder of the students.

The percentages given in column 5 of table 8.11 show that, of the superior

Table 8.10. After-graduation record—percentages of the paired accelerated and regular women students

After graduation*	104 pairs	
	Accelerated	Regular
Further schooling	27	10
Married	48	57
Full-time employment	76	79
Housewife only	13	16
Student—no employment	13	4
Unemployed—poor health		1
No record	1	3

*The accelerates averaged nine-tenths of a year younger. In view of the age differential, comparison of accelerated students in 1947 with regular as of 1946 is in certain respects fairer. In 1946, when of approximately the same age as the accelerated in 1947, 45 percent of the regular students were married and 68 percent had full-time employment. Age for age, the accelerated students thus seem ahead in such respects. As of the same time after graduation, they are only slightly behind.

students, almost twice as many of the nonaccelerated as of those who accelerated left college without a degree. With the other two groups, the percentage of the nonaccelerated students not completing their programs in the college was markedly higher. The percentages who attempted acceleration and then dropped the program were negligible and, as might be hoped in view of the program of selection, less for the superior than for others. However, it should be again mentioned that the small number of cases makes such comparisons of little significance.

The amount of acceleration was substantial; a fifth of the superior accelerates graduated in three years or less (see column 7). By the regular time for graduation, or June, 1946, over twice as many of the superior accelerates had graduated as of the superior nonaccelerates.[4]

The academic record in the initial autumn quarter, before acceleration began, was higher for each accelerated group (see column 3, table 8.12). This would suggest better background and stronger motivation. The cumulative point-hour ratios in the next column show, however, that the accelerated maintained this superiority through their concentrated remaining academic career.

The distinctive feature of the findings given in these two tables is that acceleration appears to reduce academic mortality—an outcome really understandable since, presumably, if a student sees his way clear to finish in a shorter time than usual, he is more likely to stay with his program under financial or other pressure and has less time for accidents of one sort or another to cut short his academic career. To attempt acceleration thus does not seem to lead students to overwork themselves to the point where they are likely to leave school. And at

[4]See second footnote following table 8.11.

Table 8.11. Academic outcomes of guided acceleration among women students

Students classified	Number of students	Age at entrance	Median ability*	Percentage		
				Left college	Gave up acceleration	Graduated in 3 years or less†
Entered college in 1942						
Superior:						
Accelerated	48	18-2	90	33	6	21
Regular	61	18-3	87	61		0
Difference			3	28		21
Others:*						
Accelerated	21	18-1	54	29	24	14
Regular	95	18-2	51	59		0
Difference			3	30		
Entered college in 1943						
Paired Students:						
Accelerated	12		91	33		33
Regular	12		91	50		0
Difference			0	17		33

*Among the remaining women who entered the College of Education in the autumn of 1942, some students attempted programs in addition to those invited to do so because of their general ability rating.

†By June, 1947, 63 percent of the superior accelerated students who entered college in 1942 and 25 percent of the superior regular students had graduated. The percentages for the corresponding members of the pairs who entered in 1943 were 64 and 36.

least where there has been some guidance, once a reasonable program of acceleration has been started, students seem not likely to give it up.

Relationships to Nonacademic Experience and Personality

The program of the College of Education calls for the evaluation of each student by a faculty committee at the end of the sophomore year, and sets up certain requirements for admission to junior standing. Each student is expected to show some breadth of cultural interests and knowledge of current events as indicated in part by good scores on the Cooperative Contemporary Affairs and General Culture Tests. It is considered desirable that he should have had some experience in earning money. The college also strongly urges some work experience in a settlement house, summer camp, or other type of service involving contacts with children of school age. Travel is considered desirable. Participation in extracurricular activities is urged. Advisers' ratings of each student are considered, and the attempt is made to appraise each as a total person. When the appraisal shows a lack, remedy of the deficiencies is required before junior standing is granted. For instance, a student ill informed about current events may be advised to read a desirable periodical and be checked again by test. Table 8.13 shows certain data obtained in the appraisals for junior standing for both 1942 and 1943 entrants who progressed thus far. The superior accelerated group shows medians dis-

Table 8.12. Academic record made by the students enrolled in the program of guided acceleration

Students classified	Median credit hours third June after entrance	Point-hour ratio	
		Median first quarter	Cumulative third June after entrance
Entered college in 1942			
Superior:			
Accelerated	173	2.9	2.93
Regular	146	2.73	2.78
Difference	27	0.17	0.15
Others*			
Accelerated	170	2.60	2.84
Regular	141	2.08	2.28
Difference	29	0.52	0.56
Entered college in 1943			
Paired Students:			
Accelerated	160	3.50	3.20
Regular	135	3.00	2.50
Difference	25	0.50	0.70

*See footnote marked by an asterisk appended to table 8.11.

tinctly higher on the two tests than the superior group which did not accelerate; and of the remaining cases not recommended for acceleration, those who nevertheless did expedite their progress scored higher than those who did not. Acceleration thus does not seem to have caused neglect of informative reading or other cultural experiences. On most of the additional items reported in table 8.14, the accelerated stand higher than the nonaccelerated.[5] Again, it must be emphasized that the number of cases was small, but the findings are consistently in favor of the accelerated groups. The small differences shown in tables 8.11 through 8.14 between the superior or selected accelerated students and the other accelerated students would suggest that more students might have been recommended for acceleration—and that methods of selection should be improved.

Results of Guided Acceleration in Home Economics

The material which has just been reported had to do with guided acceleration in the College of Education. A similar experiment in the School of Home Economics involved fewer cases but was similar in method and outcome. In November, 1942, records and personnel data on all nontransfer freshmen and sophomores in the School of Home Economics were examined; students who might possibly be accelerated were differentiated as those who had been in the upper third of their high school classes (sophomores and juniors had, in addition, to have cumulative point-hour ratios of 2.5 or better), who tested at entrance at the 70th percentile or

[5]That these guided accelerated students were thus active and possessed broad interests is the more significant in view of the large proportion (89 percent of the 1942 superior accelerated students) who carried heavy loads; 72 percent attended summer school, 24 percent received credit by examination.

Table 8.13. Median scores of the students accelerated and not accelerated, on two tests for junior standing

Students classified	Contemporary affairs test	General culture test	Unconditional junior standing (percent)
Superior:			
Accelerated	66	78	86
Regular	57	67	75
Others:			
Accelerated	58	53	93
Regular	45	37	81

above in general ability, were neither inadequate nor excessive in participation in activities, were not employed over fifteen hours a week, and reported themselves in good health. Students meeting these requirements were discussed with the faculty guidance committee, and those whom it considered good risks were invited to consider acceleration. Of 241 students in the two classes, 45 were invited to try acceleration and 17 did so (though some accelerated only to a slight degree), as well as 19 who volunteered. The median point-hour ratio by the end of the winter quarter was 3.19 for the first group and 2.31 for the second; the selection was thus vindicated. At that time, there were 11 students who had gained at least a quarter (three students had gained two quarters, and three were ahead three quarters). The median point-hour ratio was 3.37, all but one had been employed, and median number of activities was five. Staff ratings on all were high. By the spring of 1947, degrees in home economics were conferred upon 85 percent of those who had attempted acceleration, 46 percent of those who were invited to try acceleration but did not do so, 45 percent of those not recommended who volunteered to accelerate, and 35 percent of those not recommended who did not attempt any speed-up.

The number of cases again is small, but the consistency of all these findings on guided acceleration in two programs and their congruence with the trend of all the findings in this chapter combine to suggest that they are significant. The program of selection for and guidance in acceleration again appears vindicated in terms of total development; few showed evidence of difficulties along the way; and academic mortality was not only not increased but actually reduced.

INTERPRETATION

In general, then, individuals who have completed an undergraduate program in less than the conventional time appear not to have suffered in regard to academic work or otherwise as compared with those who took the usual time; on the contrary, those who took a longer time to complete the program presented problems in all the respects investigated. The question is how to explain such findings.

The most important factor is believed to be this: the typical undergraduate program is set at the pace of the average or slightly below-average student, and,

Table 8.14. Percentages of the students who entered college in 1942 and 1943, accelerated and not accelerated, on items of general living—facts gathered at the end of the sophomore year

Students classified	Worked for pay	Service work	Traveled	Participated in activities*		
				Some	Five or more	Held office
Superior:						
Accelerated	86	89	65	70	31	34
Regular	89	75	57	60	11	7
Others:						
Accelerated	93	85	84	90	10	30
Regular	92	88	62	55	12	9

*Information gathered from the 1945 students' yearbook. These data are only for students who entered college in 1942.

in consequence, students somewhat superior in ability and preparation find more rapid progress entirely feasible and, perhaps, even more natural for them. The difficulties of the retarded students suggest that, at least beyond a certain point, interruptions of an academic program or combination of it with substantial part-time employment may so extend the program as to handicap the student. The success of guided acceleration emphasizes the possibility that planning which recognizes individual differences in abilities, maturity, and background, and which attempts so far as possible to adapt both the academic program and other experiences to each student's best pace, may save time for many students—as well as for the institution. The second factor recurrently emerging is the per-vasively powerful influence of educational practice. Before the war, the three-quarter four-year convention was so dominant that progress at a faster rate was an isolated phenomenon. Under the pressure of wartime conditions these rigidities gave way. But even toward the end of the war, the conventions began to appear again; now they seem increasingly influential, except as the needs of the veterans continue to get modifications for them. Throughout, the conventional organiza-tion of student activities, in terms of the regular academic calendar and a four-year program, has tended to handicap all (both accelerated and retarded students) who did not conform.

However, the findings reported have dealt with certain relatively objective data. It is conceivable that although school work and campus life might be maintained in an accelerated program, there would be more subtle loss in health, emotional adjustment, or breadth of experience. Some evidence bearing on these last points will be considered later.

SUMMARY

This chapter attempts to bring together certain relatively objective data concern-ing outcomes or concomitants of progress through undergraduate college pro-grams pursued at different rates.

When students who had completed an undergraduate program during the war years in less than the conventional time from entrance to graduation were compared with those who had taken the usual time and others who had taken longer, it was found that the accelerated students entered a bit younger and the retarded somewhat older, and that on the entrance test of general ability the accelerated were slightly superior and the retarded lowest. Academic accomplishment ranked, in the same way, as best for the accelerated and poorest for the retarded. Participation in extracurricular activities was slightly better for the regular than the accelerated, but distinctly poorer for those taking longer than the usual time.

An attempt to analyze the situation was made by pairing women students who had taken three years or less for a four-year program with others of the same age and ability at entrance and in the same program who had taken the usual time; similarly, students taking five years or more were paired with regular students. Again, the accelerated were found best and the retarded poorest in academic accomplishment as well as in participation in activities, judged by the record of the total group.

In the College of Education and the School of Home Economics, trial was made of carefully selected potential accelerates in terms of ability at entrance and evidence from advisers and records as to all-round development. Only about one-third of those invited to do so tried to accelerate. The academic record of those who did was good, participation in activities was, for the most part, also good, and evidence of all-round development as shown by a variety of ratings was also superior. Most conspicuous was the fact that a much larger proportion of the students who attempted acceleration remained in the college and completed the work for a degree than of the students of equal ability who progressed at the usual rate.

Two major factors are seen to be of importance here. Academic programs appear to be paced for the average student, with the consequence that their superiors can readily and often desirably move faster. However, educational convention puts a premium on the educational lock step. Greater flexibility of programs and better guidance should then save time for both students and instructors, with even less handicap for the abler young persons.

9

A SUMMING UP

Fund for the Advancement of Education

On the basis of the evidence gathered to date on the experience of 1,350 Early Admission Scholars in the twelve participating colleges and universities over a period of five years during which two groups of Scholars have graduated, it is now possible to make much firmer judgments about the results of the experiment—and about the wisdom of early admission in general—than was the case in the summer of 1953, when the Fund published its first preliminary report on the program.

What does the evidence add up to? What were the conclusions of the independent evaluators? How do the Scholars, their Comparison students, their parents, the schools from which they came, and the colleges to which they went, feel about the Early Admission Program in particular and the idea of early admission in general? What are the implications of the results to date for secondary and higher education as a whole?

This chapter will attempt to answer these questions on the basis of the evidence accumulated thus far.

THE JUDGMENT OF THE SCHOLARS AND COMPARISON STUDENTS

In their senior essays, the 1951 and 1952 Scholars and Comparison students who successfully completed their undergraduate work were asked to express their judgment about the wisdom of early admission on the basis of their own experience and observations.

The Scholars were asked these questions:

> In retrospect, how do you feel now about the advantages and disadvantages of having entered college early? On balance, do you think it was profitable in your case?

Reprinted from *They Went to College Early,* Evaluation Report No. 2 issued by the Fund for the Advancement of Education (established by the Ford Foundation), New York, April 1957. Evaluation Report No. 1, a preliminary report entitled *Bridging the Gap Between School and College,* appeared in 1953.

What advice would you give to a friend of yours who was considering the advisability of entering college at an earlier age than usual?

Do you think the early admission idea should become a regular part of the admission policy of American colleges?

The Comparison students were asked this question:

In your opinion, what are the advantages and disavantages of acceleration? On balance, do you think the idea is wise or unwise? Under what circumstances?

The responses of the Scholars and Comparisons are shown in table 9.1.

As the table indicates, nearly nine out of ten of the Scholars who were about to graduate said that on balance it had been profitable for them to enter college early, and about eight out of ten Comparisons who were about to graduate expressed themselves as generally favorable toward the early admission idea.

Rather marked changes in attitude are observed when the answers to the four questions by the 1952 Scholars and Comparisons are compared to the responses of the 1951 group. The 1952 Scholars expressed far fewer reservations than their 1951 counterparts about early admission, whether they were asked about it as a personal experience, or in terms of advice to a friend, or in terms of a general policy for American colleges and universities. (One Scholar, in an emphatically affirmative answer to the latter question, wrote: "What I cannot understand is how early admission was once a regular part of American education and then abandoned. As you can imagine, I never miss the name of a great American who went to college early. Cotton Mather entered at twelve, Jonathan Edwards graduated at seventeen. This list could go on and on.")

The 1952 Comparison students also expressed far fewer reservations than their 1951 counterparts about the early admission idea. This increase in the "wholly favorable" category was not accompanied by any comparable shift in the proportion of students expressing wholly unfavorable judgments, except that a much smaller proportion of the 1952 Scholars rejected the idea that early admission become a regular part of the admission policy of American colleges, and a somewhat larger proportion of the 1952 Comparisons were definitely opposed to the acceleration of qualified students. Thus, the responses indicate an even stronger endorsement of the early admission idea by the 1952 Scholars and Comparisons than by their 1951 counterparts.

In their appraisal of the advantages and disadvantages of early admission, the Scholars and Comparison students were virtually in complete agreement. The advantage both cited most frequently was a much greater academic challenge in college than in high school. Fifty-eight percent of the 1951 Scholars and 82 percent of the 1952 Scholars cited this as an advantage. The corresponding figures for the Comparison students were 61 percent and 72 percent. The views expressed by the Scholars and Comparison students on this point were interesting and revealing. Many of the Scholars said that early admission to college had "rescued" them from an unchallenging high school experience. This view was expressed in several different ways. One Scholar said flatly: "The one year

Table 9.1. The overall judgment of Scholars and Comparisons about early admission

Questions and responses	1951 group %	1952 group %
Responses by the Scholars:		
Was Early Admission profitable in your case?		
Yes, very much so	42	75
Yes, with reservations	46	15
Neither profitable nor unprofitable	7	5
No, definitely not	4	3
No response	1	2
Would you advise a friend to enter college early?		
Yes, definitely	12	27
Yes, with reservations	75	61
Only in exceptional cases	8	5
No, definitely not	3	3
No response	2	4
Do you think the Early Admission idea should become a regular part of the admission policy of American colleges?		
Yes, definitely	41	66
Yes, with minor modifications	31	15
Yes, with severe limitations	12	16
No, definitely not	15	2
No response	1	1
Responses by the Comparisons:		
Do you think acceleration of qualified students is wise?		
Yes, definitely	12	32
Yes, with reservations	67	44
Only in exceptional cases	11	10
No, definitely not	9	13
No response	1	1

which I missed in high school was, as I was informed by my friends who remained there, a complete waste of time." Another said: "I loved high school because of the extracurricular activities and my friends, but I was wasting my time academically. College classes were much more of a challenge." A third put it this way: "The [Early Admission Program] picked me up when I still had great interest and ambition, which I feel I would have lost in the next two years. . . . [It] put me into a challenging intellectual atmosphere at precisely the time when I was best equipped to accept it."

The tenor of some of the Scholars' comments on this point suggested that their criticism was aimed not at their high schools but at the "lock step," which frequently keeps able students from entering college when they are ready to, regardless of chronological age or the number of years of prior schooling. This distinction was clearly made by a Scholar from a reputable high school in a large eastern city who wrote: "I found at college an intellectual challenge and satisfaction which I wanted out of high school work at that time, but which I could not seem to obtain, even though I feel that the high school I attended offered the best high school education that one could receive in _____.'' It also was made by the Scholar who wrote: "High schools are of necessity (and rightly so) geared to the average student, since he forms the majority of our population. Yet if we are to maintain our position of world leadership with any degree of dignity and self-respect at all, we must not neglect the education of those who are our future leaders and who are at present marking time in an educational atmosphere which is not challenging.''

Several of the Comparison students made the same point. One wrote: "I have known many accelerated students who would have been seriously frustrated and perhaps permanently damaged by having to spend two additional years in conventional high school.'' And another, on the basis of personal experience, wrote: "I see no reason, academically, why qualified students should not be able to accelerate their education. From my own experience, I believe that much of the time in the last year of high school is wasted in that the material could either have been taught earlier, or is repeated in college courses.

The next most frequently mentioned advantage on the part of both Scholars and Comparisons was the opportunity for acceleration, which they described in various ways—an earlier start on professional study, an earlier start on a career, an earlier marriage, or an opportunity to finish college before being called up for military service. Several of the students who cited this as an advantage mentioned that the time saved looked less significant from the vantage point of senior year than of freshman year. Pearson concluded that most of these students were more concerned with avoiding wasting time than with saving time.

The Scholars and Comparisons also agreed with respect to the major disadvantages of early admission. The most frequently cited disadvantage was that early admission makes personal and social adjustment to college more difficult. This was cited by 58 percent of the 1951 Scholars and 65 percent of the 1952 Scholars. The corresponding figures for the Comparisons were 95 percent and 85 percent. Here again the comments of the Scholars were interesting and revealing. Said one:

> On looking back over my past four years here, I am quite glad that I entered college early. However, I honestly believe I am expressing the feeling of one who has "made the grade" and not the feeling of one who has to do it over again. I sincerely believe, however, that in four years time I have gotten much more out of school than the average student, but it was a tough climb.

Another summed up the matter in these words: "That there are difficulties involved cannot be denied, and many individuals may find the adjustment problems very difficult to overcome, but for the majority I feel these will not be insuperable, or even trying.''

Several of the Scholars reported that early admission had actually enhanced their social and emotional development. As one Scholar put it: "From my first moments on campus, college represented a new and exciting experience. I had no difficulty adjusting to this new life, partly because of the sincere interest which the faculty and upperclassmen took in us. . . . The newly acquired self-responsibility was a challenge which stimulated my social and emotional maturation.''

The fact that the 1952 Scholars endorsed early admission with far fewer qualifications than the 1951 group, yet cited the personal and emotional adjustment problem as a disadvantage with much greater frequency than the 1951 group appears to be somewhat contradictory. Pearson concluded that the 1952 Scholars, in making an overall appraisal of their college experience, assigned less weight to this disadvantage than their 1951 counterparts.

The reservations expressed by the Scholars and Comparisons in qualifying their endorsement of the early admission idea were of such a nature as to indicate that they had given the questions thoughtful consideration before answering them. For example, in their answers to the questions about the wisdom of early admission, the reservations dealt not only with the advantages inherent in the program, but also with the kinds of students and the kinds of colleges where the policy was most likely to be successful. In general, both the Scholars and the Comparisons who expressed these reservations felt that the early admission policy should be adopted only by colleges capable of wise selection and proper handling of such students, and should apply only to students who demonstrated exceptional ability and a high degree of social and emotional maturity. One Scholar wrote: ''What is really needed . . . is a more effective high school system, but until the answer to this comes, colleges should provide some sort of an escape hatch for the students who are ready to handle advanced work.''

After analyzing the Scholars' reservations, Pearson concluded:

> The impression one forms in considering these comments is that the important thing is enrichment of the educational program and recognition of individual ability, rather than any particular partiality for the idea of early admission per se. These students recognize that the offering of advanced college level courses at secondary schools would probably be limited to a relatively few schools among the total number in the country. To the extent that this is possible, the need for a regular policy of early admission is limited. To the extent that this is not possible, a regular program of early admission is essential. We believe it is clear from these comments that the Scholars look upon early admission as a rather specific exception within the general framework of American education, although from their point of view the exception would be a most important one.

The qualities mentioned by both Scholars and Comparison students as desirable in applicants for early admission included mature appearance, sense of responsibility, emotional stability, self-reliance, adaptability, high motivation for college, and social maturity. Many of the students who pressed for appraisal of these qualities admitted their elusiveness and confessed their inability to describe just how an admission officer could determine their presence or absence in a specific applicant. "Their point," Pearson observed, "is that intellectual readiness for college does not presuppose emotional readiness for college and somehow the latter must be weighed in the balance."

Both Scholars and Comparison students were sharply split on the relative importance of intellectual readiness and emotional readiness. Some described the ideal student as one who is in the top 5 or 10 percent of his or her class scholastically, scores extremely high on college entrance examinations, and is active in extracurricular activities and sports. There was general agreement that if such an individual were a sophomore or a junior in high school and was frustrated by an unchallenging academic diet, he or she would be clearly admissible by these high standards. However, it was far less clear from the essays whether favorable early admission action should be taken in the case of a student who was strong intellectually but had a poorer chance of successful college adjustment. One Scholar wrote: "My own prejudice is that only intellectual adequacy to do the work is really relevant; I resent the present attempts of my own university to impose social and intellectual orthodoxy by its admission policy." Another Scholar wrote that at his college "social maturity is much less important than academic preparation." Two other students suggested that the intellectually strong youngster who was not well adjusted at secondary school was a likely prospect for early admission because he or she probably would be no worse off in college.

"Quotations such as these," Pearson observed in his report, "contrast quite sharply with the qualities of personal and social maturity which were mentioned quantitatively more often among the essays. A conceivable reconciliation of these somewhat divergent points of view is that intellectual competence is the *sine qua non* for early admission; given this, the final decision should rest on a relative assessment of the applicant's challenge and adjustment at high school and his likely challenge and adjustment at college."

The Scholars and the Comparison students were unanimous in urging a minimum of special treatment for early admission students. Many also urged that college counseling services should be improved. Reports on this aspect were very favorable on some campuses and sharply critical on others. There was a general feeling on the part of most Scholars that a strong counseling system was essential at any college admitting youthful students—not a system uniquely for them, but one which they could share with the rest of the student body.

Finally, the Scholars and the Comparison students stressed the need for a "good fit" between the individual students and the individual college. "This requirement," Pearson noted in his report, "came out in an amusing way in a number of essays where special and fervent pleas were made for confining early admission to small liberal arts colleges, or to large universities, or to highly selective colleges, or to engineering and technical schools. If one were to be guided by the sum total of these suggestions, one would conclude that early admission is a necessary feature at *all* American colleges and universities."

THE VERDICT OF THE INDEPENDENT EVALUATORS

The Pearson Evaluation

The principal conclusions reached by Pearson after his analysis of the senior essays can be summarized as follows:

1. The evidence is that adjustment difficulties were by no means limited to early admission students, although more Scholars than Comparisons reported such difficulties. The conclusion is that early admission was a contributing factor—but not the sole factor—in the existence of adjustment difficulties among the Scholars. However, although the Scholars were faced initially with a greater adjustment problem than the Comparison students, they were able to effect as successful an overall adjustment as the Comparison students.

"Borrowing from Toynbee, the response to challenge, rather than the challenge itself, becomes a measure of success of the experiment and in these terms we would record our conclusion that the experiment was a success for the students whose essays we have considered in this report."

2. The Scholars' definition of early admission as an exception to general educational practice underscores a concern that the able student will be hurt unless special arrangements are made to recognize and develop his or her ability. From this point of view, early admission or indeed any program of enrichment is viewed as giving the able student the same opportunity as that routinely offered to other students. Similarly, the problem of trying to describe the student for whom early admission would be wise is by no means dissimilar from the problem faced by the admissions officer in attempting to select candidates for regular admission. Finally, the obligation of the college to insure a successful educational experience for the early admission student differs only in detail from the college's obligation toward normal-age students.

"This suggests that the important lesson from the early admission experiment is that the American educational system cannot afford to overlook the individuality of the students with whom it deals. Whether these students are normal age or underage, or whether they have completed a formal program in secondary school is probably of less importance than their capabilities and aspirations as individuals. The contribution of the schools and the colleges to society is likely to be gauged in terms of how well these are recognized and developed, rather than in terms of formal structures and prescribed programs."

The Farnsworth Evaluation

Dr. Farnsworth and his colleagues, after studying the social and emotional adjustment of the 1951 Scholars, concluded that the Scholars adjusted to campus life as well as their Comparison students and classmates and that the reasons for failures among the Scholars were the same as for college students in general.

They suggested that the following guideposts might be helpful to admissions officers in selecting candidates for early admission, noting that most of them apply equally to the selection of regular freshmen:

a. Such students must be carefully selected on an individual basis for the individual college. They should be of the type most apt to benefit from the type of education which the college has to offer.

b. Such students should have above average academic achievement and superior intelligence.

c. Such students, except in unusual cases, should have completed the eleventh grade.

d. Personality wise, they should show evidence of emotional maturity at least consistent with their chonological age, good ability in interpersonal relations, and freedom from excessive parental pressure toward early admission. Students who have had frequent changes of schools without similar moves by the family, who come from families with severe discord or who are using college entrance as an escape from serious personal problems are poor risks.

e. Students who have had psychiatric illnesses should have had adequate treatment.

f. Students with characteriological disorders should not be admitted. However, a distinction must be made between misbehavior as representative of longstanding characteriological disorder and misbehavior as a manifestation of adolescent rebellion. These latter cases, if the difficulties have been overcome, either as a result of the natural maturing process or of psychiatric treatment, should not be excluded.

g. In the selection of students for liberal arts courses, such students should have appropriate educational values, or the capacity to acquire such values.

h. Close scrutiny should be given by large urban universities to students from rural areas.

i. In selection, it is all too easy to err in not admitting the unusually intellectually gifted student or the chronic dissenter who is not "well-rounded." While "well-rounded" students are highly desirable, if this is used as the main criterion for admission these unusual students may be passed over. Such students may make great contributions in the future. As one dean said: "There should be room in our stable for all kinds of horses."

COMMENTS OF SCHOLARS' PARENTS

The colleges and universities participating in the Early Admission Program have not made a systematic effort to determine how the Scholars' parents feel about the program, but two colleges (Goucher and Louisville) conducted special canvasses of the parents of their 1951 Scholars shortly after their graduation. These results, although based on a very small and incomplete statistical sample, tended to confirm the general impression reported by the colleges that the parents on the whole have been favorable toward the program.

In the Goucher survey, twenty-six of the twenty-seven parents responding said that if they had the choice to make again they would send their daughters to college early. Many of the parental opinions reflected the same balancing of advantages and disadvantages as the Scholar essays. One mother, who said she would again choose early admission for her daughter, remarked nonetheless that the girl had lost contact with her high school classmates and added on the drawback side: "It was, too, a lonely pinnacle of fame in the adolescent community." Another expressed the opinion that entering college early "helped to build up her self-confidence and initiative." Another wrote: "She was made more resourceful and self-reliant: had to think and act independently." And another: "I believe she matured in many ways sooner than if she had completed high school."

In the Louisville survey, eleven of the twelve responses expressed parental approval of the Early Admission Program. The one exception, written by the mother of a Scholar, said in part: "I would never influence a boy or girl again into giving up the last year in high school. . . . [My son] entered engineering school at the age of 16. He needed the chemistry, physics, and math he would have had his last year in high school. He was lost as far as the work was concerned and very unhappy. He had always made good grades. . . . As far as [my son] is concerned the early entry was not right and I've regretted it."

Another Louisville mother, who had two children in the program, wrote: "Since I wasn't sold on the Program when I first heard about it, I'm happy to have the opportunity now to say I'm wholeheartedly in favor of it since our two children have tried it. . . . They both seem happier and better adjusted at the university than they did in high school. They are certainly not either one geniuses but I really believe now that they would have been wasting their time if they had stayed in high school another year. They have even had more social life at the university."

Apart from the Goucher and Louisville surveys, a number of participating institutions have reported their general impressions on the matter of parental attitudes. Utah said it believed that most parents consider going to college early to have been a successful and valuable experience for their children. Fisk reported the reaction of parents to have been "quite favorable." Lafayette said a few of the parents felt that it would have been better for their children to have finished high school, but that most were well-satisfied with the results.

Oberlin reported that the reactions of parents have been difficult to evaluate. It noted that where a Scholar was successful the parents were highly cooperative and pleased but that where it did not work out "the reactions ranged from a mature acceptance to a projection of all the blame on the College." (In a number of these cases, it reported, the Scholars had been strongly encouraged to apply for the Fund scholarships by their parents.)

Wisconsin, on the other hand, reported that the attitude of its Scholars' parents has been "one of the most interesting and heartening aspects of early admission." The parents were pleased and grateful when their sons and daughters did well, Wisconsin added, but "what is more important, when the boys did badly the parents were extremely helpful and cooperative, and to this we probably owe many of the successful recoveries from trouble the Scholars have made. . . . It is interesting that three families have sent two Scholars each."

THE ATTITUDES OF HIGH SCHOOL PRINCIPALS

As with parental attitudes, the participating colleges have not made a systematic effort to gather data about the attitudes of the high schools from which the Scholars were chosen. However, Goucher and Louisville polled the secondary schools from which their 1951 Scholars came, and several of the other colleges have obtained, through correspondence and discussion, a general picture of the reactions of principals and guidance officers.

The available evidence suggests that the character of high school reaction is mixed, ranging from strong approval to strong disapproval, and that to some extent it is in the process of change.

Ten of the twelve participating colleges have reported to the Fund on their experience with high school principals and guidance officers, often in relation to the difficult task of Scholar selection. According to these reports, many of the college officials have encountered considerable resistance to the Early Admission Program. Sometimes this has been vocal. Sometimes, as one college commented, it has not: "The general reaction has been to ignore the plan entirely."

Many teachers and principals in secondary schools have been strongly opposed to the early departure to college of some of their best potential juniors and seniors. As one principal frankly told a college official: "We don't like the idea of the colleges taking our leaders out of high school at the end of the tenth or eleventh grade."

The dean of one of the participating colleges, reporting considerable high school resistance to the Early Admission Program, voiced the opinion that it "is based partially on a genuine concern for the emotional and social development of the individual and a belief that he will be harmed by taking him out of his chronological peers and placing him with his intellectual peers. It may also result partially from the reflection upon the job of the secondary school which is seen in the program."

This dean noted that there appeared to be a marked difference among high schools, depending on the quality of their own instruction. "Those schools which were well-established and doing very good jobs saw this as another indication of the fine work they were doing in having their students qualify for admission after only two or three years with them," he said. "On the other hand, the weaker schools tended to see this as a criticism of the programs which they were performing and a reflection that they were doing so poor a job that an additional year or two with them made little difference in the college success of the student."

Some of the colleges and universities have reported cases of active high school interest in and cooperation with the experiment. For example, one large university reported that the majority of high schools from which its Scholars came were quite enthusiastic and continued to be so, except in the case of a few Scholars who failed to stay. Another university, noting that a few high schools have sent it a large proportion of its Scholars, remarked: "Their views on the program are, of course, colored by the experience of their boys; since they have sent us applicants year after year they presumably approve the plan."

One university said that some principals in its state "have realized early admission could take some burdens from their shoulders, by removing some of the pressure for college preparation of a few students. If, for example, a boy shows potentiality as a scientist, but goes to a school which does not teach mathematics beyond algebra, early admission offers him a way to get his trigonometry, without straining the resources of the school."

A number of the participating institutions reported that high school attitudes, first largely negative, have changed, presumably as a result of experience with early admission, and that there has been a growing acceptance of its possibilities during the last few years.

Aside from these general observations by the colleges the only direct evidence as to the attitudes of high school principals and guidance officers is afforded by the results of the Goucher and Louisville surveys. The responses to these surveys ranged all the way from strong approval to strong disapproval of early admission, with most of the principals emphasizing that they felt it was wise only for students of exceptional academic ability and social maturity. For example, of the six principals responding to the Louisville survey, two said they approved of the idea, one said the wisdom of early admission depends entirely on the student concerned, another said the idea had both good and bad points, and two disapproved of the idea on the ground that the early admission student misses much by not completing high school. Following are samples of the range of comments:

> Students who enter college too young seem to lack social maturity and often are not accepted by the more mature college students. I often wonder how much these students lose by not remaining with their classes and probably taking over positions of leadership during their senior year.
>
> Whether or not it is wise for a high school student to enter college at the end of his junior year depends entirely upon the student concerned. . . . In brief, both the academic progress and the social development of the student must receive equal consideration in making the decision. In our opinion only a relatively small percentage would qualify socially.
>
> I think the [Early Admission] Program has been a distinct service to the students from this school, and I believe I would like to see the program renewed and the selections be made on an individual basis.

The pattern of responses to the Goucher survey was quite similar to that of the Louisville survey. The principals and guidance officers of high schools that had sent the largest number of students into the Early Admission Program tended to be the most favorably disposed toward it. The tenor of the replies suggested that there were two major reasons for this tendency: (1) Since the senior classes in such high schools were generally large, the Scholars were not "missed" as much as they were in small high schools; and (2) since the academic standards of these schools were generally high, the principals tended to be much less sensitive to the implication that the Scholars were offered a much greater academic challenge in college.

The reply of the scholarship counselor in a large eastern high school that has sent nine students into the Early Admission Program aptly illustrates this tendency. Asked to cite the major advantage of early admission from the student's point of view, she replied: "The student stops 'marking time' and gets on with the real work that he wants to do. If he's mature enough, he gets real satisfaction out of the greater challenge of college work." Asked to cite the major disadvantage of the program from the school's point of view, she wrote: "The school is deprived in the sense that these Early Admission students leave gaps in their class. The school no longer benefits from the stimulation of their superior work and attitudes, and generally from their participation in the extracurricular life of the school." She added, however, that "since our early admission people are so few in number, we feel no significant deprivation; and since we feel that the boys and girls themselves are benefited, we are very happy to see them succeed in college."

Principals of other large eastern high schools which have sent relatively large numbers of students into the Early Admission Program made similar observations. "Most high schools like to have bright students in their enrollment," wrote the principal of a Massachusetts high school which has furnished eight Scholars. "Occasionally key posts are left vacant (by the departure of early admission students), but they are usually filled by another capable student. Occasionally we find a brilliant student who is bored by his contemporaries; he finds their activities childish. A change in environment could be helpful."

THE VIEWS OF THE PARTICIPATING COLLEGES

In preparation for this report, the Fund asked each of the participating colleges and universities to study the records of the first two groups of Scholars to graduate and to judge whether early admission had been wise in each individual case. The results of this appraisal are shown in table 9.2.

As table 9.2 indicates, the faculty judgment at the participating institutions was that early admission was wise in the case of eight out of ten Scholars in the

Table 9.2. Opinions of participating colleges about early admission

Opinion	1951 group	1952 group
Wise	79.6%	76.4%
Opinion divided	14.6%	17.1%
Unwise	5.8%	6.5%

1951 group, and in the case of three out of four in the 1952 group. (It must be remembered that the judgments covered only those Scholars who had survived through senior year.)

The Fund also asked the participating institutions to appraise their experience under the Early Admission Program, and invited them to comment on the broad implications of the results to date for American secondary and higher education as a whole.

Excerpts from their reports follow:

The University of Chicago

The Chicago campus made adjustment easier in that there were so many students of the same age as the Scholars. For approximately ten years prior to the start of the Early Admission Program, the University of Chicago had admitted students to the College who had completed no more than two years of high school. The Early Admission Scholars who entered in 1951 and in each succeeding year were only a fraction of the total number of entering students who had not graduated from high school. I think, too, the curriculum made adjustment easier. The curriculum at the University of Chicago is arranged so as to allow each student to proceed at his own best pace. But Chicago is a large metropolitan university, and for many reasons a large university is not the ideal home for everyone, and I suppose the youth of some Scholars makes adjustment to a metropolitan campus difficult. The student body at Chicago is divided between commuting students and residential students. There is not the homogeneity in campus life that many colleges can achieve. This may have been one factor affecting the younger students, although the large number of early entrants at Chicago has made possible the development of athletics and extracurricular activities which fit their needs.

Despite all of these factors, however, I am confident that the overwhelming majority of the Scholars (and other early entrants) at Chicago have adjusted well, that they have been glad that they entered college early, and have found an intellectual stimulation from college that they would not have found during the corresponding years of high school. I see no reason to believe that the intellectual stimulation for this majority was achieved at the expense of social maladjustment [*sic*]. They have more than held their own in the social life of the campus.

Columbia College

When, in the spring of 1955, the Columbia College faculty instructed the committee responsible for admissions that up to twenty-five early admission candidates might be admitted within any one year, the action clearly had a double significance. It represents, in the first place, a formal acceptance of the desirability and practicability of early admission for qualified candidates. But the limitation of the number to be admitted reflects the special situation of Columbia College. New York City and the metropolitan area offer a rich source of student talent. We attract boys from this region as a national college which can be reached by subway. However, most of our applicants for early admission live in New York City. Our status as a national college is maintained by our capacity to draw students from beyond the confines of the metropolis. Simply adding to our representation from New York and its immediate environs will undercut the very basis on which we appeal to the highly talented youths within that area. Moreover, an increase in our New York City contingent would distort our preprofessional balance, because a high proportion of New York City applicants for early admission are premedical students of whom we already have as high a proportion as we can handle without damage to our liberal arts program.

If it were possible to secure a large number of equally able early admission candidates from the country at large, Columbia would benefit greatly. But the widespread announcement of the early admission opportunity in earlier years produced very few candidates from good schools in other urban centers, and it has been our experience that the boy from a small school, remote from an urban center, needs, when he comes to Columbia, whatever assurance and maturity his final year in high school or a year's additional growth can bestow. Our National Scholarship Program provides a direct answer to our problem here.

This is an immediate and practical response, dictated by our faith in the value of the kind of work we can do with the able students, diversified as to geographical origin and background, who come to us now. Much of the value of institutions of higher learning lies in their *distinctive* capacities to contribute to the national life.

But early admission, considered independently, poses no discernible threat to such distinctive contributions as a variety of institutions afford, and it promises to fulfill the hope of those who have tried it: to achieve a closer and more efficacious relation between the school and the college. This, at least, is our experience, and we are happy to report that Columbia and the youngsters who came early to the feast have both profited.

Fisk University

It has been made clear that the distinctly superior student coming out of the tenth or eleventh grade can succeed well with college freshman work provided the student also has good motivation and reasonable emotional maturity. The distinctly superior academic capacity of the Ford Scholars has emphasized the fact that the college needs freshman courses at different levels to meet the ability and preparation of a wide variety of students. (This variety is bound to persist in any college which does not require entrance examinations either in aptitude or achievement.)

The best of the Scholars have done so well academically that they have challenged others to keep pace with them and have challenged instructors to raise their expectation in certain courses. The leadership of the Scholars in various extracurricular activities has stimulated these organizations very distinctly. . . .

In connection with considering an appropriate curriculum for Ford Scholars, we have reviewed and rebuilt our whole general education program for freshmen and sophomores.

Goucher College

It is not easy to draw conclusions from an educational project that has been as wide flung in its implications as the Early Admission Program, but with five years of experience in it we would like to make two points: the first touching on the merits of early admission vis-à-vis admission with advanced standing, with a side look at the much-discussed question of the social adjustment of those entering as early admission students; the second on qualitative differences that have been revealed in the four early admission groups we admitted with the financial aid of The Fund for the Advancement of Education.

In our opinion it is very doubtful that the so-called enrichment programs in high school can meet as well as a college university the total intellectual and social needs of patently superior students. We say this not out of a partisan feeling for early admission but out of a realization that the superior student should feel a gravitational pull not in one or two courses alone but in all the student's educational and social pursuits. This absolute need we believe can be met by very few, if any, high schools in the country.

If we are asked by what signs we may know the superior student we would point to an outstanding educational record in high school supported by College Board aptitude and achievement scores in the 600s preferably, though some scores in the high 500s would be acceptable. These objective data we would want fortified by the recommendations of the high school principals.

Queried about social adjustment and maturity (two very different concepts, not necessarily reconcilable) we would reply that an early admission student should give evidence at entrance to college of the capacity to catch up in the space of two years with those who will be her college classmates. If the student is intellectually ready for college we think she should be admitted even if there will be some periods of social and personal strain ahead of her (and we would believe that in almost every case they would be inevitable). We are convinced that as these stem from superior ability and differentness, the early admission student has a better chance of meeting them more happily in a setting where the intellectual is not considered a "freak" or a young Einstein. We believe that the ampler ether of college or university will serve to help the student with superior endowment to wait on the maturing processes of time without vulgarizing herself by seeking mere conformity or by denigrating her intellectual resources by calling them "compensations." In other words we believe that social maturity can be sooner and better achieved by the superior student with less waste of spirit in college than in high school.

As to the best time of entrance to college for the patently superior student we are at this point almost inclined to say the end of the tenth year, though there is a possible danger of shortchanging the student in her preparation for college work in the sciences and mathematics. Our inclination toward the tenth year has been influenced by the facts (1) that some of our tenth-year students have been among our best; (2) that a lack of intellectual challenge may result in a dulling of intellectual interests and/or in a failure of habits of industry, which failure spread over two years in high school blights performance and attitude in college; and (3) that the longer a student is entrenched in the extracurricular life of her high school the harder it is to extricate herself without cries of woe from those who are more interested in the extra dividends paid by high office in the senior year than by the intellectual and, we believe, total achievement of the student in question.

The second observation we wish to make is one which bears on the question of qualitative differences within early admission groups. We believe that after five years of experience in selecting early admission students for admission we are better informed about what constitutes what we call, reverting to an earlier terminology, a "true Ford," or an early admission student whom we would define as one who by the end of the first by second year of college has (1) made a good beginning in self-knowledge (and discipline); (2) revealed purposefulness in planning and execution; and, above everything else, (3) shown a sensitivity to form and plan and order, this last in the high sense of Schiller's "*heilige Ordnung.*"

But even developing expertness in selection has not increased our yield of "true Fords" in each class. Always they number about one-third of the group. What makes the difference between those equally endowed in mental acuity is a question we cannot yet answer, if we ever can. But henceforth we shall be studying subjective classifications, seeing how far they correlate with objective data.

Using the three criteria mentioned above in the qualitative description of a "true Ford" we think we can divide by the end of the *third* year each early admission class into three groups: the first in patent possession of those qualities; the second group definitely above average in their grasp of their value but not ("yet" might be added parenthetically since self-education will be carried on beyond graduation) in possession of them; the third group, average in their ability to see order or to give form and order to their plans and ideas. It should be recognized that these three classifications are *not* based on such objective data as grade point averages or College Board scores, but depend ultimately on our judgment of the student in the light of value criteria. But the classifications can yield interesting objective data. We intend to study and report on our findings next year.

Lafayette College

Lafayette College feels that the Early Admission Program has been a success. The record of the achievement of the Ford scholars in academic work and extra activities is an excellent one. For this reason, the College plans to continue to admit qualified students even though they have not been graduated from secondary school.

Even though the groups to be admitted to college under this program will probably never be large, the Early Admission Program does offer an excellent opportunity to the young man who is more mature intellectually, socially, and emotionally than his age group. If he is desirous of accelerating his educational program, it is evident that he can do so without losing any of the advantages of college life.

University of Louisville

It is the opinion of all persons concerned with the Early Admission Program that it has been most successful. The University of Louisville has admitted students to its College of Arts and Sciences after three years of high school since 1934, and that program will continue. There is no definite arrangement for financial assistance to such students except that which the Student Aid Committee is able to give them if they need help.

From our experience with the Early Admission Program during the past four years, we have learned that a good student, after three years of high school, can do a good job in college if he is well adjusted emotionally and socially before he comes.

The program has caused us to examine the aspects of our program that affect all students. We are now trying to locate within our own students the superior student and to do more for him. . . . It is our hope that much more can be done to give more public recognition to these superior students and also to enrich our academic offerings to them.

One of the main implications of the Program for secondary and higher education generally is that more should be done to identify the superior student and to enrich his educational program.

Oberlin College

There still seem to be some real difficulties in attracting and selecting appropriate students for early admission. There is still considerable resistance on the part of many secondary school educators to the early admission principle. This is based partially on a genuine concern for the emotional and social development of the individual and a belief that he will be harmed by taking him out of his chronological peers and placing him with his intellectual peers. It may also result partially from the reflection upon the job of the secondary school which is seen in the program. Still a third difficulty in the way of attracting the proper students for the program lies in the fact that the schools which have given most publicity to the Early Admission Program have been the better high schools and preparatory schools which are doing a relatively effective job in their own right. The student of superior ability who is stuck in a second-rate high school may not even hear about the Early Admission Program, yet he is the person who could benefit most from being selected for such advancement.

The results of the Early Admission Program at Oberlin were carefully reviewed during this past year and the faculty took action this spring to continue to admit students who had a minimum of two years of high school work and who, in the opinion of the director of admissions, were ready for admission to college. There are, of course, broad differences of opinion about the advisability of such a program among our faculty, but enough of them felt it had been sufficiently successful to continue on the above-mentioned basis. No special scholarship program will be offered for these early admission students who may be admitted in succeeding classes, but they will be permitted to compete for any of the regular admissions office scholarships open to four-year students.

The general success of the Early Admission Program certainly suggests the lack of adequate provision in the vast majority of our secondary schools and colleges for the truly superior student. It would appear that there is a considerable number of students who are marking time in many high schools during their last one or two years there. If they are gaining much educationally, it may very possibly be because they are educating themselves as a result of their intellectual curiosity rather than because of anything the school itself is doing to educate them. At the same time it would appear that many students coming out of four years of experience in good secondary schools may very well be marking time educationally in the first year or two spent in college. The basic implication I see in the results of the Early Admission Program is the tremendous need for better integration of secondary and college education and more provision for the education of the superior student at both of these levels.

Shimer College

Shimer feels that the Early Admission Program has very real value for the preprofessional student. Faced with a long program of specialization, the early entrant finds that his program is accelerated to such an extent that he may begin his professional training at least a year earlier than the student who finishes high school before entering college.

In some measure, the admission program at Shimer will undergo a slight change as a result of this recent experience. Probably the percentage of students under the Early Admission Program will be somewhat decreased, with an even greater emphasis on the student who is particularly qualified, both in terms of academic preparatioṅ and social adjustment. The administration and faculty of the college believe strongly in the Early Admission Program, and every effort is being made by the college to secure financial underwriting for early entrant scholarships.

While it is doubtful that this program with its limitation in numbers will specifically affect the structure of the American education system, it would seem that there is adequate evidence that the qualified student can perform successfully in college without the usually prescribed sixteen Carnegie units. This evidence should lead to some revision of admission policy on the part of many colleges and universities since it is evident that neither the sixteen units are absolutely required, nor are specifically required high school course groupings absolutely necessary.

University of Utah

In summary, those of us who have been close to the Early Admission Program at the University of Utah view the program after four years as a successful and valuable experience. We believe, moreover, that this attitude is shared by a great majority of the Scholars and their parents and by a growing number of high school administrators and teachers.

We believe the problem of the abler student to be especially serious and difficult of solution in situations like ours, where state law requires all young people to remain in school until they are eighteen or have been graduated from high school and where a high school diploma, with rare exceptions, is a guarantee of university or college admission. It will become increasingly acute in the next decade with the great increase in students entering our gates. However, it seems to us that the University of Utah with its geographically homogeneous population and its potentially close relationships with the schools from which its students come has a very special opportunity and challenge to do something about it.

Our special situation is but one illustration of the many striking differences among our higher institutions, even among the small number of institutions engaged in the early admission experiment, and points out again that there are no simple answers, let alone a single one, to the problem. However, we believe that there are some general implications from our experience for secondary and higher education and for the Fund in planning its future program. We believe that, theoretically at least, admission with advanced standing would be sounder psychologically for the students than early admission and better in its effect upon the high schools. However, only a handful of schools in our state could possibly carry out such a program, and even in them the problems of staff and finance would be very great. The same lack of resources would confront any major effort in behalf of the individual student such as is carried on in the Portland experiment.

Under our circumstances the early admission program was the best immediate answer. It caused the least disruption; except for the scholarships it cost relatively little; and, as we have seen, it has been quite successful. However, it has serious disadvantages. It inevitably serves too few of the students we are trying to help; attractive scholarships play too great a part; the high schools are too little involved; and the ultimate effect upon secondary education is negative rather than positive.

This last is probably the most important point. To the student, the parents, the schools themselves, and the public the inference is inescapable that the senior year in high school is a waste of time. For the student, high school education is a truncated rather than an integrated and completed educational and social experience. The tendency for the school, if it is not simply hostile to the whole business, is to feel that it can do nothing special for the abler student and to pass the responsibility on to the college or the university.

Yet both acceleration and enrichment were desirable and even necessary for our better students. . . . One way to achieve the desired results for all might be for the schools to reconsider a plan once in effect, if not now, in certain systems. This plan provided a faster track for the better students, which began in the seventh grade, eliminated the eighth grade, and permitted them to complete a full senior high school program a year early and in sufficient numbers to retain the values of their peer group. If such acceleration were combined with a rich program of basic academic subjects and if the higher institutions were alert and flexible in the handling of the students when they entered, great good might result. The success of any such program would depend ultimately upon adequate counseling based upon a conviction that individual differences make it as democratic and vital to identify and serve the needs of the student of high ability as the student of low.

University of Wisconsin

The question is often asked, "Should the colleges make a general practice of accepting students who have not finished high school?" or its converse, "Should high schools make a general practice of recommending such students to college?" As they stand, these questions receive a qualified negative answer; our experience shows that early admission demands what appears to be an unusual combination of intellectual and social precocity. It is probably not as rare as it seems on the surface; there may be as many as a fifth of most high school classes who could make the grade. But the vast majority of these would probably gain nothing by early admission, and the principals have undoubtedly been wise when they have hesitated in recommending many applicants. On the other hand, there are a few boys who have almost certainly gained more from college than they would have from their last years of high school; a wise principal will be able to pick them, and the ideal situation would be that in which the original suggestion came from the school rather than the individual student or his parents. Unfortunately, not every teacher's judgment is infallible, and the method of selection remains a problem.

As they make their decision, they must take into account the matter of finances. The Scholars have had much less pressure on them to earn part of their way than the majority of their fellow students, and this has undoubtedly been an important factor in their success: at least two who have been dropped failed partly because they were trying too hard to earn money on the side. This is not easy for boys of 16, for even in the summer they cannot get jobs at respectable pay. For the past two years the stipends for freshman and sophomore Scholars have averaged $540, of which $500 must be used for tuition and fees by out-of-state students; Wisconsin students pay $180. About a fifth of the students accepted have decided that they could not afford to take advantage of the offer. We feel that any early admission student must be assured of sufficient financial support, either from his family or from scholarship aid, before he accepts the award; he cannot rely on being able to pay his own way until his junior year. After that, of course, he is in the same position as any other student.

With all these restrictions, intellectual, moral, and financial, it is clear that early admission is only advisable for a tiny proportion of high school students, and that it accents more problems than it answers. It has long been patent that most high schools cannot really push their ablest students, and that the students consequently are apt to lose their enthusiasm in the boredom of waiting for their fellows to catch up with them. Two of the Scholars, one in each of the first two classes, compressed high school and college into five years and graduated as members of Phi Beta Kappa; the very fact that this is possible points to the waste of time which must often take place. Some of this waste can, perhaps, be avoided; some schools have honor classes, a few are able to have a general standard high enough to keep all but the very ablest stimulated. Some duplication of courses might be avoided, especially in the sciences and American history; many colleges allow a student to take work at an advanced level in certain fields if he can show he is qualified, and good high school teaching should certainly be encouraged in this way. Even if the number of years of school and college is not reduced, there is certainly a need to keep able students working at full capacity. Early admission can do this for a few, but the solution on a large scale must be sought elsewhere.

In sum, early admission has offered a partial solution to the problems of getting the best from able students and of shortening the cruelly long period necessary for technical training. The solution is only partial because probably only a very few students have the balanced development of intelligence, personality, and savoir-faire it demands. At Wisconsin it seems to have been generally quite successful, and it could be more so if we had better techniques of selection and enough Scholars so that each one would not feel himself to be something quite apart from the ordinary university student. It will probably always be expensive, and there will always be some failures among the Scholars who embark on this course, but the benefit to the successful is very great.

Yale University

It seems to be true that the Yale environment presented a more difficult adjustment problem to the Scholars than did many of the other colleges in which the early admissions Scholars matriculated. The fact that almost all of the boys were from high schools and many from relatively small schools no doubt made more difficult their adjustment to a fairly sizeable campus in an urban center.

. . . the 1952 group seems to have made a more successful adjustment to the Yale environment. This can be attributed both to the fact that the adjustment factor was more in our minds when we admitted the second group, and perhaps too, to the fact that they were in no way isolated during their first year on our campus as were the 1951 Scholars.

Yale University felt that it had received maximum benefit from the Early Admission Program as sponsored by the Fund for the Advancement of Education after its first two years of participation. From that experience the university decided to adopt as part of its admissions program measures which would give qualified students desiring to enter college from their junior year in school a chance to do so. To quote from the catalogue of Yale for 1955–56: "Although an applicant is normally expected to have completed four years of secondary school work for entrance, an exception will occasionally be made for a candidate of unusual promise and maturity who has completed three years." No particular scholarship arrangements are made for this group other than those made for all applicants for financial aid. The university does not make a special effort to find and encourage Early Admission applications.

Yale feels that early admissions should be part of the policy of every college and university. It does not, however, feel that a specific number of places should be reserved for early admission candidates in each class, nor that a university such as our own should make special effort to attract such Scholars other than having as its policy the admission of those duly qualified.

THE FUTURE OF EARLY ADMISSION

In *Bridging the Gap Between School and College*, the Fund said that the preliminary results of the Early Admission Program were "decidedly encouraging." On the basis of the evidence presented in this report, it now feels that the results to date have been impressive.

Although the period of Fund support has ended, eleven of the twelve colleges participating in the experiment have incorporated the early admission idea into their regular admissions policy. (Wisconsin has not yet taken any action on the matter.) At least one of the colleges—Goucher—has set up a special scholarship program for early admission students. At the other colleges, early admission students are permitted to compete for scholarship aid on equal terms with other entering freshmen.

There are some indications that the early admission idea is gaining wider acceptance. The College Entrance Examination Board reports that 29 of its 169 member colleges had early admission programs in the academic year 1955–56. Only six of these were participants in the Fund-supported experiment. It is interesting to note that 27 of the 29 also had programs of advanced placement, thus providing able high school students two different kinds of opportunity for college-level work before graduation.

It is much too early yet to predict the future of the early admission idea, but the evidence in this report clearly indicates that under the proper circumstances it represents a promising approach to the problem of enabling the very best students to realize their full potential. The risks of entering college early have been the subject of much popular concern, and properly so. But too little thought has been given to the risks run by an able student in an unchallenging environment in *not* entering college early. As one of the Scholars wrote in his senior essay: "There is some danger that a young student's talents will be harmed by being thrust among older students who do not accept him. But the greater danger is that he will be allowed to stagnate in secondary school and will arrive in college lacking imagination and ambition, these having been 'educated' out of him. The harm to him and society is great."

Richard Pearson observed in his report that "the important lesson from the Early Admission experiment is that the American educational system cannot afford to overlook the individuality of the students with whom it deals. Whether these students are normal age or underage, or whether they have completed a formal program in secondary school is probably of less importance than their capabilities and aspirations as individuals. The contribution of the schools and colleges to society is likely to be gauged in terms of how well these are recognized and developed, rather than in terms of formal structures and prescribed programs."

Yet there is some danger that in the decades ahead, when American colleges and universities become engrossed in the problems attendant upon steeply rising enrollments, the capabilities and aspirations of the "unusual" student are likely to be neglected. College admissions officers, confronted with the happy prospect of having many more applications for admission than there are places to be filled, may well tend to "play it safe" and to avoid the risks involved in admitting unconventional students, particularly those who are younger than most and who have had a less-than-normal high school preparation. It will be all too easy to say, "We'll get them next year anyhow, and another year in high school won't hurt them." But the evidence clearly indicates that the superior student *can* be hurt by being detained in an intellectual environment he or she has outgrown. As one Scholar wrote in his senior essay: "I don't advocate anything so radical as a society composed exclusively of eggheads, but it seems downright cruel to force a gifted child to suffer needless years of boredom (and boredom can be suffering, I know) when he can have an opportunity (whether or not he utilizes it is obviously up to him) to meet some fine minds on a college faculty which might be able to salvage at least part of his intellectual potential before the habit of mental laziness has completely encrusted him."

The notion that the superior student does not need special attention because he is bright enough to look out for himself is still widely prevalent, but an increasing number of thoughtful educators and laymen have begun to challenge it and the assumption that regardless of ability and energy each student must move with his chronological age group through eight years of elementary school, four years of high school, and four years of college. Coupled with this has been a critical reexamination of the meaning of educational equality in a democratic society—a questioning as to whether it means equal amounts of education for all or equal opportunity for each individual to develop his or her talents as fully and freely as possible.

There is also a growing awareness that the health and vigor of our society—and indeed even its very life—depend on making the most of all the capacities of all of our people. And it has become increasingly clear that if we are to make the most of these capacities, we must not fail to provide for the fullest possible development of our ablest young people. The Fund for the Advancement of Education believes that the Early Admission experiment has clearly demonstrated its promise as a means to that end.

10

HIGH SCHOOL PERFORMANCE OF UNDERAGE PUPILS INITIALLY ADMITTED TO KINDERGARTEN ON THE BASIS OF PHYSICAL AND PSYCHOLOGICAL EXAMINATIONS

James R. Hobson

INTRODUCTION

Logically, if we are to provide for individual differences after a child enters school, it seems reasonable to recognize some of the more basic and obvious differences as he or she approaches school age and to develop an elastic system of school admission based upon those differences which are objectively measurable and which do not, in the main, depend upon environment and training. In fact, early admission may be the ideal method of acceleration.

The Brookline Plan of Underage Admission

For the past thirty-five years, the public schools of Brookline have admitted to kindergarten all educable children who have attained a minimum chronological age of 4 years 9 months as of 1 October. For the first fifteen of these years, children from three to nine months or more below this age were admitted on trial following an individual psychological examination by the Department of Child Placement and a physical and health examination administered by the medical director. Approximately 115 children were admitted annually under this plan and individual records of the later school performance of all children so admitted have been carefully kept. The results of early research undertaken to appraise the validity of the criteria used showed:

1. A significantly high positive relationship between mental age at entrance and

Reprinted by permission of the managing editor, from *Educational and Psychological Measurement*. Originally published 1963 in *Educational and Psychological Measurement* 23(1): 159–70.

both teachers' marks and standardized achievement test results through grade four.

2. Average marks and achievement test results of the underage group higher than those of the other children in every grade except kindergarten, where the marks of the underage children were slightly lower on the average despite higher average ratings on standardized reading readiness tests.

Later Studies

The results (Hobson 1948) of ten years' operation of this elastic system of admission confirmed both conclusions of the earlier study and further indicated:

1. that the margin of average superiority of the selected underage children increased as they progressed through the eight grades of elementary school;
2. that the least successful group of underage children were those admitted with an M.A. rating of 5–0, which was the minimum requirement;
3. that the next least successful group was composed of those children more than six months underage, although some individuals in this group were very successful;
4. that underage children originally admitted by test not only exceeded their fellows scholastically on the average but were referred less often for emotional, social, and other personality maladjustments; and
5. that, because of lower ages for school admission in large communities nearby and the frequent changes of residence in a metropolitan area, by grade six there were more underage children who had moved in than there were in the group originally admitted by test. By grade eight there were nearly twice as many, and nearly half of the group admitted by test had departed. As a result of this research, the minimum M.A. required for admittion on trial was raised to 5–2 and the privilege of early admittion was limited to those within six months of the required minimum chronological age for all children. This plan has been followed for several years.

THE CURRENT INVESTIGATION

The three main purposes of the present study are:

1. to compare high school scholastic performance of underage children, originally admitted to kindergarten by test (ABT), with performance of the others in their class;
2. to compare high school activity participation by underage, test-screened children and their classmates; and
3. to gain some idea as to the relative success in college admissions of the two groups.

Table 10.1. Percentages of academic and extracurricular distinctions of underage, test-screened pupils and others in ten graduating classes combined

	Total N*	Honor graduates			Elected to Alpha Pi		
		Boys	Girls	Total	Boys	Girls	Total
Underage, test-screened	550	18.8	25.4	22.7	12.9	18.7	16.4
Others	3,891	8.4	15.0	11.9	5.8	8.7	7.3
Difference		10.4	10.4	10.8	7.1	10.0	9.1

*There were 224 boys and 326 girls graduated (of 1,165 originally admitted to kindergarten in the underage, test-screened group). The "Others" group was made up of 1,863 boys and 2,028 girls.

Two general investigations were made. The first was a comparison of distinctions received by the 550 underage test-screened children graduates in ten classes and the 3,891 other pupils in those classes. The distinctions chosen were: (1) graduation with honors (which denotes an all A and B record in grades eleven and twelve); and (2) election to Alpha Pi, an undergraduate honorary society for which the criteria of selection are participation and prominence in extracurricular activities as well as excellence in scholarship (the latter alone does not suffice). The second study was a more detailed analysis of two early classes whose scholastic performance through elementary school was reported in detail in an earlier article (Hobson 1948). Analyses are made of scholastic performance in high school, participation in extracurricular activity, and data on college admissions.

COMPARISON OF DISTINCTIONS RECEIVED

A complete summary of the comparative distinctions received by the underage graduates who were originally admitted by test and the other graduates over a ten-year period is presented in table 10.1. It should be noted that there is an important factor which has some bearing on the performance of underage children as compared with those of their older classmates. Because of lower entrance ages in some cities near Brookline, we have by grade six as many underage children who have moved into town after grade one as we have who were originally admitted by test to kindergarten, and by grade nine we have twice as many. The study reported in 1948 showed that these children as a group were in every grade (two to eight inclusive) more successful scholastically than the older children in the class but less successful than the underage children originally selected by test. In this study these children are in every case included in the "other" classmates with whom the underage accelerates are compared.

The data in table 10.1 show that the underage boys and girls exceeded their older fellows in the percentage who graduated with honor by a margin statistically significant beyond the 1 percent level of confidence.

For election to Alpha Pi, at least one-third of the points presented as evidence of eligibility for membership must come from participation in extracurricular activities. The data summarized in table 10.1 show that the percentage of underage boys and girls gaining election to Alpha Pi exceeded that of the other boys and girls by a substantial margin, again yielding a difference significant beyond the 1 percent level of confidence.

These data indicate that underage children originally admitted to kindergarten on the basis of psychological and physical examinations are certainly not at a disadvantage during their high school years so far as honors and distinctions at graduation are concerned. Both criteria indicate the previously reported superiority of the experimental group holds throughout the public school years of these pupils.

COMPARATIVE SCHOLASTIC PERFORMANCE OF UNDERAGE AND OTHER GRADUATES IN TWO CLASSES

Since the elementary school records of the classes which graduated in 1946 and 1947 had been analyzed in some detail in the 1948 study, it seemed fitting to choose these two classes as the ones to be studied in detail through their high school years. The criterion of academic success was GPA in the sixteen standard high school courses. Table 10.2 presents these analyses.

In order to present the comparative scholastic performance of the underage and other graduates by means of a single index, marks were translated into a point rating scale used in many secondary schools and colleges in which an "A" counts four points, a "B" three, a "C" two, and a "D" one point. The differences in the class of 1947 are all significant at about the 1 percent level of confidence and beyond. Those in the class of 1946 will permit rejection of the null hypothesis at somewhere between the 5 percent to 10 percent level of confidence, chiefly because of the small number of underage boys in the class of 1946. If the comparison is based upon the separate course marks received by the two groups during the four high school years, the differences are all significant beyond the 1 percent level of confidence.

EXTRACURRICULAR ACTIVITY PARTICIPATION OF UNDERAGE AND OTHER GRADUATES IN TWO CLASSES

As stated previously, the second main purpose of the present study was to investigate and informally analyze the comparative high school extracurricular activity participation of two groups. Since the activity record of each graduate is published with his picture in the yearbook and since this record is checked by the yearbook staff and reviewed by the faculty sponsors, the data published can be

Table 10.2. Four-year academic point ratings of underage, test-screened graduates and others in two classes

		Class of 1946				Class of 1947		
	Total *N**	Boys	Girls	Total	Total *N**	Boys	Girls	Total
Underage, test-screened	39	2.43	2.52	2.49	52	2.53	2.73	2.64
Others	336	2.22	2.33	2.29	388	2.18	2.38	2.28
Difference		.21	.19	.20		.35	.35	.36

*The class of 1946 was made up of 12 boys and 27 girls in the experimental group; 139 boys and 197 girls in the control group. In the class of 1947 there were 20 boys and 32 girls in the former, 197 boys and 191 girls in the latter groups.

considered more than ordinarily reliable. The time and opportunity for participation in extracurricular activities may be limited by out-of-school hours employment. Such employment is listed and counted as an extracurricular activity.

The data on extracurricular activity participation of the classes of 1946 and 1947 are shown in table 10.3.

The data in table 10.3 show that the underage boys and girls of both classes exceed their classmates of the same sex by a substantial margin in average number of extracurricular activities engaged in over the four-year period. Both the underage and other girls exceeded both underage and other boys both years as well. The most significant fact for the purpose of this study was the revelation that the underage boys and girls of both classes taken as one group had an average of 18.8 extracurricular activities compared to an average of 12.1 activities per student among the other graduates in the two classes—a ratio of more than three to two. The underage boys exceeded the other boys by a difference that is significant at about the 2 percent level of confidence. The wide margin by which underage girls exceeded the other girls is significant far beyond the 1 percent level of confidence.

Apparently the accelerated status and youth of the underage children originally admitted by test was no handicap to them in extracurricular activity participation. Judging from the data on election to Alpha Pi, it appeared that they were able to achieve more than their share of success and prominence in these activities.

A detailed analysis of the kinds of extracurricular activities engaged in by the underage and other graduates would make an interesting study in itself, but that is too lengthy an undertaking to be included in this paper. An informal analysis of the activities engaged in by the two groups of graduates shows no discernible differences in the kinds of activities undertaken by the underage and other girls. While 126 of the 224 underage boys took part in athletics, it appears from a subjective analysis of all ten classes of graduates that the underage boys seldom achieved eminence in the contact sports.

In any event the data in tables 10.1 and 10.3 will support the generalization that the underage boys and girls were more universally active and successful in

Table 10.3. Extracurricular activity participation of underage (ABT)* and other graduates in the classes of 1946 and 1947

	Underage				Other			
	Boys		Girls		Boys		Girls	
	Number of activities		Number of activities		Number of activities		Number of activities	
Year	Total	Mean	Total	Mean	Total	Mean	Total	Mean
Class of 1946	138	11.58	583	19.33	1145	8.79	3023	14.85
Class of 1947	222	11.50	826	26.22	1841	8.55	3228	15.62
Both years combined	360	11.53	1409	22.89	2986	8.69	6251	15.24
S.D.		7.43		14.13		7.83		11.33
Difference		2.84		7.65				
Both sexes combined	N = 1,769		Av. = 18.8		N = 9,237		Av. = 12.1	

*ABT = Admitted by test.

extracurricular activity participations and that a larger share of them achieved distinction in these activities than was true of their classmates.

POSTSECONDARY SCHOOL ADMISSIONS OF UNDERAGE GRADUATES (ABT) IN THE CLASSES OF 1946 AND 1947 COMPARED WITH OTHER GRADUATES

The data in regard to college admissions for the classes of 1946 and 1947 are shown in table 10.4, broken down into regular four-year colleges which are fully accredited and other advanced institutions which include junior colleges, business and other specialized schools, and some of the newer colleges which have not as yet qualified for full accreditation.

The data in table 10.4 show that a significantly larger percentage of underage boys and girls went on to postsecondary education. If only four-year accredited colleges are considered, the margin is even greater: 22.6 percent more ABT boys and 21 percent more ABT girls went on to such colleges than was true of their fellows. It may also be noted that, despite the entrance into the armed forces of about one-third of both the ABT and other boys in the class of 1946, for the two-year period the boys in each category exceeded the girls in percentage gaining admission to four-year colleges. If 1947 is taken as a more normal year, the margin is sizeable. This is undoubtedly a reflection of the greater tendency of boys to prepare for entrance into the professions and the greater tendency for girls to prepare for business, homemaking, and shorter-term occupational specialties.

The percentage of both ABT and other girls substantially exceeded that of boys in their category in the matter of total postsecondary school attendance. However, the ABT boys exceeded the older girls for the two-year period despite the loss to the armed forces in 1946. The data presented in table 10.4 will amply

Table 10.4. Admission to postsecondary schools of underage (ABT) and other graduates of the classes of 1946 and 1947

| | | Underage (ABT) | | | | Other | | | |
| | | 4-year colleges | | Other institutions | | | 4-year colleges | | Other institutions |
Class	En.	N	%	N	%	En.	N	%	N	%
Boys										
1946*	12	6	50.0	1	8.3	140	36	25.7	26	18.6
1947	20	13	65.0	2	10.0	216	95	44.0	26	12.0
Total	32	19	59.4	3	9.4	356	131	36.8	52	14.6
Difference			22.6							
Girls										
1946*	30	15	50.0	6	20.0	205	66	32.2	68	33.2
1947	32	19	59.4	10	31.3	203	72	35.5	59	29.1
Total	62	34	54.8	16	25.8	408	138	33.8	127	31.1
Difference			21.0							

*4 ABT and 45 other boys of the class of 1946 entered the Armed forces of the U.S. shortly before or immediately after graduation. These percentages are 33.3 and 32.1, respectively.

support the generalization that a larger percentage of underage accelerates in the classes of 1946 and 1947 gained admission to first-class colleges for the purpose of continuing their education than was true of their fellows.

A NECESSARY MAJOR ASSUMPTION

This has been an objective report of factual material recorded on permanent records in the archives of Brookline High School. In arriving at the conclusions summarized below it has been necessary to make only one major assumption, namely, that no selective factor affecting the results of this research is involved in the moving away from Brookline of more than half of the underage children originally admitted by test before their graduation. The data in the 1944 study showed an average of 117 underage pupils per year admitted to kindergarten by tests and 115 per year completing grade one. The question is—are the talents and other personality traits of the 55 per year who remained to graduate approximately the same on the average as those of the 60 who have departed. Brookline is an expensive town in which to own property. Consequently, a great deal of the moving is occasioned by successful people in business or the professions buying homes in Newton, Needham, or Wellesley, Massachusetts, and moving from their rented apartments in Brookline. The children of successful people moving to homes of their own should compare favorably in the traits that make for success in school as compared to the children of families which stay put. While subjectively one might think that families whose children are particularly happy and successful in school might tend to avoid moving while a child is in high school, actually the attrition during the high school years in the case of the classes of 1946 and 1947 was approximately 60 percent of what it had been during the last four years of elementary school. The class of 1946 lost twelve underage accelerates in grades five to eight inclusive and fourteen in grades nine to twelve inclusive, while in the class of 1947 the figures were twenty-five and eight, respectively.

CONCLUSIONS

The following conclusions appear to be supported by the data detailed in the preceding sections of this report.

1. The scholastic superiority in elementary school of underage children, originally admitted to school on the basis of physical and psychological examinations, is continued and somewhat increased through high school. This conclusion is supported by the statistically significant margin by which both boys and girls in the underage (ABT) groups achieved higher GPAs and by the percentage graduated with honor.
2. Underage accelerates (ABT) engaged in a significantly larger average number of extracurricular activities over the four-year period. Their activity participation was not overly weighted with activities of a scholastic nature. Athletic and social honors and elective positions came in for their full share of underage participation.
3. In the matter of honors, awards, and distinctions at graduation the underage (ABT) boys and girls exceeded their fellows by a ratio of about two to one.
4. A significantly larger percentage of underage (ABT) graduates sought and gained admission to accredited four-year colleges of superior standing than was true of their classmates of the same. sex.
5. Initial acceleration, of children who are within a few months of the usual minimum age for admission to school and who can demonstrate, in physical and psychological examinations, physical fitness and mental maturity which will insure their being under no serious initial handicap as compared with the average of their older classmates, is the ideal means of making initial provision for individual differences. It avoids the break in the continuity of the educative process which is inherent in any system of grade-skipping or double promotion after a child has attended school. It is a step in providing for gifted children and saves a year for the candidate for the professions who faces a long period of graduate and postgraduate study after college.

REFERENCES

Ammons, M. P., and Goodlad, J. I. 1955. When to begin: Dimensions of the first grade entrance age problem. *Childhood Education* 32: 21–26.

Anderson, E. E. (ed.). 1961. *Research on the academically talented student.* Washington, D.C.: National Education Association.

Beall, R. H., and Holmes, M. 1938. Identifying mature and immature first-year entrants. *Newer Practices in Reading in the Elementary School* (Bulletin of the Department of Elementary School Principals, National Education Association) July: 257–58.

Birch, J. W. 1954. Early school admission for mentally advanced children. *Exceptional Children* 21: 84–87.

Carter, L. 1955. The effect of early school entrance on the scholastic achievement of elementary school children in the Austin public schools. *Journal of Educational Research* 50: 91–103.

Cone, H. R. 1955. Brookline admits them early. *Nation's Schools* 55(3): 46–47.

Dwyer, P. S. 1939. Correlation between age at entrance and success in college. *Journal of Educational Psychology* 30: 251–64.

Edmiston, R. W., and Holohan, C. E. 1946. Measures predictive of first-grade achievement. *School and Society* 63: 268–69.

Forester, J. J. 1955. At what age should a child start school? *School Executive* 74: 80–81.

Gates, A. I. 1937. The necessary mental age for beginning reading. *Elementary School Journal* 37: 497–98.

Gelles, H. M., and Coulson, M. C. 1959. At what age is a child ready for school? *School Executive* 78: 29–31.

Gray, W. S. (ed.). 1940. *Reading in general education.* Washington, D.C.: American Council on Education.

Handy, A. E. 1931. Admission of underage pupils. *American School Board Journal* 83(2): 46.

Handy, A. E. 1938. Are underage children successes in school? *American School Board Journal* 97(4): 31–32.

Harrison, M. L. 1936. *Reading readiness.* Boston: Houghton Mifflin.

Hausman, E. J. 1940. Ready for first grade? *School Executive* 59(2): 25–26.

Hildreth, G. H. 1946. Age standards for first grade entrance. *Childhood Education* 23: 22–27.

Hobson, J. R. 1948. Mental age as a workable criterion for school admission. *Elementary School Journal* 48: 312–21.

Kazienko, L. W. 1954. Beginner grade influence on school progress. *Educational Administration and Supervision* 40: 219–28.

Keys, N. 1938. *Underage student in high school and college.* Berkeley: University of California Press.

King, I. B. 1955. Effect of age of entrance into grade one upon achievement in elementary school. *Elementary School Journal* 55: 331–36.

Knight, J., and Manuel, H. T. 1930. Age of school entrance and subsequent school record. *School and Society* 32: 24–26.

Lehman, H. C. 1953. *Age and achievement.* Princeton: Princeton University Press.

Manwiller, C. E. 1936. Follow-up of pupils tested for placement in grade one before the chronological age of six. Pittsburgh Schools, No. 10: 86–95.

Miller, V. V. 1957. Academic achievement and social adjustment of children young for their grade placement. *Elementary School Journal* 57: 257–63.

Monderer, J. H. 1953. An evaluation of the Nebraska program of early entrance to elementary school. Ph.D. thesis, University of Nebrasks. Abstract: 1954. *Dissertation Abstracts* 14(1): 633.

Nemzek, C. L., and Finch, F. H. 1939. Relationship between age at entrance to elementary school and achievement in the secondary school. *School and Society* 49: 778–79.

Partington, H. M. 1937. Relation between first-grade entrance age and success in the first six grades. *National Elementary Principal* 16: 298–302.

Patterson, H. 1934. Chronological age of highly intelligent freshmen. *Peabody Journal of Education* 12: 19–20.

Pauly, F. R. 1951. Sex differences and legal schools entrance age. *Journal of Educational Research* 45: 1–9.

Shannon, D. C. 1957. What research says about acceleration. *Phi Delta Kappan* 22: 70–72.

Smith, J. 1951. The success of some young children in the Lincoln, Nebraska public schools. Master's thesis, University of Nebraska.

Terman, L. M. 1954. The discovery and encouragement of exceptional talent. *American Psychologist* 9: 221–30.

Washburne, C. 1939. Introduction to *Child development and the curriculum, Part 1*. Bloomington, Ill.: Public School Publishing Company.

Wilson, F. T. 1954. Educators' opinions about the acceleration of gifted students. *School and Society* 80: 120–22.

Worcester, D. A. 1956. *The education of children of above average mentality*. Lincoln: University of Nebraska Press.

Wright, G. S. 1946. Permissive school entrance ages in local school systems. *School Life* 18: 20.

11

IDENTIFYING AND NURTURING THE INTELLECTUALLY GIFTED

Julian C. Stanley

The main point of this article is that most of the supplemental educational procedures called "enrichment" and given overly glamorous titles are, even at best, potentially dangerous if not accompanied or followed by acceleration of placement in subject matter and/or grade. To state it more simply, for highly precocious youngsters acceleration seems to me vastly preferable to most types of enrichment. This appears to be especially true where mathematics and mathematics-related subjects are concerned.

But what do I mean by "enrichment" and "acceleration"? Unless we agree on the differences between such processes, my points may be obscured in the minds of those who consider enrichment to be a form of acceleration and acceleration as being enriching. To me, *enrichment* is any educational procedure beyond the usual ones for the subject or grade or age that does not accelerate or retard the student's placement in the subject or grade. Admittedly, some ambiguity remains after this definition, because it does not tell what is usual for the subject, grade, or age. Illustrations of four types of enrichment may produce better agreement.

One of these forms of enrichment—unfortunately, it is quite commonly used—is what might be termed *busywork*. It consists of more of the same, greater in quantity than is required of the average student in the class but no different in level. One of our most mathematically precocious boys, an eighth-grader with an IQ of 187 who had already skipped a grade, was required by his Algebra I teacher to work every problem in each chapter rather than just the odd-numbered ones. He could have completed the whole course with distinction in a very few hours without needing to work many problems, but his teacher was trying to hold him for 180 fifty-minute periods. It is a pity that at the beginning of the school year he was not allowed to take a standardized algebra test, learn the few points he did not already know, and move on to Algebra II

Reprinted with permission of editors, *Gifted Child Quarterly* and *Phi Delta Kappan*. Published 1976 in *Phi Delta Kappan* 58(3): 234–37 and *Gifted Child Quarterly* 20(1): 66–75, 41. The GCQ title is "The case for extreme educational acceleration of intellectually brilliant youths."

within a few days. At the end of the seventh grade, a boy less able than he scored above the 99.8th percentile on a standardized algebra test (missing only two items out of forty) without ever having had the course called "algebra." Another boy, more brilliant than either, scored forty out of forty when still a seventh grader. These are not typical youngsters, of course, but in three years of math talent searching in Maryland we have found more than 200 others rather like them.

There is a happy ending to the story of the boy oppressed by busywork in his beginning algebra course. After the eighth grade he studied all of his mathematics part time at the college level, for credit. This took him through college algebra and trigonometry, calculus, advanced calculus, and linear algebra with an initial B and subsequent As. He also completed an introduction to computer science in the Johns Hopkins day school with a grade of A at age 12. Furthermore, he completed college chemistry through two semesters of organic chemistry with As. At age 15 years and 2 months he became a full-time student at Johns Hopkins, having sophomore status because of thirty-nine credits already earned and living happily in a dormitory. As an electrical engineering major he completed the first college year with eight As and only one B and finished the junior year at age 16.

Though this boy did manage to turn the usually stultifying effects of busywork into great motivation to detour further such obstacles and forge ahead, it would be difficult to make a general case for this type of enrichment.

A second type often used is what I shall term *irrelevant academic enrichment*. It consists of setting up a special subject or activity meant to enrich the educational lives of some group of intellectually talented students. It pays no attention to the specific nature of their talents. If the activity is, for example, a special class in social studies, it may be meant for all high-IQ youths. The math whiz may enjoy it as a temporary relief from the general boredom of school, but it will not ameliorate his or her situation in the slow-paced math class. It may be essentially irrelevant to his or her main academic interests.

My third type of enrichment, *cultural*, might also be considered irrelevant to the direct academic needs of intellectually gifted students, but it seems much more worthwhile. The special social studies class already used as an illustration of irrelevant academic enrichment merely introduces earlier what should, in a good school, be available at a later grade level. Cultural enrichment means supplying aspects of the performing arts such as music, art, drama, dance, and creative writing or offering systematic instruction in foreign languages before it is usually made available. This can serve the unmet needs of many students, however, not just those with high IQs or special intellectual talents such as great mathematical reasoning ability or superb mechanical comprehension. Nevertheless, if supplied specifically for those students talented in one or more of the performing arts or in languages, cultural enrichment becomes merely a type of "relevant enrichment," which I describe next.

If a student is given advanced material or higher-level treatment of in-grade topics in areas of his or her special aptitudes, the enrichment might be said to be "relevant" to those abilities. For example, mathematically able youths might have a unified, integrated modern mathematics curriculum from kindergarten through, say, grade seven, in lieu of the usual mathematics sequence for those eight grades. This could be splendid, but imagine the boredom that would surely result if as eighth graders such students were dumped into a regular Algebra I class.

If the special mathematics curriculum extended from kindergarten through the twelfth grade, it would be crucial that students completing it well should not begin in college with the standard introductory mathematics courses there. The same considerations apply in English, science, or social science curricula. The more relevant and excellent the enrichment, the more it calls for acceleration of subject matter or grade placement later. Otherwise, it just puts off the boredom awhile and virtually guarantees that eventually it will be more severe.

Thus in my taxonomy there are four main types of enrichment: busywork, irrelevant academic enrichment, cultural enrichment, and relevant academic enrichment. All of these except cultural enrichment may be viewed as horizontal, because they are usually tied closely to a particular grade or narrow age range and are not meant to affect the age-in-grade status of the participating students.

By contrast, academic acceleration is vertical, because it means moving the student up into the higher school level of a subject in which he or she excels, or into a higher grade than the chronological age of the student would ordinarily warrant. If a seventh-grader is allowed to take algebra, usually at least an eighth-grade subject, that is subject-matter acceleration. If a student is allowed to skip a grade, that is grade acceleration.

Often these two types of acceleration should go together. For example, if a high school student scores well enough on the calculus test of the national Advanced Placement Program, he (or she) will earn quite a few credits that would be accepted by many colleges. At Johns Hopkins he or she would be ready to take advanced calculus upon entry, and would also have 27 percent of the credits needed to complete the freshman year. Passing three or four Advanced Placement courses will give sophomore status at a number of colleges such as Harvard.

Entering college before completing high school is another example of grade-skipping. We helped a boy who was only 11½ years old to become a full-time college student, quite successfully, at the end of the sixth grade. He skipped grades seven through twelve. Two 13-year-old boys entered Johns Hopkins right out of the eighth grade. A 14-year-old enrolled at the end of the ninth grade. Another 14-year-old enrolled as a college sophomore after skipping four grades. He is scheduled to complete the B.A. degree a few days after his seventeenth birthday. It will be illuminating to see in some detail how he accomplished this remarkable speed-up.

We first heard of this boy, whom I shall call Sean, in the fall of 1971. As a sixth-grader whose twelfth birthday came that 4 December, he was rather old in grade. According to local rules, he could have been a seventh-grader, but his parents had moved to Baltimore from another section of the country that had more restrictive entering regulations. Sean had greatly impressed the teachers in the elementary school he attended, so during the summer following the fifth grade he participated in a special computer science project conducted by the Maryland Academy of Sciences. Through local newspaper publicity the academy heard of our new programs for mathematically precocious youths. It recommended Sean to us, thereby making him the first participant in a five-year study funded by the Spencer Foundation, although before the study began we had enrolled two 13-year-olds as regular freshmen at Johns Hopkins.

Sean proved to be exceptionally able both quantitatively and verbally, but especially with respect to mathematical reasoning ability. He had not yet learned much mathematics, however. For example, he did not know the rule for dividing one common fraction by another (that is, invert the second fraction and then multiply), but learned the rule and its proof quickly—as Professor Higgins said in *My Fair Lady,* "with the speed of summer lightning."

Sean was not in a high enough grade that year to enter our first mathematics competition, which was restricted to seventh and eighth and underage ninth graders. It was not until we formed our first fast-mathematics class in June, 1972, that he, then 12½ years old, began to get special educational facilitation from us. The story of that class is told in chapter 6 of our *Mathematical Talent* book, which appeared in 1974 and covered the background and first year of the study. The class continued until August, 1973, and Sean was one of its two stars. He completed four and one-half years of precalculus mathematics well in sixty two-hour Saturday mornings, compared with the 810 forty-five- or fifty-minute periods usually required for Algebra I through III, plane geometry, trigonometry, and analytic geometry.

Sean skipped the seventh grade, which in Baltimore County is the first year of junior high school, and in the eighth grade took no mathematics other than the Saturday morning class. Also, during the second semester of the eighth grade he was given released time to take the introduction to computer science course at Johns Hopkins. He found this fascinating and at age 13 readily made a final grade of A.

While still 13 years old, Sean skipped the ninth and tenth grades and became an eleventh grader at a large surburban public high school. There he took calculus with twelfth graders, won a letter on the wrestling team, was the science and math whiz on the school's television academic quiz team, tutored a brilliant seventh grader through two and one-half years of algebra and a year of plane geometry in eight months, played a good game of golf, and took some college courses on the side (set theory, economics, and political science). He even successfully managed the campaign of a 14-year-old friend for the presidency of the student council. This left time to prepare for the Advanced Placement Program examination in calculus and, entirely by studying on his own, also in physics. He won fourteen college credits via those two exams.

During the summer after completing the eleventh grade, Sean took a year of college chemistry at Johns Hopkins—as usual, earning good grades. That enabled him to enter Johns Hopkins in the fall of 1974 with thirty-four credits and therefore sophomore status. He lived at home and commuted to the campus with his mother, who took a position at Johns Hopkins in order to make this easier (14-year-olds aren't permitted to drive automobiles, no matter how far along in college they may be). During the first semester he took *advanced* calculus, number theory, *sophomore* physics, and American government, making As on the two math courses and Bs on the other two courses. Also, he began to get involved in campus politics. He got along well socially and emotionally. As he told an Associated Press reporter who asked about this, "Either social considerations take a poor second to intellectual ones, or there are no negative social effects. . . . The most significant aspect of my life is having skipped grades."

Let us recapitulate here. Sean began by being "enriched" in the Academy of Science summer program for brilliant elementary school pupils. That served as a good background for the college course in computer science, which was intended to be both enriching and accelerative. The fast-mathematics class provided radical acceleration, because it telescoped into one year of Saturday mornings four and one-half years of precalculus mathematics. Skipping four grades was also highly accelerative, as were the college courses taken and the Advanced Placement exams passed.

Sean is unusually bright, of course, and extremely well motivated, but he is by no means the ablest youth we have found. He has done the most different accelerative things, however. By contrast, another mathematically and verbally brilliant boy simply took a college course each semester or summer term from age 12 to age 15. Besides that, he skipped the second, eleventh, and twelfth grades. This combination of college courses and grade skipping enabled him to enter Johns Hopkins at age 15 years 2 months with thirty-nine college credits— that is, 30 percent of the way through the sophomore year. Another boy skipped grades eight, eleven, and twelve, took seventeen credits of college courses, and earned eight college credits in calculus via the Advanced Placement exam. In the fall of 1974 he entered Johns Hopkins at barely 15 years of age with 83 percent of the freshman year completed.

Many students in the study, including some girls, are *eager* to move ahead faster than the usual age-in-grade lock step. They do so with ease and pleasure. We find that the combination of great ability and personal eagerness to accelerate educationally virtually guarantees success. Nearly all of our forty-four early entrants to college thus far have done very well in their studies and social and emotional development. Only one performed poorly initially, and even he improved rather soon. This brilliant but headstrong 14-year-old had signed up for a heavy load of difficult courses and then would not study enough during his first year of college. Compared with the academic and personal record of the typical Johns Hopkins student, the early entrants have been truly outstanding.

Perhaps our most interestingly different course has been college calculus for two hours on Saturday mornings to supplement high school calculus, so that students can do well on the higher level of the Advanced Placement calculus exam. With a class composed mainly of well-above-average tenth graders, but with one student only 11 years old, this went along so well from September, 1974, until February that by then everyone in the group knew more calculus than most college students learn in two semesters. By early May only nine college students in 1,000 score higher than the lowest-scoring one of the thirteen students in this class—and that wasn't the 11-year-old! All of these special students scored excellently on the higher level (BC) of the national Advanced Placement Program examination in calculus in May, 1975, and earned a year of college calculus credit. Nine of them earned the highest score reported—that is, five on a five-point scale, meaning "extremely well qualified to enter college Calculus III." Three earned fours, and one earned a three. A new class with twenty-three students began in the fall of 1975. All of them were eleventh or twelfth graders, some as young as 15 years old.

Recently we had an extreme example of what powerful predictors of achievement their scores on difficult tests can be for intellectually gifted youths. The mathematics department at Johns Hopkins conducted a test competition for eleventh graders. We heard about it only a week before the test date and got permission to tell some of our participants. We hastily located the names and addresses of nineteen persons who as eighth graders three years earlier had scored high on the SAT-M in our first talent search. These were not our very best, because most of those had moved along beyond the eleventh grade; several of them were already in college. Of these nineteen, ten came for the test. Seven of them had not been identified by their high school mathematics teachers, and one of the three so identified was a member of our calculus class whose father teaches mathematics at Johns Hopkins.

Fifty-one students entered the contest, and their scores ranged from 140 down to 2. One of our group, not nominated by his teachers, was far ahead of anyone else with 140 points. The math professor's son ranked second with 112 points. Another of our group ranked third with 91 points. The highest scorer not in our group ranked fourth with 82 points. The other seven nominated by us ranked down only to 23.5 out of the 51. Isn't it a bit frightening that a single score from a test administered three years earlier identified high math achievers much better than did teachers who have known their students for at least seven months?[1]

This finding is congruent, however, with Lewis Terman's discovery of many years ago that teachers are not good at identifying students with extremely high IQs. Apparently the math classes simply do not tap the best abilities of mathematically brilliant students, whereas the difficult test does. There's a moral in this for those who lean too heavily on teachers' recommendations where intellectually

---

[1]For details, see my article, "Test Better Finder of Great Math Talent Than Teachers Are," in *American Psychologist,* April, 1976, pp. 313, 314.

gifted children are concerned. In selecting early entrants in our study, we pay far more attention to scores on advanced tests and other evidence of marked precocity than we do to school grades or recommendations, because most of the high school courses are not pitched at an appropriate level of difficulty and challenge for such students.

It should be no surprise that educational acceleration works well when highly able, splendidly motivated students are given a variety of ways to accomplish it. From Terman's monumental *Genetic Studies of Genius* and Sidney Pressey's definitive 1949 monograph on *Educational Acceleration* through the experiences of the University of Chicago, Shimer College, the Ford Foundation's large early-entrance study of the 1950s, Worcester's and Hobson's work, and Simon's Rock College, up to the radical accelerative techniques we are developing, it is clear that acceleration can work much better than so-called academic enrichment for those students who really want it. Counter-examples are rare and likely to be atypical. For every William Sidis who renounces intellectual pursuits because of extreme—and apparently quite unwise—parental pressures, there are many persons such as Norbert Wiener and Sean who benefit greatly from the time saved, frustration avoided, and stimulation gained.

We believe that concentrating efforts on preparing "teachers of the gifted" to enrich curricula is, while far better than nothing, a relatively ineffective and costly way to help the ablest student. At least, such teachers should help provide the smorgasbord of accelerative opportunities and counseling in their use that many such students need.[2]

The procedures that we propose are not expensive. Most of them actually save the school system time and money. One does not need a large appropriation in order to encourage grade-skipping, identify students ready to move through mathematics courses at a faster-than-usual rate, encourage early graduation from high school, help certain students enroll for courses in nearby colleges or by correspondence study, promote Advanced Placement exams, or even set up special fast-math courses. More than money, they take zeal and a distinctive point of view.

Persons who hear about our study usually ask, "But what about the social and emotional development of the students who become accelerated?" We often counter with, "What about the intellectual and emotional development and future success of students who yearn for acceleration but are denied it?" For more than six years we have been studying the social and emotional development of youths accelerated in a variety of ways. If the acceleration is by their own choice, they look good indeed. Part of the problem is in the minds of those skeptics who automatically assume that one's social and emotional peers are one's agemates. Performance of gifted youngsters, including ours, on such personality measures

---

[2]For more about this, see Daniel P. Keating, ed., *Intellectual Talent: Research and Development* (Baltimore, Md.: Johns Hopkins University Press, 1976).

as the California Psychological Inventory shows that emotionally they are more like bright persons several years older than themselves than they are like their own agemates. There is considerable variability, of course, but on the average they are better matched socially and emotionally with able students who are older. Thus, just as their intellectual peers are not their agemates, their social and emotional peers aren't either. For clarity of discourse, it would seem wise not to use the word "peer" in this type of argument without prefacing it with one or more modifiers.

Another question often asked us is, "Why do you start with 12- and 13-year-olds who reason superbly mathematically? That is awfully narrow. Why not be broader?" Well, neither mathematics as a field nor our various procedures is "narrow." Mathematics undergirds many of man's highest endeavors. In a sense, it is probably the most generally useful subject (although, of course, some philosophers would argue about that statement). We try to approach talent in mathematics comprehensively, but we deliberately chose to specialize in this area where great precocity often occurs because one can be brilliant in mathematics without yet having had many of the usual life experiences of an adolescent or adult. Also, because of this precocity, many students in school are horribly bored. Imagine having to serve time in first-year algebra for 180 fifty-minute periods when one knows the subject well the first day of class! That is by no means an uncommon occurrence, and it may partially explain the lack of interest in mathematics among many bright persons.

My own motivation to help accelerate the mathematical progress of fine mathematical reasoners grew out of my early background. It seems sensible to specialize in what one knows and likes best. Many educational researchers dislike mathematics. Of course, they should concentrate elsewhere.

With more than 2,000 mathematically able boys and girls already identified, we do not have time and facilities to look for latent talent or potential achievers, worthy though that pursuit surely is. We leave that to the many persons who prefer to specialize in identification and facilitation of underachievers, "late bloomers," and the "disadvantaged gifted." Aside from some concern about sex differences in mathematical precocity, we have not tried to screen in a set percent of any group. From socioeconomic and ethnic standpoints, however, the high scorers have been a varied lot.

A well-known quotation from Thomas Gray's famous elegy sums up the case for seeking talent and nurturing it:

> Full many a gem of purest ray serene
> The dark unfathomed caves of ocean bear;
> Full many a flower is born to blush unseen,
> And waste its sweetness on the desert air.

Another poet tells us that ". . . a man's reach should exceed his grasp, or what's a heaven for?"

It is our responsibility and opportunity to help prevent the potential Miltons, Einsteins, and Wieners from coming to the "mute inglorious" ends that Gray viewed in that country churchyard long ago. The problem has changed little, but the prospects are much better now. Surely we can greatly extend both the reach and the grasp of our brilliant youths, or what's an educational system for?

IV
Symposium

12

EDUCATIONAL ACCELERATION OF INTELLECTUALLY TALENTED YOUTHS: PROLONGED DISCUSSION BY A VARIED GROUP OF PROFESSIONALS

Sanford J. Cohn, William C. George, Julian C. Stanley, editors

ABSTRACT

For many years various forms of educational acceleration have been used. James Fenimore Cooper entered Yale College at age 13, Norbert Wiener was graduated from a village high school in Massachusetts at age 11 and Tufts College (Phi Beta Kappa) at age 14, and the brilliant young Princeton University mathematician Charles Fefferman simply entered college at 14 without a high school diploma and received his Ph.D. degree at barely 20. Entering school early, skipping grades, moving ahead fast in a subject such as mathematics, taking college courses part time while still in secondary school, doubling up to be graduated from high school early, leaving high school for college without a diploma, completing college in less than eight semesters, earning a master's degree concurrently with the bachelor's, and myriad variations of these enable a relatively few students to break the age-in-grade lock step that characterizes most schools and colleges, both public and private, in the United States.

It appears that not a single substantial study has ever shown acceleration to be harmful to the typical accelerant who is intellectually able enough to warrant the use of such procedures. On the average the results are decidedly beneficial, whereas the withholding of acceleration from able, well-motivated youths is likely to harm their academic, social, and emotional development. Most evidence against acceleration is of the ''I knew a student who . . .'' variety.

In April of 1977 the time seemed ripe for some of the best educational and psychological thinkers from a variety of backgrounds and viewpoints to examine this belief system and to try to ascertain its causes, consequences, and possible antidotes. By having a lengthy, spirited exchange of facts and opinions among some twenty professionals, each of whom summarized his or her own position briefly, and the audience, it was possible to explore the issues and to move toward resolving them. Such discussion seems never to have been staged before on nearly the scale of this symposium. Aided by background material furnished by the organizer (Julian C. Stanley), each symposiast prepared a brief position paper and read it at the symposium. The names and the addresses of those professionals follow:

Dr. Anne Anastasi, Professor of Psychology, Fordham University, New York, New York 10458.

Dr. Scarvia B. Anderson, Director and Senior Vice-President, Educational Testing Service, Room 1040, 3445 Peachtree Road, N.E., Atlanta, Georgia 30326.

Dr. Alvia Y. Branch, Social Science Research Council, 605 Third Ave., New York, New York 10016.

Dr. Stephen P. Daurio, Assistant Professor of Psychology, St. John's University, Staten Island, New York, New York 10301.

Dr. Virginia Z. Ehrlich, Project Director, Gifted Child Studies, 40 Seventh Ave., S., New York, New York 10014.

Dr. Lynn H. Fox, Associate Professor of Education and Coordinator of the Intellectually Gifted Child Study Group (IGCSG), Evening College and Summer Session, The Johns Hopkins University, Baltimore, Maryland 21218.

Mr. William C. George, Director, Office of Talent Identification and Development (OTID), and Associate Director, Study of Mathematically Precocious Youth (SMPY), The Johns Hopkins University, Baltimore, Maryland 21218.

Dr. E. Glenadine Gibb, Professor of Mathematics Education, The University of Texas, Austin, Texas 78712.

Dr. Marvin Gold, Department Chairman, School of Special Education, The University of South Alabama, Mobile, Alabama 36688.

Dr. Robert J. Havighurst, Professor of Education, The University of Chicago, 5885 Kimbark Ave., Chicago, Illinois 60637.

Dr. David M. Jackson, Co-Director, National Institute on Gifted and Talented, 11539 Maple Ridge Road, Reston, Virginia 22090.

Dr. Nancy E. Jackson, Developmental Psychology Laboratory, The University of Washington, Seattle, Washington 98195.

Dr. H. Thomas James, President of the Spencer Foundation, 875 N. Michigan Ave., Chicago, Illinois 60611.

Dr. Elizabeth I. Kearney, Curriculum Specialist, Gifted Program, Pasadena Unified School District, 351 S. Hudson Ave., Pasadena, California 91109.

Dr. Daniel P. Keating, Associate Professor of Child Development, Institute of Child Development, University of Minnesota, Minneapolis, Minnesota 55455.

Dr. Albert K. Kurtz, State Consultant and former Professor of Psychology, 1810 Ivy Lane, Winter Park, Florida 32792.

Mr. Leroy Owens, Anchorage Public Schools, Anchorage, Alaska 99503.

Dr. Ellis B. Page, Professor of Education, Duke University, Durham, North Carolina 22706. Formerly he was at the University of Connecticut.

Dr. Joseph S. Renzulli, Professor of Educational Psychology. The University of Connecticut, Storrs, Connecticut 06268.[1]

[1]EDITORS' NOTE: Professor Renzulli was unable to attend the symposium. He did provide the editors with a position paper, however. It has been inserted at the point where he would have spoken.

Dr. Dorothy A. Sisk, Formerly Director, Office of the Gifted and Talented, Department of Health, Education, and Welfare, Washington, D.C. 20202.[2] Currently Professor of Special Education, University of South Florida, Tampa, Florida 33620.

Dr. Julian C. Stanley, Professor of Psychology and Director of the Study of Mathematically Precocious Youth (SMPY), The Johns Hopkins University, Baltimore, Maryland 21218.

Dr. Joan S. Stark, Dean of the School of Education, The University of Michigan, Ann Arbor, Michigan 48104.

The symposium was begun by Julian C. Stanley.[3]

STANLEY: I'm delighted to welcome you today to the Symposium on Educational Acceleration of Intellectually Talented Youths. This is a prolonged discussion by some twenty professionals from various persuasions and several points of view. We are fortunate to have them come together here. The participants are divided into four groups. Each person within a given group will present a short position paper and then there will be a discussion among the members of that group. We will then go on to the next group. After these papers have been presented, there will be time for full-scale discussion with the audience.

The introduction to the symposium will be given by Dr. H. Thomas James, who is President of the Spencer Foundation and who prior to that time was the Dean of the School of Education at Stanford University. Dr. James:

INTRODUCTORY COMMENTS

H. Thomas James

When I left Stanford University in 1970 to join the Spencer Foundation we talked at length about how a foundation with modest resources might be most effective in the improvement of education. We had noted the pendulum-like swings of interest so characteristic of the world of education and decided that one way to be useful was to try to find a countercyclical position from government funding. With government funding at an all-time high for studies and assistance to the handicapped, the disadvantaged, and the variously deprived child, we were pleased to find early opportunities to fund studies of the mathematically and scientifically precocious, as well as the verbally and humanistically gifted children. Last year after our first six years of operation we asked a distinguished scholar of the field to review our investments in studies of the gifted. He noted that the field of talent study virtually had been dormant, and pointed out three

[2]EDITORS' NOTE: Dr. Sisk was asked to write a position paper that would serve to close the discussion by integrating various viewpoints.

[3]EDITORS' NOTE: The organizer and chairperson of this symposium was Julian C. Stanley.

independent events that suggested it sprang to life again in the early 1970s. "The first was the development of the Study of Mathematically Precocious Youth at The Johns Hopkins University by Julian C. Stanley and his colleagues. The second was a bequest to the American Psychological Foundation by Mrs. Esther Katz Rosen, who directed that the income from the endowment should be used for the study of gifted children. The third was a too-long-delayed follow-up of the Terman gifted children in 1972." Since then other indicators of reviving interest are appearing, notably the Social Science Research Council's series of conferences that may be indicating a sustained interest by that illustrious body in the study of talent, and a recent "Tuesday Morning at the White House" discussion of giftedness, which in turn may signal more funding from government sources for this field of study and practice.

Our society is deeply ambivalent about its two most fundamental values, liberty and equality. On the one hand we argue for the libertarian right of each individual to develop his or her capacities to the highest possible level. On the other we argue for the egalitarian right of equal opportunity for all. In recent decades the egalitarian emphasis, especially in the political arena, seems to have gained. Yet we live in a vastly complex technological society with insatiable demands for talented people to keep it running. Talent does not develop in a vacuum; it needs nurturing, and to ignore its nurture is to imperil our way of life.

Elbert Hubbard once said, "There is something that is much more scarce, something finer far, something rarer than ability. It is the ability to recognize ability." I am most happy to be in this company, where at least we are learning better ways to look for the very able, and perhaps how best to recognize and nurture great talent. I look forward with great interest to the discussion to follow.

STANLEY: Thank you, Dr. James. We go now to the first group of panelists, those who will give background on the gifted and the creative. The first speaker in that group is a distinguished educator from the University of Chicago. One would have to be extraordinarily insensitive to educational trends not to have heard repeatedly of Robert J. Havighurst over the years. We are especially pleased to have him on the program, because he is one of the true pioneers in facilitating the education of intellectually gifted youths. Dr. Havighurst:

THE GIFTED AND THE CREATIVE: ACCELERATION OR ENRICHMENT?
Robert J. Havighurst

In order to discuss this topic usefully, we need both a quantitative and a qualitative definition of the group of children and youths to whom we refer. If we use a broad definition of the "intellectually gifted," we might speak of 10 percent of an age cohort, or some 350,000 boys and girls of a given age. In that case, most educators would say that the emphasis should be upon enrichment of the educative experience, with perhaps as much as a one-year acceleration in progress through the school grades. But *we* must use a much more selective definition.

Following Stanley, we may speak of the "intellectually talented" as a subgroup of those 12- and 13-year-olds who score in the top 5 percent of their grade on national norms in both mathematical and verbal reasoning. Those boys and girls then take the College Entrance Examination Board's Scholastic Aptitude Test (SAT), and some 10 percent of them score higher on this test than does the average college-bound male twelfth grader. Thus we select about 0.5 percent of the group who at age 12 or 13 are "intellectually talented" in mathematics—that is, the top 1 in 200. If we add another equal-sized group who score equally high in science but not so high in mathematics, we get about 1 percent of the age group, or 35,000 boys and girls whom we define as "intellectually talented."

For this group I would argue that three or more years of acceleration by the age of about 15 are useful. That is, this group might enter college as freshmen at the age of 15, or with sophomore standing at the age of 16. This would assume that these youngsters had completed high school level courses in mathematics, science, and English, or had passed examinations for such courses. As for enrichment, this group probably would have experienced some of what Stanley calls "relevant" enrichment, which would encompass special work in mathematics or science or some other academic subject area in which such students were specially interested.

For those young people in the top 10 percent on tests of knowledge and aptitude, who are often called "gifted" but are not in the top 1 or 2 percent, I would argue for what Stanley calls "cultural" and "relevant" enrichment plus one or two years of acceleration. The acceleration might be gained by skipping one or more grades, or by taking "advanced placement" courses in high school that would permit entrance to college with up to a year of college credit.

This would leave those just below the top 1 percent in a category that would be treated according to their social maturity and motivation for academic work.

The contention of many educators who oppose "radical" acceleration on the ground that it may damage the social and emotional development of the students who are accelerated is an important issue. Often there are disadvantages to academic acceleration of three or more years, especially during early adolescence, and these must be weighed against the disadvantages to intellectual development of "holding back" a gifted student.

The pros and cons of acceleration should be explored by any conscientious educator, perhaps by reading the case studies of young people (Hollingworth 1942; Hildreth 1938, 1954; Strang 1956) and also by reading the few autobiographies that are available. An especially good autobiography is that of Norbert Wiener (Wiener 1953), the mathematician who was a child prodigy and was ambivalent about his boyhood experience. The autobiography of John Stuart Mill (Mill 1908) and his biography by Packe (1954) also are useful in this connection.

References

Hildreth, G. H. 1938. Characteristics of young gifted children. *Journal of Genetic Psychology* 53: 287–311.

―――. 1954. Three gifted children: A developmental study. *Journal of Genetic Psychology* 85: 250–57.

Hollingworth, L. S. 1942. *Children above 180 IQ Stanford-Binet: Origin and development.* Yonkers-on-Hudson, N.Y.: World Book.

Mill, J. S. 1908. *Autobiography.* London: Longmans-Green.

Packe, M. S. J. 1954. *The life of John Stuart Mill.* New York: Macmillan.

Strang, R. 1956. Gifted adolescents' views of growing up. *Journal of Exceptional Children* 23: 10–15.

Wiener, N. 1953. *Ex-Prodigy: My childhood and youth.* New York: Simon and Schuster. (Also available as Paperback No. 19 from the M.I.T. Press, Massachusetts Institute of Technology, Cambridge, Mass. 02142.)

STANLEY: Thank you, Dr. Havighurst. I am delighted that Bob has pointed out that educational acceleration is a matter of degree rather than just a qualitative difference. At the Johns Hopkins University in May of 1977 five very young persons received bachelor's degrees, three of them at age 17, one at age 18, and one at age 19. They accelerated anywhere from three to five and one-half years. At one of the more distinguished New York City colleges, a young man who became 15 years old on 24 March 1977 received his B.S. degree in mathematics, summa cum laude. His accomplishments included a three-year National Science Foundation graduate fellowship and an almost perfect score on the Graduate Record Examinations in advanced mathematics. All degrees of acceleration are represented on a continuum ranging from moderate acceleration to great acceleration. So far as we are concerned there are no magical or mystical gaps in that continuum.

The next speaker on the general panel of "The Gifted and the Creative" is a distinguished worker and professor in the field of gifted-child education who is closely associated with the administrative and executive responsibilities of the Association for the Gifted (TAG), which is a division of the Council on Exceptional Children. He is the past editor of a newly emerging journal published by the Association for the Gifted, called *Talents and Gifts*. He is the publisher and founding editor of a much-needed new journal for parents and teachers called *G/C/T* (Gifted/Creative/and Talented Children). I am pleased to present Professor Marvin Gold from the University of South Alabama. Dr. Gold:

ACCELERATION: SIMPLISTIC GIMMICKRY
Marvin J. Gold

Often I am asked "Why hasn't gifted-child education progressed any faster than it has?" I usually respond, "There are several reasons, undoubtedly, but I am certain that heading up the list is overdependence on one or another of three words: enrichment, segregation, and acceleration.'' Adherents of each term have in their way done much to slow the progress of gifted-child education.

The problem with the term *enrichment* is that it conveys no meaning. Indeed, as one administrator opined, "Enrichment is that term educators hide behind when they don't want anyone to know they are not doing anything for the gifted." To some, enrichment means learning to type in the fourth grade; to others, mastering Haiku; to others still, it connotes twenty spelling words instead of ten, two compositions in lieu of one.

Segregation implies the setting apart for all or part of a day, a year, or an academic career. It could be partial or it could be total.

Acceleration refers to some form of "speeding up" (e.g., early admissions, double promotions, ungraded primaries or junior high schools, entering college early). A wide variety of options is possible.

When one talks about the educational value of the above three alternatives (and from this point on, I shall confine myself to the concept of acceleration only) it is like talking about the value of a hammer: straight against a nail into one beam to be joined to another there is some significant value to the hammer's effect; against an infant's skull, the hammer's drive would be of questionable worth. The problem then lies not in the tool, acceleration, but in the product to be built, curriculum.

Unfortunately, too often school administrators seize upon an overly simplistic approach to gifted-child education and look for an administratively manageable answer. Grabbing hold of acceleration, a "how" device for implementation, it is quite easy to forget the "what" of the educational effort, the curriculum.

Complex concepts such as futurism, productive thinking, creativity, leadership training, critical thinking, and the like all become second-class citizens in the educational country where quick simple answers are likely to rule unchallenged.

I am not against acceleration any more than I am against the hammer or motherhood or the flag. Decent parenting or a flag that has meaning are certainly most worthwhile, as worthwhile as is acceleration that moves a gifted child's education forward meaningfully. Biological motherhood or phony patriotism, however, is as meaningless as the "speeding up on something" that has little value within the world of education.

Let's attend to the "what" of education first and look at the implementing methods, the "how," second. Otherwise, we are forcing ourselves to live with some form of simplistic gimmickry.

STANLEY: Thank you, Dr. Gold. One person who was unable to attend is Professor Joseph Renzulli of the University of Connecticut, who has been instrumental in defining the term *enrichment* and its implications. It is quite unfortunate that Joe is not with us, because he has written extensively on the meaning of enrichment. [Dr. Renzulli provided the editors with the following position paper concerning educational acceleration.]

SOME CONCERNS ABOUT EDUCATIONAL
ACCELERATION FOR INTELLECTUALLY TALENTED YOUTH
Or
ARE TREADMILLS REALLY DIFFERENT
IF WE RUN THEM AT A FASTER RATE?
Joseph S. Renzulli

Although it would be foolish to argue against acceleration as one potentially valuable approach for meeting the needs of intellectually gifted youth, I have a few basic concerns about this practice and therefore would like to suggest a great deal of caution and selectivity in its use. It is certainly not a panacea for meeting the needs of all gifted youngsters and, in fact, under certain circumstances it may fail to respect some of the characteristics that bring gifted and talented persons to our attention as creative and productive individuals.

My major concern about acceleration is that it does not represent a radical or imaginative departure from the usual type of educational programming provided for almost all youngsters in the vast majority of their learning experiences. In other words, acceleration is basically a means for quantitative rather than qualitative differentiation.

Let us begin by analyzing briefly a typical learning situation. Almost all traditional learning experiences are characterized by the step-by-step pursuit of curricular material that is planned and administered by the teacher. Students engage in predetermined exercises with generally prescribed procedures for problem solving and generally agreed upon standards of acceptability for success. Thus, the curriculum from the early grades through most college-level courses consists of one long progression of exercises, and the student is cast mainly in the role of an "exercise learner." Needless to say, many exciting and potentially worthwhile experiences can emerge from this traditional approach to instruction. It is important, however, to keep in mind that there are at least a few alternatives to a constant and continuous diet of prescribed and predetermined exercises.

Now let us take a look at the practice of acceleration. My main concern here is whether or not we are removing youngsters from one exercise-learning situation and placing them in another similar situation, albeit at a somewhat more advanced level. Unless appropriate modifications are made in the *ways* in which advanced courses are taught, the student still is cast in the role of exercise learner. If such courses are planned and administered by the teacher and if they consist mainly of a succession of prescribed and presented exercises with agreed-upon solutions, then I fail to see how an accelerated course differs qualitatively from the regular curriculum. To paraphrase Gertrude Stein, "A course is a course is a course."

Placing youngsters in advanced level courses obviously respects a very important characteristic of the learner. This characteristic is a more quickly developed capacity to comprehend material, to deal with higher levels of conceptualization and abstraction, to process larger amounts of information, and to reach higher levels of generalization more rapidly and with greater degrees of understanding than does the learner of average ability. Though these certainly are admirable goals for intellectually gifted youngsters, two additional dimensions of the learner must be taken into account if we are to have total respect for *all* of the capacities of gifted and talented persons. The first of these dimensions is sustained interest in a particular discipline, topic, or even a single event. As an instructor marches along from one exercise to another, putting students through the hoops that are listed on the course outline, I wonder if there is sufficient time or opportunity for an individual student to pursue a particular topic that may provoke an unusual personal interest.

A second dimension of the learner that should be respected in qualitatively different educational situations is the preferred learning style of the individual. This dimension is concerned with the way(s) in which a person would like to become involved with certain topics. Being involved as an exercise learner is the *sine qua non* of most course-oriented situations, and it is the rare course indeed that allows an individual to investigate a topic in a manner that approaches *real* inquiry about *real* problems.[4] Gifted persons who have attained recognition in their respective fields almost always have been characterized by high levels of task commitment that have been brought to bear on real problems. If educational institutions are to approximate the *modus operandi* of truly gifted individuals, then learning opportunities must go beyond mere course work (however advanced), and these opportunities must be characterized by experiences that are in direct opposition to presented exercises.

Acceleration has many obvious values, especially in the acquisition of basic concepts, investigative methodology, and the fundamental principles of subject-matter areas. This is especially true for areas that are highly structured and sequential in concept complexity such as mathematics, computer programming, and physics. But unless additional provisions are made for individual investigative activity, then I am afraid that we are guilty simply of turning up the rate of speed on the exercise treadmills.

STANLEY: Another person who was not able to come because of other commitments is Professor Halbert Robinson of the University of Washington at Seattle. Hal has a fascinating program for finding intellectually brilliant youngsters in the preschool years and studying them longitudinally to see what they and their families are like and how they develop. We are fortunate to have as a substitute for Dr. Robinson a person working directly in his laboratory with these youngsters, Dr. Nancy Jackson:

---

[4]Space does not permit a detailed discussion of what is meant by "real inquiry" and "real problems." The interested reader is referred to Renzulli, J.S. 1977. *The enrichment triad model: A guide for developing defensible programs for the gifted and talented.* Wethersfield, Ct.: Creative Learning Press.

PLACEMENT ACCORDING TO READINESS[5]
Halbert B. Robinson, Nancy E. Jackson, Wendy C. Roedell

Few fundamental principles of human behavior are as logically compelling and empirically verifiable as the dicta (1) that learning is facilitated by an appropriate match between the material to be learned and the learner's level of relevant cognitive organization; and (2) that there exist substantial differences in performance on any learning task among individuals of the same chronological age. The notion that each child is, at any given moment, ready for some kinds of learning experiences and not for others is obvious. Equally incontrovertible is the notion that such readiness is correlated imperfectly with chronological age.

Sensible educational programs certainly must take cognizance of these fundamentals. Many do. Those with a single, well-defined goal (e.g., to teach children to swim, play a musical instrument, or speak a foreign language) rarely give much prominence to chronological age. Learners generally are grouped by competence, and tasks typically are tailored to their levels of mastery. A ski instructor who placed all 6-year-olds in Snowplow I and all 12-year-olds in Advanced Parallel soon would learn the error of his or her ways.

It is, rather, the broadly based educational programs with multiple, often ill-defined goals, that magnify chronological age as *the* major criterion for class placement. As goals of the educational enterprise have proliferated, the age-graded lock step increasingly has become the norm. Without denying the complexities of the issues involved in our efforts to deal with the "whole child," and indeed the "whole society," we have been blinded to a broad range of intra- and inter-individual differences; we often fail to see specific and easily defined trees because we are so busy examining ambiguous forests with ill-defined boundaries.

The Child Development Research Group at the University of Washington has undertaken a set of projects concerned with identifying and nurturing young children who display extraordinary intellectual abilities. By age 5, the usual criterion for kindergarten entrance, a typical child in our program is reading at the level of the average fourth grader and is about as proficient in mathematics as is the average beginning second grader. This child's fine-motor skills are average, and his or her social skills also are judged to be about average. To place this child in an average kindergarten surely would lead to inappropriate matches with respect to some important areas of development; placing him or her in the third or fourth grade would lead to equally distressing mismatches with respect to other important areas.

Although difficult, the problems posed by intra- and inter-individual differences are not impossible to resolve. Other speakers today have reviewed the evidence on such topics as early admission, enrichment, and acceleration. The

[5]While Dr. Jackson presented this paper at the symposium, it represents not only her position but also that of her two colleagues, Drs. Robinson and Roedell.

overwhelming weight of the evidence indicates that placement according to readiness rather than age facilitates learning as well as the general adjustment of the children. We cannot, of course, pretend that we know all that we need to know about the long-term social, emotional, and cognitive consequences of placing children according to indices of readiness. The data, however, have been consistently encouraging.

A final thought concerns the formulation of the topic we are here to discuss: the educational acceleration of intellectually talented youths. I wonder why we are concerned with the idea of acceleration at all. I have never known a gifted child whose education in the area of his or her "gift" seemed truly accelerated. I have known a very few such children lucky enough to have parents and teachers who allowed them to proceed at their own pace, but most have had to deal with systematic, and, I think, unconscionable attempts to *decelerate* their education. The costs of such practice to the children and to society, I believe, have been very substantial. I submit that we should at this point be attending to the detrimental effects of continuing to decelerate the educational progress of intellectually talented young people.

STANLEY: Thank you, Dr. Jackson. Incidentally, when the Spencer Foundation began a few years ago, one of its first actions was sponsoring the Study of Mathematically Precocious Youth that we run at Johns Hopkins, later Lynn Fox's Intellectually Gifted Child Study Group, and also this important project at the University of Washington.

The next speaker earned her Ph.D. in social psychology at Harvard University. She is a staff member of the Social Science Research Council as well as the staff associate there who works with the committee on gifted children that the Social Science Research Council recently set up with some of the income from the Rosen bequest that Dr. James mentioned. We are delighted to have Dr. Alvia Branch with us today. Dr. Branch:

SELECTION OF APPROPRIATE CRITERIA AND COMPARISON GROUPS FOR USE IN THE EVALUATION OF EDUCATIONAL PROVISIONS FOR THE GIFTED AND TALENTED
Alvia Y. Branch

This paper does not take a position with respect to the superiority of either acceleration or enrichment as a means of providing for the educational needs of gifted and talented students. Rather, it points to research and evaluation that are needed to assist teachers, administrators, and parents in making better-informed choices between these alternatives. Because acceleration (particularly the "radical" acceleration of relatively young students) has met with the greatest resistance and, in this sense, bears the greatest onus of proof, most of the comments contained herein are directed toward issues related to the educational acceleration of gifted and talented students. The major argument to be presented is that many individuals involved in assessing the effectiveness of acceleration have chosen strategies that are overly conservative in view of the intensity of the resistance they must counter. This conservatism is reflected both in the selection of comparison groups and in the selection of criteria for use in determining the extent to which successful educational facilitation has been achieved.

When we consider that the image in need of correction entails lives horribly distorted in service to the development of a single "gift," comparisons of the academic achievements of accelerated students versus those of (1) their classmates and (2) their agemates (both unselected for ability) do not constitute a sufficient counter. Equal or greater academic achievement among the accelerates might be expected solely on the basis of intellectual ability. Yet, most research into the effects of acceleration has made precisely these comparisons, belaboring a point that many opponents would be willing to concede. The only comparison potentially capable of generating data that can chip away at the bulk of resistance to acceleration is a comparison between comparably "gifted" students, accelerated and nonaccelerated. It seems feasible to make such comparisons in terms of scientific requirements and in terms of ethical considerations. Because of the scarcity of funds, many gifted students (regardless of ability levels) will not be exposed to qualitatively different and appropriate educational experiences. It is therefore appropriate to monitor the development of both groups, those who are and those who are not receiving such provisions, and then to make relevant comparisons of their experiences. Only in this way can credible statements be made concerning the effectiveness of any intervention, whether enrichment or acceleration.

In addition to the correct comparison group, one needs to be concerned with the question being asked of the comparison. With respect to the criteria used in determining the success or failure of an intervention, many studies have employed one or a combination of the following: (1) ability to master courses in advanced subject matter, (2) demonstrations of "no psychological damage," and (3) demonstration of a high degree of participation in extracurricular activities. Of these, the latter two come closest to confronting the essence of the resistance. In order to increase the likelihood of greater acceptance of acceleration as a means of providing for the educational needs of the intellectually talented, however, one needs to go beyond the demonstration of "no psychological damage" toward demonstrating psychological benefit in excess of risk. The type of study indicated would follow closely the lives of children identified as gifted regardless of whether they were subsequently successful, and would allow the researcher to do both of the following:

1. Investigate the possibility of substantially damaging effects resulting from lack of attention to the educational needs of the gifted. In order to be most convincing, an investigation of this kind would involve comparisons of accel-

erated and nonaccelerated gifted students, or gifted students whose educations have or have not been facilitated. As it stands, available biographical data on the lives of geniuses or prodigies most often recount triumph in the face of lack of attention to their special needs.

2. Look explicitly for positive effects of an accelerated or otherwise facilitated education. The emphasis of studies of this kind should be on in-depth analyses of personality and social variables thought to be associated with movement toward the fulfillment of potential. Again, comparisons would be made with students of equal ability whose educations have not been facilitated.

Clearly, Terman and Oden's discussion of the experience of the As (most successful) and Cs (least successful) among the men in the sample (see Oden 1968) approximates the kind of study being advocated here. Future studies along these lines, however, would be designed with sufficient controls to permit confident attribution of outcome differentials to the effects of acceleration.

Reference

Oden, M. H. 1968. The fulfillment of promise: 40-year follow-up of the Terman gifted group. *Genetic Psychology Monographs* 77 (First half, Feb.): 3–93.

STANLEY: Thank you, Dr. Branch. Those are important methodological and theoretical considerations. We all know that the typical attitude of the public toward the gifted for hundreds of years has been to expect almost impossibly great performances from them, to fault special treatment when even a single exception to the rule of good development comes up, and (as Dr. Branch points out so cogently) to preserve the status quo by not worrying about how stultifying that might be. The problem of the control group always has been great and always will be great in research of this kind. Even a series of seemingly definitive studies will not convince certain groups of people that they are wrong, however, because those persons have an emotional commitment to their stereotypic attitudes. On the other hand, such studies presumably will help spike some of the more irrational arguments as ''arguments'' and perhaps will help some persons who really are uncertain to make up their minds about the situation. Terman led the way in this endeavor.

The final speaker on the general panel concerning the gifted and creative is a remarkable young man who is a fourth-year doctoral student in psychology at Johns Hopkins, having come there from a bachelor's degree in psychology at Yale four years ago. He found time, at great personal sacrifice, to do a comprehensive background paper for this symposium covering hundreds of references in the area of giftedness with special attention to acceleration and enrichment. [See chapter 2.] Mr. Stephen P. Daurio:[6]

[6]EDITORS' NOTE: Mr. Daurio currently is an assistant professor of psychology at the Staten Island Campus of St. John's University.

EDUCATIONAL ACCELERATION OF
INTELLECTUALLY TALENTED YOUTHS
Stephen P. Daurio

The controversy over whether to enrich or to accelerate the education of intellectually able students appears to be an artifact of chronological age grading in American schools. The question arises, "What if students were grouped according to mental age or special abilities instead of chronological age?" A likely outcome would be the end of the enrichment-acceleration debate because, theoretically, all students would be working according to their level of intellectual ability rather than at an assumed ability level based on chronological age. Why then has this seemingly obvious solution not been adopted?

The answer apparently lies in the following two considerations. First, educators tend to associate age grading with educational reform and to support the idea that it is better for children to interact with same-aged peers in school and in play. According to the historian Joseph Kett, who served on the President's Science Advisory Committee in 1974, age segregation started in the mid-nineteenth century as a *by-product* of the educational reform movement led by Horace Mann and Henry Barnard (Kett 1974). Similarly, age grading was coincidental with American industrialization and antedated the rising tide of immigration by only a few years. Age grading also was well suited to the Americanization of immigrants' children, following the great "melting pot" tradition. Moreover, during times of economic prosperity educational certification offered a kind of ticket for upwardly mobile poor children. Elementary schools, and later high schools, provided practical training demanded by increased specialization in industry. Conversely, during the depression of the 1930s, age grading was defended as a "cure" for unemployment. Thus, despite the fact that many educators believed over the years that age grading served the best interests of educational reform, the fact remains that age grading also served the *economic* and *political* needs of a growing nation. Since it is difficult to disentangle these utilitarian goals from better-intentioned goals such as reform, the value of the age grade lock step has yet to be proved for today's students. Considering the relative recency of this "tradition," that is, approximately one hundred years or less, the value of age grading is called into question even more.

The second observation involves educators' excessive concern over potential social and emotional maladjustment following acceleration. It seems a disproportionate amount of caution vis-à-vis acceleration stems from the rather unfortunate case of William James Sidis; Leta Hollingworth (1929), Catharine Cox Miles (1946), and, more recently, Kathleen Montour (1977, 1978), and H. Zuckerman (1977) have documented counter-examples of successful prodigies whose lifetime adjustments and professional careers were outstanding. In addition, the ongoing Study of Mathematically Precocious Youth at The Johns Hopkins University (Stanley 1976, Keating 1976) reports successful college experiences for over ninety-five young men and women who entered college at least one and as many as seven years early. In fact, a recent extensive review of the acceleration literature failed to turn up a single substantive study that refuted the appropriateness of acceleration for intellectually able youngsters who were eager to move ahead at rates faster than the conventional lock step would allow.

Educators' concern over social and emotional adjustment also might be due to what Frank Laycock (1964) calls their "selective" use of evidence despite the wealth of "representative" literature supporting acceleration. According to Laycock, "Administrators have reported the cases they remember best, while psychologists have insisted upon good samples." In other words, administrators' reluctance to endorse acceleration may well simply reflect their individual biases in this matter.

Whatever the reason acceleration meets opposition in schools, the unwarranted disregard of empiricism concerning the effects of acceleration ought not jeopardize the education of intellectually talented youths.

References

Hollingworth, L. S. 1929. *Gifted children: Their nature and nurture*. New York: Macmillan.

Keating, D. P. (ed.). 1976. *Intellectual talent: Research and development*. Baltimore, Md.: The Johns Hopkins University Press.

Kett, J. 1974. History of age grouping in America. In J. S. Coleman (chairman) et al. (eds.), *Youth: Transition to adulthood, a report to the panel on youth of the President's Science Advisory Committee*. Chicago: University of Chicago Press.

Laycock, F. 1964. Acceleration for the gifted? A brief note on the use of evidence. *Perceptual and Motor Skills* 19: 1006.

Miles, C. C. 1946. Gifted children. In L. Carmichael (ed.), *Manual of child psychology*. New York: Wiley.

Montour, K. M. 1977. William James Sidis: The broken twig. *American Psychologist* 32(4, Apr.): 265–79.

————. 1978. The highly precocious: How well did they succeed? In J. C. Stanley, W. C. George, and C. H. Solano (eds.), *Educational programs and intellectual prodigies*. Baltimore, Md.: SMPY, Department of Psychology, The Johns Hopkins University, pp. 47–61.

Stanley, J. C. 1976. Concern for intellectually talented youths: How it originated and fluctuated. *Journal of Clinical Child Psychology* 5(3, Winter): 38–42.

Zuckerman, H. 1977. *Scientific elite: Nobel Laureates in the United States*. New York, N.Y.: Free Press, especially pp. 89–91.

STANLEY: Thank you, Mr. Daurio. Steve was an integral part of the Study of Verbally Gifted Youths (SVGY), conducted at The Johns Hopkins University from 1972 to 1977 with support from the Spencer Foundation. That study was independent of Lynn Fox's Intellectually Gifted Child Study Group (IGCSG) and also of the Study of Mathematically Precocious Youth (SMPY). Although we have interacted over the years, the studies were conducted and funded separately.

SVGY did not continue beyond 1977, so SMPY and IGCSG have taken over some of the verbal component.

Having heard six speakers, we now have a few minutes for some interaction among them before going on to the next panel. The speakers, as you recall, were Drs. James, Havighurst, Gold, Jackson, and Branch, and Mr. Daurio. I will ask first if any member of that particular panel has a comment that he or she would like to make about any other paper presented by a panel member. Dr. Havighurst:

HAVIGHURST: The papers presented to this point in the symposium are concerned somewhat with the problem of social and emotional development. It seems to me that anybody who is tending strongly toward substantial acceleration, that is acceleration of three or more years for the highly talented youth, ought to read the life stories of as many past prodigies as possible. I read quite a lot about John Stuart Mill, who was reading Latin at the age of 5, and about Norbert Wiener, one of the relatively contemporary prodigies who eventually became a professor of mathematics at MIT and developed the science of cybernetics. Both of these people achieved high levels of success. But I must say, however, as I read their autobiographies, I had the feeling that they went through a lot of difficulty during the first ten to twenty years of their lives. I wonder if there is any possible way of helping such people to avoid some of the problems of social and emotional adjustment. I remember reading that Norbert Wiener was picked on a bit by the other children when he was 8 years old and in the sixth grade in one of the suburbs of Boston. He said that his motherly teacher would take him on her lap in this sixth grade and start comforting him in front of the class. He didn't know what to make of it at the time (I guess in a way he appreciated that motherly attention). You can see, however, his problem of interacting with people five or six years older than he, when he was treated this way. It is certainly not an easy experience to grow up socially and emotionally when one is that far advanced intellectually.

STANLEY: Thank you, Dr. Havighurst. There seem to be two types of prodigies, the pushed, propelled, programmed type of which Mill, Wiener, and Sidis are great examples, and the largely self-propelling types such as those with whom we work at Johns Hopkins. The latter don't get much strong, systematic facilitation during the early years. We are fortunate to have on the panel today the mother (Joan Stark) of one of the three 17-year-olds who will graduate from Johns Hopkins in May of 1977 (with a three-year graduate National Science Foundation Fellowship) and who are beginning distinguished research careers already. Her son, Eugene, probably is not a highly programmed person except in the general sense of being from a bright, cultured family. You will hear from her later. In the meantime, Dr. Thomas James has a comment. Dr. James:

JAMES: I'd need to know a lot more than I do now about the discomforts of the normal child during that period of development, before I could get greatly concerned about the issues Dr. Havighurst has raised.

STANLEY: It is interesting that if you read Packe's biography of John Stuart Mill, you'll find that the somewhat dyspeptic, middle-aged Mill remembered his childhood incorrectly. As Packe finds it, the evidence from Mill's childhood is that he was a rather happy youngster, but Mill's report seems to have been colored by fatigue, his wife's death, and other midlife crises. Dr. Nancy Jackson:

JACKSON: My reaction is similar to that of Dr. James in that I would like to know not only more about the recollections of childhood that the normal child might have, but also the recollections of the extremely unusual person such as Wiener or Sidis, whether or not they were accelerated. I think that the problems they experienced may have been independent of their acceleration and may have come from being very different from the normal run of people. When we are relying on case-study literature, we can't separate these two things.

BRANCH: I also would like to point out along those same lines that we have a very select body of material. We have autobiographies of those people who made it; the autobiographies of those who were defeated at some point along the way are not available to us, so we don't really know how to interpret these experiences. We need to know more about the experiences of those people who aren't quite so prodigious, for example, those within the upper 5 percent. We really know a lot less about them than we do about the very spectacular cases.[7]

STANLEY: The recent biography of Sir Francis Galton[8] shows that he had almost the same identity crisis at age 20 that John Stuart Mill had, but that his upbringing had been substantially different in many respects from Mill's. Perhaps, a function of great intellect is having to come to terms with oneself at some time in the developmental process. Before Freud, geniuses were allowed to have a nervous breakdown every now and then and just go take a rest cure at one of the inexpensive spas to get over it. The great physicist Max Born and his wife had them rather regularly throughout their lives.[9] It was expected that people who led complex, difficult, hard-pushing lives would cave in psychologically occasionally. Nowadays one doesn't dare do it, for fear of falling into the "Eagleton" syndrome—that is, of being considered mentally ill. Mr. William George:

GEORGE: I think another important consideration must involve what might have been, had the person *not* been accelerated. Studies carried out in the 1950s by the Fund for the Advancement of Education of the Ford Foundation show that although there were some problems of initial adjustment in entering college early, these were temporary. In addition, these problems were no different in magnitude from adjustment problems encountered by the typical college student. Mr. Daurio's point about eagerness to move ahead is well taken. Almost all of the accelerative options developed by SMPY involve a bridging mechanism between junior high school and college, with eagerness a primary self-selection criterion. I think one also has to look at what the consequences of a solution

---

[7]EDITORS' NOTE: Kathleen Montour has followed up some less-famous prodigies and found that, by their own standards, most of them led successful lives. See references for Montour listed at the end of chapter 1.

[8]The reader is referred to Forrest, D. W. 1974. *Francis Galton: The life and work of a Victorian genius.* New York, N.Y.: Taplinger Publishing Company.

[9]EDITORS' NOTE: See Born, M. (ed.). 1971. *The Born-Einstein letters: The correspondence between Albert Einstein and Max and Hedwig Born, 1916–1955.* New York: Walker and Company.

might be if a youngster hadn't accelerated. Educational acceleration may not be a perfect solution, but what would have been the options or alternatives for that individual if he or she hadn't moved ahead? They may have been much more restricting and harmful.

ANASTASI: There is a hazard in putting too much emphasis on the published biographies of eminent people. There are bound to be selective factors in the publication itself. A person who is very talented, who has achieved eminence, and who also was very maladjusted, is much more newsworthy; he or she has more dramatic appeal than the person who wasn't maladjusted. This applies both to an author who decides to write a biography (his or her own or someone else's) and to the publisher who chooses the more newsworthy characters for publication.[10]

STANLEY: The next panel group consists of people who work in school systems. The first speaker is Dr. Elizabeth Kearney, who is the coordinator for the Mentally Gifted Minor program in the Pasadena, California, public schools. Liz is extremely well qualified for that position and has had a great deal of experience in an unusually favorable environment where there is a longstanding tradition of caring for the gifted. Dr. Kearney:

ACCELERATION: A VARIED APPROACH
Elizabeth I. Kearney

The term *acceleration* has triggered emotional responses for a number of years. Yet, there are numerous ways to accelerate the learning process, and many of those methods are supported by the same individuals who voiced a reluctance to "accelerate a child." Because semantics plays an important role in this issue, many educators in California avoid using the term while actually implementing the process.

Dr. Julian Stanley stated that academic acceleration allows students to advance through subject areas at a rate that may, or may not, alter their progress through the grade structure. With this view in mind, directors of programs in California have tried to provide many channels of acceleration for the identified gifted (California State Department of Education 1971).

Pasadena introduced its first class for the gifted at the Grant School under the direction of Miss Grace Ball (Director of Special Programs) the year after the first volume of Lewis M. Terman's famous *Genetic Studies of Genius* appeared—i.e., in 1926 (see Kearney and Brockie 1978). The teachers stressed an educational process that allowed students to explore in depth and at advanced levels those areas in which they were academically accelerated while keeping

---

[10]EDITORS' NOTE: But see references for Montour listed at the end of chapter 1.

them with their chronological peers for the major portion of the school day. Grant School was staffed by teachers willing to serve as facilitators and mentors, and, according to Miss Celia Johnson (one of the first teachers in the program), "The children were happy, and the parents endorsed the plan enthusiastically." Despite parental support, however, public pressure resulted in the school's closure in 1943. Subsequently, less isolating means were sought to provide for the needs of the gifted in the population.

The 1950s saw the end of another plan. The "6-4-4" plan provided a grade grouping (K-6, 7-10, and 11-14) that was most beneficial to the gifted because they could take classes one or more years beyond their grade level as a matter of course. Unfortunately for this new concept, community college districts formed and the plan disappeared.

By 1963 the state had set up a funded program for gifted students, and a research project funded by the Cooperative Research Branch of the United States Office of Education was underway. This $249,000 grant aided in the development and demonstration of special program prototypes. Model demonstration centers were established in six school districts. Materials and curricula were prepared to aid educators interested in providing acceleration, special classes, and counseling programs for the gifted. Project Talent (the title of the project)[11] ran from 1963 to 1966 in the Davis Joint Unified, Lompoc Unified, Los Angeles Unified, Pasadena Unified, Ravenswood City, and San Juan Unified school districts. The results were published in a series of booklets and subject-matter guides.

One of these publications, *Acceleration Programs for Intellectually Gifted Pupils* (Robeck 1968), set forth the results. The following report was made on the portion of the research program conducted in Pasadena: "The high achievement and the successful adjustments made by accelerants . . . confirmed the reports of . . . other studies. Standardized test results should be studied in relation to pupils' progress . . . to determine the level of academic talent needed for success in the program. Characteristics of pupils, such as motivation, that are not measured by standardized tests but which play important roles in pupils' success . . . should be identified for use as guides by those responsible for the selection of participants, . . . and the purpose and function of counseling should be delineated. . . ." It was noted that a follow-up study should be conducted, but unfortunately, none was.[12]

Money shortages promote innovation, and this is sometimes an advantage. The need to provide suitable educational opportunities, coupled with an inability to fund major projects, has resulted in programs that provide acceleration by permitting students to change courses, take Advanced Placement Program courses, enroll in advanced classes, do independent research, take seminars, work independently under the direction of mentors from the school staff and/or

[11]Not to be confused with John C. Flanagan's national longitudinal study.

[12]EDITORS' NOTE: The Study of Mathematically Precocious Youth is perhaps the first large longitudinal intervention study of this kind.

the community, be graduated early, and/or serve as career interns prior to graduation. By using a variety of approaches to acceleration, schools throughout California have been able to insure that the brightest of their students are being given an opportunity to receive an education truly designed to meet their needs.

References

California State Department of Education. 1971. *Principles, objectives, and curricula for programs in the education of mentally gifted minors: Kindergarten through grade twelve.* Sacramento: California State Department of Education.

Kearney, E. I., and Brockie, J. S. 1978. Educating gifted children in California. In J. C. Stanley, W. C. George, and C. H. Solano (eds.), *Educational programs and intellectual prodigies.* Baltimore, Md. 21218: SMPY, Dept. of Psychology, The Johns Hopkins University, pp. 18–28.

Robeck, M. C. 1968. *Acceleration programs for intellectually gifted pupils.* Sacramento: California State Department of Education, pp. 107–08.

STANLEY: Thank you, Dr. Kearney. Our next speaker is from the New York City public schools. She coordinates programs for the gifted there. Dr. Virginia Z. Ehrlich:

ACCELERATION AND ENRICHMENT FOR THE GIFTED IN NEW YORK CITY PUBLIC SCHOOLS
Virginia Z. Ehrlich

With a population of over one million children, the New York City public school system has opportunities for educational experimentation that are available to few other communities, our major competitor being California, clear across the country. New York's concerns for the gifted are recorded as early as 1899. We had rapid-advancement classes shortly after that, in which two semesters of work were completed in one semester. It was in the New York City public school system that Leta S. Hollingworth conducted her studies for the gifted at Public School 500 Manhattan, known as the Speyer School. The practices of the city reflect Terman's position on acceleration, that such children should be promoted rapidly enough to permit college entrance by the age of 17 at the latest, and that a majority would be better off to enter at age 16.

A combination of both grade and academic acceleration seems feasible. In fact, this is the method the city has used successfully for many years, together with enrichment. The general policy states that it is not desirable to accelerate a child more than one year in elementary school and one year in junior high school. Acceleration at both levels often is accomplished by completing the work of two years in one. In the elementary school this usually occurs by combining grades seven, eight, and nine into a special-progress class that completes the work in two years. We used to have a three-year senior high school, Townsend Harris, but it was discontinued, much to the regret of its alumni and prospective students. Early admission to kindergarten is not commonly practiced. Since 1974 the Astor Program, which I have directed, has introduced the practice of accepting gifted children to kindergarten at age 4 years, instead of at age 4 years and 8 months, as previously required. Currently, local school districts are considering extension of this practice into their regular procedures. Our specialized high schools, honors programs in our academic high schools, and special-skills programs in our vocational high schools all rely heavily on academic acceleration combined with enrichment. These programs also take advantage of the College Board's Advanced Placement Program examinations for obtaining college credit while the student, technically, still is attending high school.

Enrichment is practiced at all levels as well. At the elementary level, we have homogeneously grouped classes for the intellectually gifted, usually in grades four, five, and six and sometimes in grades one to three. Special pull-out programs in selected subjects also are available for many curriculum areas. At the junior high level special enrichment classes are homogeneously grouped. In these classes enrichment in the usual curriculum areas is provided; foreign languages are added to the curriculum. New York City's specialized high schools and honors programs provide many opportunities for enrichment within subject-matter areas or by including additional curriculum areas at higher levels of difficulty (very often at the college level). Of course, this may be considered academic acceleration as well.

Another facet of our public education system is summer and evening classes at the college level. This makes another type of acceleration possible. Plans for reducing the eight years of high school and college to six or seven years are being considered in many quarters. At the college and graduate levels, there is also a trend toward shortening the educational certification process. A few years ago, in cooperation with the New York Law School, City College undertook a program to accelerate the training of lawyers by reducing the seven-year sequence to six.

Like many cities in the country, New York City increasingly has resisted programs for grade acceleration. The disbanding of Townsend Harris High School, the limited use of acceleration in the elementary school, and the discouragement of accelerated special-program classes all are indications of the city's vulnerability to the prevalent opposition to grade acceleration, in spite of results of research studies that support the concept. It is my belief that lay response and resistance to the concept of acceleration in grade is based on uninformed emphasis on the sad lives that a few outstanding personalities have led and on our own inadequate presentation of the case for acceleration. We have not made clear the difference between the moderate acceleration recommended by Terman and others, and implicit in studies favoring acceleration, and the unnatural race through intellectual experience to which Mill, Wiener, Sidis, and others were subjected by their "pushy" parents. Nor do I think we have made clear the advantages of intellectual acceleration as it relates to the child's ability within the framework of the normal environment of age peers. The problem, in part, lies with the establishment's inability to restructure itself so that it can deal with each student as an individual in terms of his or her unique patterns of capacities and needs.

STANLEY: Thank you, Dr. Ehrlich. The next speaker has pioneered in work with the National and State Level Leadership Training Institutes (N/S-LTI) on Gifted and Talented. Many of you are familiar with that far-reaching program. I present Dr. David Jackson:

A POSSIBLE ECONOMIC CORRELATION OF
ACCELERATION FOR THE INDIVIDUAL AND FOR SOCIETY
David M. Jackson

It is the purpose of this brief paper to raise some economic questions about the consequences of acceleration both to the individual and to society in general. I believe the case for acceleration is well made in the research literature provided by Professor Stanley for this symposium,[13] and that our current need is for arguments to convince educators, parents, and others that they should act to assist larger numbers of well-qualified young people to move much more rapidly through the formal educational system. Thus, I seek arguments in the economic sphere in hopes of reducing professional and parental resistance to acceleration. What follows is an attempt to develop some economic arguments from possibilities that exist as a result of the operations of the Advanced Placement Program of the College Entrance Examination Board.

The Advanced Placement Program offers an existing practical means by which a boy or girl of high ability and achievement can accelerate his or her progress in formal education. Grades of "3" or better on three or more Advanced Placement examinations are sufficient in the case of many colleges and universities to support an offer of sophomore standing to the entering student.[14] How many 17-year-olds currently are using this method of acceleration? College

[13]EDITORS' NOTE: Before the symposium, panel participants were sent a packet of material that included the most substantive articles to date written about acceleration and enrichment as strategies for educating gifted youngsters. The articles included in the packet were as follows:

(a) Daurio (see chapter 2);
(b) Fund for the Advancement of Education. 1957. *They went to college early.* New York: Fund for the Advancement of Education of the Ford Foundation, pp. 60–91 only;
(c) Hobson, J. R. 1963. High school performance of underage pupils initially admitted to kindergarten on the basis of physical and psychological examinations. *Educational and Psychological Measurement* 23(1): 159–70; and
(d) Terman, L. M., and Oden, M. H. 1940. The gifted child grows up. *Genetic studies of genius.* vol. IV, chapter 20 (pp. 264–81).

[14]EDITORS' NOTE: Of course, an individual who plans to garner advanced standing credits for college via any of the nineteen or so Advanced Placement Program examinations that are offered nationwide each May needs to plan carefully in advance with the college(s) to which he or she applies. Standards as to what scores on which specific tests will *guarantee* credit vary from institution to institution, and often from department to department within an institution.

Board records support an estimate of 3,000 in 1976. If we assume that 2 percent, or 80,000 students of the age cohort of about four million could do so, the current rate is estimated at only 3.75 percent of that potential number.

What are some of the possible economic consequences of raising this number? Each individual who saves one year of college attendance, at an average cost of $7,500, and instead is gainfully employed for one year at a salary of $193 per week will pay federal income tax of a little more than $2,000. Thus, if the other 96.25 percent (77,000 students) of those capable of one year's acceleration followed this pattern, the federal treasury would gain $154 million. Gains to the 77,000 individuals ($7,500 in savings plus about $7,500 in net earnings) would amount to more than a billion dollars for the one year!

To specify the economic consequences of this pattern of acceleration precisely, studies are needed on questions such as these:

1. How many accelerated students work for a year before college? What is their employment experience, in terms of wages, types of work, etc.?
2. How many accelerated students enter the labor market after completing one or two degrees? What is their employment experience in terms of wages, types of work, etc.?
3. What is the incidence of frustration among students who are capable of using this method of acceleration, but who do not do so? In how many cases does frustration lead to dropping out?
4. Do accelerated students persist longer in graduate study than equally able nonaccelerated students?

There seems little doubt, however, that acceleration of the type cited leads to considerable redistribution of funds, to the advantage of students, their families, and probably society.

STANLEY: Thank you Dr. Jackson. We have been reminded repeatedly that we need good fiscal arguments for the value of acceleration, rather than the many arguments for getting more money to work with the gifted in special, expensive programs. Your brief analysis is eye-opening.

Dr. Frank Williams, an educational consultant in Salem, Oregon, was unable to be with us. We are fortunate to have as his substitute Mr. Leroy Owens, who is the evaluator of one of Dr. Williams's district projects in Anchorage, Alaska. Mr. Owens:

PROGRAMS FOR THE GIFTED AND TALENTED IN ANCHORAGE, ALASKA
Leroy Owens

I would like to share with you what Frank Williams would have said. In Alaska we borrow paid consultants through a talent bank. We asked Frank to work with us in an evaluative position at the initiation of Anchorage's program for gifted and talented. What follows are some of the bad and good experiences we had at the beginning of that project. We share them in hopes that some of you might be able to interact with us and share some of your problems as well.

At the beginning of the program we felt strongly, and still do, that there is much we don't know about this area. Consequently, we can do considerable harm with our good intentions by attempting to help in regular classroom settings students who are in some distinct ways quite different from their peers. In Anchorage, we have tried to conceptualize a program that would give some continuity among the identification of students, the training of teachers, and the evaluation of the program. The large amount of research on gifted individuals has resulted in a list of multiple abilities that differentiate the gifted from typical learners. Special needs of the gifted are the result of their differentiating characteristics, and an analysis of these characteristics could provide a model for identifying, developing, and evaluating those persons who participate in educational programs designed for the gifted and talented. Programs for gifted students will be most effective in meeting their educational needs and nurturing high level abilities only if identification and selection criteria are related to development and treatment conditions. The latter, in turn, must be evaluated by appropriate procedures. While all students have unique needs, there are some generalizations that can be made about the needs that appear to be the result of multiple-ability giftedness. It is these generalized needs of the gifted that have served as an articulated model joining together selection with treatment and evaluation in our Anchorage program.

The project in Anchorage extends the earlier work of Frank Williams in which he analyzed characteristics and needs of talented individuals on two dimensions: cognitive versus affective processes; and, convergent versus divergent conditions. This general notion represents a common conceptual thread not only throughout the training program for teachers, but also in the identification procedures for students and the evaluation at the end of the program. We have identified seven characteristics from Williams's research. Three of them rest in the cognitive domain (fluid thinking, original thinking, and elaborative thinking); and four rest in the affective domain (curiosity, risk-taking or courage, complexity of challenge, and imagination or intuition). We are focusing on those seven student behaviors within a program that deals with three content areas (language, arithmetic, and science) in our pilot program.

There are nearly 2,000 students who could be identified as gifted, if we used the rather loose state guidelines that would allow us to identify up to 5 percent of our students. We felt strongly at the beginning of the program that no single existing test adequately could measure all the variables about which we were concerned. We identify students via a hierarchical process starting with nominations, followed by some very specific testing. Finally, a committee performs the actual selection using criteria that allow them to compensate for the weaknesses in the tests we use. As you can see, we still have a lot of difficulties with this process, but it's developing.

STANLEY: I'll not joust with the next speaker, an old friend and former graduate student of mine. You know her as a leading executive, professional, and author of a number of important tests. The School and College Ability Tests (SCAT) and the Sequential Tests of Educational Progress (STEP) were largely influenced by her. She is now senior vice president of the Educational Testing Service (ETS) and the director of its Southern office in Atlanta, Georgia. Dr. Scarvia Anderson:

SUPER STUDENTS, AVERAGE SCHOOLS
Scarvia B. Anderson

I remember a few years ago going to a junior high school in New York City to give a workshop on errors of measurement or something equally irrelevant— "irrelevant" in the face of more pressing problems for a school lacking a piano, books with copyrights later than the early 1900s, an adequate counseling staff, or any regularly credentialed mathematics teachers even in the so-called mathematics honors program. Notions that exceptionally able boys and girls would be identified there, much less the controversy of which is better, enrichment or accelerative opportunities for them, would be about as irrelevant as my workshop was.

Pianos and books are relatively easy to come by. Highly competent and dedicated personnel are not, especially in such a specialized field. Yet any large-scale provisions for the intellectually gifted are going to have to depend on the availability in, or to, local school districts of personnel with skills in measurement, counseling, guidance, instruction, and even public relations for the intellectually talented. Complementary personnel are needed with skills in the following:

1. early identification of extraordinary intellectual talent;
2. guidance for the talented toward appropriate activities in light of such factors as their levels of cognitive and emotional development, interests, and family pressures;
3. identification and development of internal and external sources of intellectual stimulation and enrichment for these students; and
4. provision of such intellectual stimulation locally in at least some educational areas.

Julian Stanley has said that teacher judgments of mathematical talent are woefully invalid. [EDITORS' NOTE: e.g., see Stanley 1976.] He and his colleagues have gone to their own formal and informal identification systems that are relatively independent of the schools. One suspects, too, that one of the reasons the SMPY staff is so dedicated to acceleration rather than enrichment is mistrust of the ability of many local teachers to provide true enrichment as opposed to "Mickey Mouse" activities. Acceleration offers greater opportunity for use of experts outside the system, or at least teachers acknowledged to be at higher levels within the system.

In addition to the problems of the competence of local school personnel to deal with highly gifted students, their families, and other institutions, there are also subtler issues on the local scene, issues of attitudes. It is well known, anecdotally at any rate, that some teachers feel threatened by students who are brighter in any respect than they are. In school systems where there are large numbers of low achievers, there may be resistance and resentment if money and effort are "diverted" away from those judged "most needy." In many communities, too, high achievers must contend with negative peer pressures and hostilities.

To summarize these brief remarks, as we discuss the role of school systems in furthering the development of intellectually gifted students, we must keep before us the realities of what the average school system *can* do now and temper our expectations for the future to the personnel and contextual problems that will have to be overcome if local environments for the gifted are to be invigorating rather than stultifying.

Reference

Stanley, J. C. 1976. Tests better finder of great math talent than teachers are. *American Psychologist* 31(4, Apr.): 313–14.

STANLEY: Thank you, Dr. Anderson. The final speaker on this portion of the panel is a distinguished educational psychologist, the president of the Division of Educational Psychology of the American Psychological Association, and a former editor of the *Educational Psychologist*. He is Professor Ellis B. Page of the University of Connecticut, a measurement specialist. Dr. Page:

ACCELERATION VERSUS ENRICHMENT: THEORETICAL PERSPECTIVES
Ellis B. Page

Let us consider the issue of acceleration versus enrichment from some theoretical perspectives. When we do so I will argue that we find ourselves concerned with two of the most traditional problems of psychology. Furthermore, we may be on the threshold of some useful new understandings about them.

In thinking fundamentally about programs for the gifted, a dilemma exists if we take for granted that talents stem either from the genes or from the environment or from some combination and/or interaction of genes and environment. I talent comes from the environment (nurture), isn't it unfair to give the gifted any additional opportunities, whether by acceleration or enrichment? Doesn't this simply compound the basic unfairness of their already advantaged environment

On the other hand, if talent comes entirely from heredity (nature), why are special programs necessary? That is, if the environment is unimportant in determining the outcome, then why do anything at all environmentally to accommodate individual differences? From this reasoning it seems that we can defend programs for the gifted best, if defense is our purpose, if we assume some combination of nature and nurture, and especially if we assume some interaction of nature and nurture. To be intellectually defensible, a program for the gifted must not be equally appropriate for the less gifted. Perhaps we can accept the following statement as a core agreement: the gifted are innately different in ability from the average, and this innate difference by itself is not adequate to assure their maximum contribution to society or to their own fulfillment. So, in a sense, we must be interactionists, if we believe in special programs. I mean *interactionist* in an especially technical, statistical sense.

As people interested in such programs, let us consider now a more parochial question. Which sort of help promises optimal achievement? Here we have run into problems that are both theoretical and practical. The most coherent and informed arguments against acceleration are based on the study of individual profiles, that is, when we accelerate a child by grade-skipping we typically promote the whole child; all of the gifted child goes to college, not just his unusual mathematical ability. It is quite true that our standard for inclusion of Mary in a program for gifted artists would not necessarily entitle her to inclusion in a program for gifted mathematicians or poets or historians. On the other hand, many of these more intellectual fields do correlate substantially with each other. Both test scores and grades for different areas of study show, in at least a moderately significant range, correlation matrices that are overwhelmingly positive. If we choose the top youngsters for their scores on the first factor in such a matrix, we shall indeed have students who are in the superior range for most academic subjects and who seldom fall below average in anything intellectual. The question remains, how superior? And how can we face the realization that during any specific educational experience we shall not have the ideal set of students at any moment in any practicable program, simply because of their profile differences? Gradually, we begin to see that we are dealing here with one of the most ancient problems in scientific psychology, second only to the basic nature-nurture problem of general ability. This is the problem of whether intelligence consists of one central trait or a cluster of many parts. In more technical jargon the problem becomes whether something like Spearman's g should be the central consideration, or whether something like Thurstone's primary mental abilities should play the central role in determining educational policy. In principle, pure g seems to argue for acceleration of the whole child. Purely separate traits seem to argue for enrichment to deal with the specific talent.

Since this is such a traditional problem we may well ask what new perspectives we can bring to it. Having faced the importance of the two major considerations, the nature-nurture of general ability and the separation of traits, I believe that now we are in an unprecedented position to cast light upon them. We have three principal advantages over our predecessors: first, the availability of huge masses of test information; second, newly improved multivariate strategies and relatively inexpensive computer power; and third, emerging new methodologies in behavior genetics and related fields. This is no place to detail these advantages, but let me just cite one line of research. Workers at the University of Birmingham in England and elsewhere have been employing techniques involving identical and fraternal twins and various educational scores to test the hypothesis that performance on verbal tasks, for example, has genetically different sources from performance on mathematical tasks. The tentative evidence is that they are indeed differently loaded, however much they share a set of common gene loci. Other investigators have been developing strategies to break down the ordinarily observed correlation matrix into component parts to locate factors that are genetic versus those that are environmental in origin, rather than simply accepting phenotypic, that is the observed, correlations. At the University of Connecticut, in cooperation with researchers elsewhere, we hope to explore some of the largest sets of "twin" data ever examined, taking advantage of some advanced mathematical techniques to make our estimations. Again, these technical possibilities are beyond the scope of the discussion this morning.

My principal message here is that in gifted-child education we should not continue to ignore the fundamental question of the origin and structure of talents. The sooner we support research and achieve deeper insights into these origins and structures, the sooner we will be able to design rationally defensible and effective programs for these youngsters. These children represent the most important resource we have for developing future solutions to the complex problems that beset us.

STANLEY: Thank you, Dr. Page; a session such as this wouldn't be complete without some consideration of the nature-nurture aspects of talents. You have heard the second panel consisting of Drs. Kearney, Ehrlich, David Jackson, Owens, Anderson, and Page. Rather than hazard using all of the time for the panelists to interact with each other, I will start off with an invitation to members of the audience to address questions to any member of the panel who has spoken already.

JAMES ALTSCHULD:[15] My question is addressed to Mr. Daurio. In the research studies that you cited on acceleration, were the criteria the broader type that Dr. Ehrlich was describing in her talk, or were they the narrower types of criteria that Dr. Ehrlich suggested should be broadened?

DAURIO: The research literature that I reviewed included both psychological and educational research spanning at least the last fifty years. Within that category there is literature in specific areas, and literature in general areas.

[15]Audience questioner: James Altschuld, Ohio State University, Center for Vocational Education, 1960 Kenny Road, Columbus, Ohio 43210.

Acceleration is both broadly defined and narrowly defined, so both types were included. The studies that I mentioned, done by the three individuals (Leta Hollingworth, Catharine Cox Miles, and Kathleen Montour) were case histories of successful prodigies of unusual general intellectual ability, so they would be described as case histories based on the more narrowly specified criteria.

GEORGE ROSS:[16]   I'd like to address Dr. Leroy Owens. In our school system as we sample students we ask them if they feel they are especially talented in certain areas. It is amazing the proportions of students who feel they are especially talented. What problems have you had in your program with those students who feel they are especially talented but who are not included in the program?

OWENS: We have a hierarchy for identification to allow all students who feel that they are gifted to identify themselves at the beginning. I think we do have a problem in being certain ourselves that we know what giftedness is. When we select even on the basis of a set of multiple criteria, the tests themselves become the definition of giftedness. I think that is too bad, because the tests we've used are not always the best.

RACQUEL S. MAVALAYSAY:[17]   I would like to address this question to Dr. Branch. She suggests that there should be studies to probe possible damage to gifted children caused by inattention. This led me to wonder what kinds of cautions should be observed in such investigations to preclude any expectations from biasing the results. Since those who will be conducting the investigations are likely to be the same people who will be interested in finding evidence of damage, how will you control for their expectations?

BRANCH: This might be a stated objective in future studies. I don't maintain that it is necessarily the case that negligence of the gifted results in substantial effects. I do think that the studies that we have are selective. We have the case histories of those individuals who made it. We know nothing about the people who've exhibited some level of ability at some point and who later dropped out as they proceeded through the educational system. What I would advocate is a more adequate job of sampling people at an early point and following them through, whether or not they receive special attention. We won't know who will be facilitated or damaged at some later point in life, but broader sampling of people with initial ability will avoid biasing the outcome one way or the other.

BETTY WATTS:[18]   A number of speakers made reference to parental and public reaction against acceleration or enrichment. I'm wondering if any of the speakers has knowledge of any systemic variation between ethnic groups in the United States with respect to attitudes toward acceleration or enrichment?

STANLEY: Not in terms of ethnic groups, but in terms of sex, because the

---

[16]Audience questioner: George Ross, Cedar Rapids Community Schools, Cedar Rapids, Iowa 52401.
[17]Audience questioner: Racquel S. Mavalaysay, Acadia University, Wolfville, Nova Scotia.
[18]Audience questioner: Betty Watts, Schonell Educational Research Center, University of Queensland, Australia.

propensity for radical acceleration through the schools among math-talented youths seems to be restricted largely to males.

HAVIGHURST: In the Terman study there were roughly equal numbers of men and women, but the "A group" perhaps contained men who wanted to achieve outstanding accomplishments. But such desires are not necessarily accelerative in nature.

STANLEY: One of the differences between our study and Terman's is that we go all out to offer educational opportunities. We have a "smorgasbord" of various educational accelerative possibilities, so when participants in our study don't accelerate, it is because they don't want to accelerate. Terman, on the other hand, was determinedly noninterventional except in fairly minor ways. He corresponded with youths who wrote him and occasionally he referred to them as his geniuses or the like, but he did not intend to change the pattern of acceleration. We really don't have substantial information on what happens when opportunities for considerable acceleration are created in various alternative ways according to the desires of the individuals concerned.

JAMES: There is an indicator in the traditional pattern of expenditures for the handicapped and the gifted in state legislatures, about $20 for the handicapped to $1 for the gifted. At the federal level it has run a little more sharply against the gifted, about $100 for the handicapped for every dollar earmarked for the gifted. One consequence of this expenditure pattern is a very deep value implanted in our society that we help the underdog but remain pretty wary of someone who has the initial advantage of intellectual talent.

STANLEY: We now go to the third panel, which will focus on the mathematical and physical sciences. The first speaker will be Mr. William C. George, who is the associate director and the only full-time staff member of the Study of Mathematically Precocious Youth (SMPY) at The Johns Hopkins University. He performs the managerial tasks and much of the consulting work. The others at SMPY are a professor (I), graduate students, and so forth, who are only part time. Mr. George:

ACCELERATION AND THE
EXCELLENT MATHEMATICAL REASONER
William C. George

As specialists in educating the gifted, we recognize that no two individuals are identical. Learning rates, academic skills, ability levels, and social and maturational levels vary from individual to individual. Still, many persons insist on an age-grade lock step for our educational system.

At the Study of Mathematically Precocious Youth (SMPY) of The Johns Hopkins University we have observed that educational acceleration of able youths who are *eager* to move ahead fast seems to enhance their academic ability, motivation, career aspirations, social awareness, self-concept, and creative potential. For example, a young man whom I shall call Alex was graduated from The Johns Hopkins University in May of 1977 at the age of 17¾ years. He is one of five young men in SMPY's program graduated from Hopkins during the 1976–77 school year who ranged in age from 17 to 19. If Alex had remained in the sequential lock step, he would have just graduated from high school in June of 1977. Before attending Johns Hopkins Alex skipped three grades, took seven college courses, and earned the top grade (five) on the difficult BC level Advanced Placement Program calculus examination. He was one of five SMPY participants at Johns Hopkins or elsewhere graduating during the 1976–77 school year who earned a three-year National Science Foundation (NSF) Predoctoral Scholarship with which to do graduate study. While still an undergraduate he solved a difficult computer problem that had remained unsolved even among experts for a number of years.

Another individual, Tom, also is an NSF winner who graduated from Johns Hopkins in May of 1977. At age 18 Tom received his B.A. in theoretical physics with high honors (GPA = 3.93). In March of the same year he presented a professional paper on "quarks" at an invitational inter-American conference on theoretical physics in Texas. Both Alex and Tom were elected to Phi Beta Kappa. Would either of them have found equally challenging and stimulating educational opportunities had they remained in high school? That seems overwhelmingly improbable.

Among the many forms of accelerative facilitation for intellectually gifted youths, subject-matter acceleration is especially appropriate in the area of mathematics (George and Denham 1976, Stanley 1976b, Fox 1974, 1976) and probably for the physical sciences as well (Cohn in press, Cohn and George 1977). Because of the sequential nature of mathematics it is easy for students highly talented in math to telescope the learning time for the precalculus sequence into one or two years, while preventing boredom from occurring. We at SMPY have demonstrated that fast-paced mathematics classes are an effective and stimulating way for individuals to learn mathematics. All of the twenty-eight students who attended the second fast-math class from September 1973 to June 1974 completed at least calculus by the end of their senior year in high school. For many of them this would not have been feasible without our program. Sells (in press) has shown that mathematics acts as a filter to self-select individuals, especially girls, out of professional careers. At least thirteen students in the above mentioned class had completed the math sequence through calculus III and differential equations at the college level before they were 18. Seven presently are attending major universities such as MIT, Princeton, and Johns Hopkins. In the fall of 1977 another two entered college two years early. Individuals choosing not to major in mathematics or the mathematical sciences still retain a solid background with which to pursue other fields of interest such as electrical engineering, the natural sciences, and even economics.

The type of acceleration will vary according to the needs of the student, his or her desire to move ahead, and the school situation. Acceleration is an alternative that we at SMPY believe many students would select if given the opportunity. By slowing down the natural learning rates of highly able reasoners one extinguishes academic motivation and adjustment in precisely those curricular areas where individual ability and interest are strong. Appropriate enrichment as defined by Stanley (1976a) eventually should lead to academic acceleration at some later stage in secondary school. Lehman (1953) points out the importance of early professional work and its positive relationship to creative potential.

Would you insist that a student who can get a perfect score on the Cooperative Mathematics Test—Algebra I before studying the subject still should take 180 fifty-minute periods of formal algebra I instruction? Some school systems do. Sixty-five percent of 278 seventh or underage eighth graders from SMPY's talent search who took a standardized algebra I test scored at least as high as 39 percent of the eighth graders in a national sample did *after* having completed a school year of algebra I. Our group, however, was fifteen months younger and had studied no algebra per se. Thirty-six of that group scored in the upper 5 percent of the national norm group.

As demonstrated by programs in states such as Illinois, Maryland, Minnesota, Nebraska, and Pennsylvania, administrative flexibility and acceleration should be important components of any school's program. In conclusion, acceleration and appropriate enrichment when blended together permit an eager, well-qualified student to proceed at a stimulating pace and at an appropriately high level of abstraction through a curriculum that he or she might not otherwise ever pursue well.

References

Cohn, S. J. In press. Individualizing science curricula for the gifted. Accepted for publication by the *Gifted Child Quarterly*.

————, and George, W. C. 1977. Chemistry and the mathematically talented: Origins and relationships. Paper presented at the annual meeting of the National Association for Gifted Children in San Diego, California, in October.

Fox, L. H. 1974. A mathematics program for fostering precocious achievement. In J. C. Stanley, D. P. Keating, and L. H. Fox (eds.), *Mathematical talent: Discovery, description, and development*. Baltimore, Md.: The Johns Hopkins University Press, pp. 101–25.

————. 1976. Sex differences in mathematical precocity: Bridging the gap. In D. P. Keating (ed.), *Intellectual talent: Research and development*. Baltimore, Md.: The Johns Hopkins University Press, pp. 183–214.

George, W. C., and Denham, S. A. 1976. Curriculum experimentation for the mathematically talented. In D. P. Keating (ed.), *Intellectual talent: Research and development*. Baltimore, Md.: The Johns Hopkins University Press, pp. 103–31.

Lehman, H. C. 1953. *Age and achievement*. Princeton, N.J.: Princeton University Press.

Sells, L. W. In press. The mathematics filter and the education of women. In L. H. Fox, L. E. Brody, and D. H. Tobin (eds.), *Women and the mathematical mystique*. Baltimore, Md: The Johns Hopkins University Press.

Stanley, J. C. 1976a. Identifying and nurturing the intellectually gifted. *Phi Delta Kappan* 58(3): 234–37.

———. 1976b. Special fast-mathematics classes taught by college professors to fourth-through twelfth-graders. In D. P. Keating (ed.), *Intellectual talent: Research and development*. Baltimore, Md.: The Johns Hopkins University Press, pp. 132–59.

STANLEY: The first book that came out of the Study of Mathematically Precocious Youth was entitled *Mathematical Talent* and subtitled *Discovery, Description, and Development*. The editors of that volume were Julian C. Stanley, Daniel P. Keating, and Lynn H. Fox. Both Dan and Lynn earned their doctorates under my direction while helping get SMPY started several years ago. Since 1974 both have been working on their own projects, Lynn at Johns Hopkins and Dan at the University of Minnesota. Our next speaker is Dr. Fox, a specialist particularly in the area of sex differences as related to mathematical aptitude and achievement. She also is the founder and project coordinator of the Intellectually Gifted Child Study Group in the Evening College and Summer Session of The Johns Hopkins University. Dr. Fox:

SEXISM, DEMOCRACY, AND THE ACCELERATION VERSUS ENRICHMENT CONTROVERSY
Lynn H. Fox

If we define *enrichment* as the provision for learning experiences that develop higher processes of thinking and creativity in a subject area and define *acceleration* as the adjustment of learning time to meet the individual capabilities of the students, they are complementary rather than conflicting goals. If we assume that the major goal of educational programs for the gifted is to meet their learning needs, both enrichment and acceleration are necessary. Thus, the gifted learner can proceed at a faster pace, to a higher level of content and more abstract and evaluative thinking than his or her age peers.

At the risk of overgeneralizing, we can conclude that the controversy over enrichment versus acceleration is partly a function of the specific curriculum for a given content area. By and large, the acceleration of learning in science and mathematics leads to higher levels of abstraction, more creative thinking, and more difficult content. In social studies and language arts the hierarchy of curriculum is less clear (Fox 1979).

Another dimension of the acceleration versus enrichment argument involves the administrative level for instruction. Teaching a gifted student concepts of computer science, algebra, logic, a foreign language, and so forth as a supplement to in-grade work at the elementary, middle school, or junior high school level, without any high school or college credit, is likely to be called enrichment. If the same student studied the same content in a course at the high school or college level for credit, it would be called acceleration. Acceleration typically leads to either early graduation from high school or entrance to college with advanced standing or earned credit, whereas enrichment implies that the student is exposed to the higher-level material without receiving formal credit. Thus, the student may be forced to repeat the material at a later time.

Although few schools or school systems provide for or encourage accelerative experiences in mathematics and science, acceleration of learning by very able youngsters does occur within and outside school settings (Fox 1974a, 1976a). SMPY repeatedly has found students at grade seven who already know most of the content of a first-year algebra course before they have taken it in school (Fox 1974b). This natural acceleration is due to great mathematical reasoning ability and independent study at home in systematic or unsystematic ways. Unfortunately, students who have a deep interest and curiosity that leads to such accelerated learning are penalized by the rigidity of schools that fail to provide diagnostic-prescriptive teaching strategies. Thus, well-motivated students typically are forced to waste hours of their time "learning" something they already know.

A few students rebel successfully against the system and are allowed to move ahead in their studies at school. A few students find they can double up on science and mathematics courses in high school or take courses in the summer and, eventually, speed their progress. Such students are likely to be male and from homes where education is valued but parents are willing and able to trust their own judgments over those of the school authorities. Thus, failure to provide systematic accelerative experiences in school for talented youths probably contributes to sex differences in later achievement (Fox 1976c). In one study, 48 percent of a group of mathematically gifted boys managed to accelerate their math progress in school by at least half a year, whereas only 16 percent of a comparable group of girls accelerated their progress (Fox 1976b). A group of girls who participated in a program to encourage acceleration after grade seven were, by the tenth grade, as accelerated as the boys and significantly more accelerated than the other female group (Fox 1977). It seems likely that some disadvantaged gifted males also are held back by the system. Failure to provide accelerated experiences within school settings may actually be sexist and undemocratic.

References

Fox, L. H. 1974a. Facilitating the educational development of mathematically precocious youth. In J. C. Stanley, D. P. Keating, and L. H. Fox (eds.), *Mathematical talent: Discovery, description, and development*. Baltimore, Md.: The Johns Hopkins University Press, pp. 47–69.

————. 1974b. A mathematics program for fostering precocious achievement. Ibid., pp. 101–25.

————. 1976a. Identification and program planning: Models and methods. In D. P.

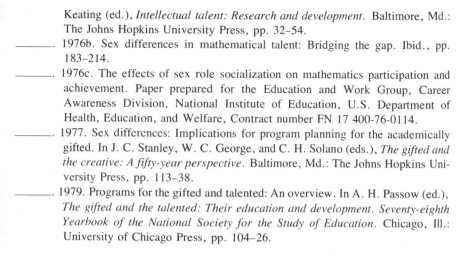

Keating (ed.), *Intellectual talent: Research and development.* Baltimore, Md.: The Johns Hopkins University Press, pp. 32–54.

_____. 1976b. Sex differences in mathematical talent: Bridging the gap. Ibid., pp. 183–214.

_____. 1976c. The effects of sex role socialization on mathematics participation and achievement. Paper prepared for the Education and Work Group, Career Awareness Division, National Institute of Education, U.S. Department of Health, Education, and Welfare, Contract number FN 17 400-76-0114.

_____. 1977. Sex differences: Implications for program planning for the academically gifted. In J. C. Stanley, W. C. George, and C. H. Solano (eds.), *The gifted and the creative: A fifty-year perspective.* Baltimore, Md.: The Johns Hopkins University Press, pp. 113–38.

_____. 1979. Programs for the gifted and talented: An overview. In A. H. Passow (ed.), *The gifted and the talented: Their education and development. Seventy-eighth Yearbook of the National Society for the Study of Education.* Chicago, Ill.: University of Chicago Press, pp. 104–26.

STANLEY: Thank you, Dr. Fox. The next speaker is Dr. Daniel P. Keating, who is the editor of a book that came out in 1976 from The Johns Hopkins University Press called *Intellectual talent: Research and development.* It was the second volume in SMPY's *Studies of Intellectual Precocity* series. Dr. Keating:

THE ACCELERATION/ENRICHMENT DEBATE: BASIC ISSUES
Daniel P. Keating

It is remarkably easy to become lost in a discussion of the relative merits and demerits of educational adjustments that are termed *accelerative*, and others that are termed *enriching*. What we risk losing are two important things: a useful perspective of the overall goals for the education of highly able students, and a sense of what it is possible to achieve in the real world of the schools as they exist in the present. Since other symposiasts undoubtedly will address many of the important issues involved in the acceleration/enrichment controversy, I would like to make some simple (but I hope important) observations from the perspectives noted above.

If we step back for a moment and ask ourselves what is the single most compelling difference between gifted or high-ability students and more average students, it is quite obvious that it is the rate at which they are able to acquire and integrate new information, especially if the information is meaningful: high-ability students learn faster. Evidence for this comes from long years of classroom experience with such students, from laboratory classroom studies that have been carefully controlled and conducted (Keating 1976; Stanley, Keating, and Fox 1974), and from experimental laboratory studies that indicate moderate

rate advantages even for very basic information-processing parameters (Keating and Bobbitt 1978). A major goal for all students should be to expose them on a fairly regular basis to novel, challenging, and educationally relevant material. If this is to be accomplished for high-ability students, a higher density of subject matter per time unit will be required. Any educational facilitation that can provide for high-ability students is appropriate, and whether we choose to label this "acceleration" or "enrichment" is an administrative rather than an educational decision.

This brings us directly to the second constraint, which is that such adjustments do need to be made within the confines of the school, if we are to have practical and continuing programs in the foreseeable future. The implication is that such administrative matters are far from trivial. In counseling with high-ability students, a great deal of time must be spent on just such arrangements. The most feasible adjustment for the vast majority of students is to move them ahead directly so that they have a reasonable chance of seeing material that meets the criteria of being novel, challenging, and educationally relevant.

Thus, for the vast majority of students, acceleration in the administrative as well as the educational sense will be the best option. We should not, however, cease efforts in other kinds of educational reforms that also will benefit their learning process. But such efforts should not divert us from doing meaningful things for current students. In particular, we often hear of the solution for such students being found in curriculum reform. Although such reform might be desirable, there should be differences in the rate of exposure to any curriculum, because individual differences among and within students surely will remain.

Much of the acceleration/enrichment debate concentrates on a separable issue, however—the possible *harmful* effects of moving ahead. These criticisms are reasonably arranged in two categories: possible negative effects on other areas of development, such as social or affective; and possible negative implications for mathematics or science learning per se, the usual concerns being gaps in skills or superficiality. As for the social-emotional concerns, it seems time to abandon them unless and until some solid reliable evidence is forthcoming that indicates real dangers in well-run programs. The evidence to date is that, try as we might, we cannot detect such harm, although much research has been conducted along these lines (see chapter 2). One may question the accuracy of the research, of course (e.g., how to measure affective or social development effectively), but without some solid evidence of problems in this area, it seems unwise to abandon helpful measures because there *may* be problems elsewhere. A cost-benefit ratio works heavily in favor of active intervention on this issue, while orthodoxy alone argues against intervention.

A similar situation exists for the second concern, mathematics or science learning per se. Gaps in skills need to be demonstrated rather than asserted, and to my knowledge no convincing negative evidence exists here either. It certainly does not show up in the performance of the SMPY students (Keating 1976, Stanley, Keating, and Fox 1974).

The issue of superficiality is more difficult to dispel, principally because it is harder to define operationally. This argument *can* be an infinite regress, that is, one can meet each specific criticism with a demonstration, only to have it supplanted by another criticism demanding additional demonstration.

Criticism: These students are learning only specific rules for a given subject which they do not understand, and thus will lack ability to learn subsequent material.

Demonstration: They continue to do very well in subsequent courses, even difficult ones.

Criticism: They are learning only techniques, but do not have a good overall conceptualization of the subject matter.

Demonstration: Even in advanced, college-level theoretical courses, they outperform many bright but nonaccelerated students. And so on.

Eventually one can place the bar on the hurdle so high that no one can jump it, and we gain little knowledge from having done so. One specific criticism, for example, is that budding mathematicians may be deflected from following pure mathematics because of an accelerated program. This is a valid potential research topic, but one that will be difficult to pursue because of the very low base-rate of pure mathematicians in the population (e.g., less than 500 new Ph.D. recipients in pure mathematics each year), a point often overlooked. Longitudinal follow-up studies by SMPY eventually may address this question, however.

Let me conclude by observing that well-run programs to facilitate academic talent through accelerative adjustments have substantial benefits but relatively few demonstrable costs. Like any educational technique, however, acceleration is subject to abuse. Important components of well-run programs include selection appropriate to the particular facilitation under consideration, excellent and continuing counseling, and enthusiastic, competent teachers. A discussion of these components is beyond the scope of this paper, but if they are present, there is good evidence to support the contention that such facilitation will be beneficial to students currently. We should continue to seek the *best* route for educating such students, but accelerative adjustments are the closest contemporary approximation.

References

Keating, D. P. (ed.). 1976. *Intellectual talent: Research and development*. Baltimore, Md.: The Johns Hopkins University Press.

———, and Bobbitt, B. L. 1978. Individual and developmental differences in cognitive-processing components of mental ability. *Child Development* 49: 155–67.

Stanley, J. C., Keating, D. P., and Fox, L. H. (eds.). 1974. *Mathematical talent: Discovery, description, and development*. Baltimore, Md.: The Johns Hopkins University Press.

STANLEY: Thank you, Dr. Keating. Our next speaker is a recent past-president of the National Council of Teachers of Mathematics and a professor of mathematics education at the University of Texas. I have known her for a number of years, ever since she was a graduate student in mathematics education at the University of Wisconsin. Dr. E. Glenadine Gibb:

EDUCATIONAL ACCELERATION OF INTELLECTUALLY TALENTED YOUTHS: THE *MATHEMATICAL* AND PHYSICAL SCIENCES
E. Glenadine Gibb

Should the talented in mathematics be provided with programs of enrichment or should these students have the opportunity to choose among the several modes of acceleration commonly defined as skipping grades, fast-paced mathematics courses, enrollment in college courses, early admission to college, advanced placement in a mathematics program, and the like?

I support a program of enrichment with depth and horizontal development followed by acceleration as deemed desirable. My rationale for this position includes some specifications: the nature of the enrichment, the needs for effectiveness in mathematics, and the shortcomings of acceleration supported by research that otherwise might purport to support acceleration as the optimal management system for the education of these talented youths.

Divergent production is a necessary ability for success in mathematics. Creativity is also a commonly identified trait of students in programs for the mathematically gifted. Such programs place greater emphasis on advanced conceptualization not easily grasped by those similar in age but of lesser ability; on the development of higher-level cognitive processes; on opportunities for divergent production; and on fostering creativity, including questioning, experimentation, devising new approaches, and testing results. At the same time, such programs should not become sterile, pedantic, and too intellectual. They should be designed for appropriateness of the maturity and interests of the learner, whether at the elementary, secondary, or collegiate level.

Programs that the gifted can be expected to encounter, if accelerated, are designed for the mainstream student at that level. Although evidence from research supports the success of talented students in such courses, one must be reminded that for the most part these evaluations reflect a student's ability to perform on traditional, convergent-production tasks. These evaluations can be expected to neglect an important component of giftedness, that of divergent-production tasks. Reducing the student's learning of mathematics to mere logic is an effective way to stifle creative mathematical thought. A student whose creativity is stifled may not continue in mathematics long enough to learn to enjoy it and to contribute his or her talents to the field. Furthermore, students who have experienced programs of acceleration have been found to have superficial mathematical understandings and insights and to have gaps in their programs of study.[19] They also have been denied the opportunity to develop their innate abilities of divergent thinking and creativity, abilities that are characteristic of talented people and particularly of mathematicians and scientists. Indeed, they have had the opportunity to study "average" material sooner, only to have an "average" education.[20]

If, however, programs of enrichment merely produce "more of the same," and are irrelevant to the student's development of higher intellectual processes, then support of acceleration in the average, mainstream program becomes a more likely alternative compared to that which can be expected to bore the student and reduce his or her intellectual activity from brilliance to mediocrity.

May we not debate the issue of enrichment versus acceleration? Special content properly organized and presented can be achieved in any number of environments and management systems. The more difficult problems of research and development lie in quality curriculum enrichment—enrichment that provides the needed depth and stimulation for the intellectual ability of gifted mathematics students at their levels of maturation and interest.

STANLEY: Thank you, Dr. Gibb, for those heuristic suggestions. I might say that in SMPY's experience, the holes in the background theory doesn't hold up empirically at all. The youngsters who move fast do learn the material and show up, for instance on the Graduate Record Examination's advanced exam in the field of mathematics, making virtually perfect scores as early as age 14.

Dr. Anne Anastasi, the final speaker on this panel, is the long-term leader in the field of psychology of individual differences in the United States. The author of two distinguished textbooks in that area, she is a recent past president of the American Psychological Association. Dr. Anastasi:

SOME REFLECTIONS ON THE ACCELERATION-ENRICHMENT CONTROVERSY

Anne Anastasi

Let me begin by underscoring a point made by several speakers: acceleration and enrichment are neither unitary nor mutually exclusive approaches to the education of gifted children. There are many variants of each and many combinations of the two. Several examples can be found in the Study of Mathematically Precocious Youth, conducted by Julian Stanley and his associates,

---

[19]EDITORS' NOTE: After an extensive review of the literature, Daurio found no such evidence.
[20]EDITORS' NOTE: Certainly, those students who were graduated from The Johns Hopkins University or elsewhere five and one-half to seven years early did not have an "average" educational experience. Surely, for example, the depth and rigor of a good college course in mathematics will surpass most of what is called secondary school mathematics enrichment.

as well as in Elizabeth Kearney's description of the California programs, to cite only two illustrations. The optimal variant or combination depends not only on the intellectual, emotional, and physical variables of the individual child but also on the child's own interests, wishes, and initial response to the program. I trust that no one would recommend continuing a program of acceleration, enrichment, or both if it clearly makes the child unhappy. I would urge not moderation but rather individualization.

Acceleration never ought to mean "pushing." It should mean "stop pulling back." In the same spirit, enrichment activities should fit the child's interests and utilize his or her strengths. From the standpoint of mental health, the individual should be given opportunities to pursue activities that interest him or her and in which he (she) can succeed. But notice that the more closely the content of enrichment matches individual interests and talents, the closer it approaches acceleration. If a child already is mathematically talented, enriching his or her program with more math places that child even farther ahead of age and grade peers in this area.

Suppose, on the other hand, that the content of enrichment is chosen with the opposite goal in mind—that of broadening the scope of the child's activities. In this connection it is noteworthy that large-scale surveys consistently have shown gifted children as a group to have characteristically broad interests. In some cases they even run the risk of diffusing their energies too widely and hence need help in focusing and channeling their activities. Some advocates of enrichment, however, seem to imply that we should seek out an area in which the child shows little interest and talent, and "enrich" the child's life by providing more in that area. This is a form of lateral enrichment based on the spinach theory. You give it to the child because it's supposed to be good for him (her). I don't think I need to spell out what such an approach is likely to do both to the child's liking for the area and to his or her mental health.

In order to cope with the continuing knowledge explosion in all fields, we need specialization and an early focusing of educational efforts. The person who sets out to be a Renaissance man today is likely to end up as a dilettante. Formal education, based on what is known at the time, should be completed as early as possible. Otherwise, much will have to be unlearned after graduation. The rapid accumulation of knowledge makes lifelong education essential for leadership in any intellectual field. The process of growing to maturity in today's world includes a succession of choices between what we can and what we cannot afford to master—between what can and what cannot be fit into one lifetime.

STANLEY: Thank you, Dr. Anastasi, for those perceptive remarks. We are fortunate to have as one of our symposiasts Dr. Joan S. Stark, who is the director of the program in higher education at Syracuse University.[21] I knew her a few

[21]EDITORS' NOTE: In the fall of 1978 Dr. Stark became Dean of the School of Education at the University of Michigan.

years ago as an assistant dean at Goucher College and from October of 1971 through her son, Eugene. Dr. Stark has had a distinguished career in her own right. As a student at Syracuse University she majored in the science area and was elected to Phi Beta Kappa in her junior year. Her son, Eugene, who was graduated from Johns Hopkins as an electrical engineering major at age 17, won a National Science Foundation Fellowship to work toward the doctorate at MIT. He has done remarkable research work at both General Electric and Bell Telephone Laboratories during the summertime. I will yield the floor to Dr. Stark to tell you whatever she wants to share about either her general views of giftedness or her special views about her role as the mother of an extremely accelerated physical scientist. Dr. Stark:

REMARKS ABOUT PRECOCITY AND COLLEGE COURSES
Joan S. Stark

This paper is written from my dual vantage point as (1) a college administrator and educational researcher who has done some minor studies of educational acceleration in the distant past, and (2) the mother of a radically accelerated student. I intend to suggest two areas of investigation that seem not to have been pursued in Professor Stanley's SMPY program but that I believe are important in learning to facilitate the progress of gifted youths who enter college at a young age. Not surprisingly, the matters that I believe merit investigation relate to my concerns about the education of students who pursue college studies at the typical age as well.

My first proposal is that an apprenticeship program as a method of meeting initial acceleration needs of brilliant youth might be superior to the pursuit of a random selection of college courses on a part- or full-time basis. This hypothesis is based on assumptions that some college teachers are better suited than others to deal with intellectually talented students and that these teachers can be identified by their attitudes toward students and toward the educational process.

The efforts of SMPY are based largely on the assumption that early college work is better for brilliant youths and the project has demonstrated that selected students can progress well at a young age. College work is presumed better because it is more stimulating intellectually than that which normally can be pursued in junior high or high school. Additionally, there is evidence that some high school teachers are not receptive to the needs of talented youth or, on the basis of negative stereotypes, they may even be antagonistic or threatened. Research done by the SMPY investigators indicates, too, that the success of junior high youths in accelerated mathematics classes is greatly facilitated by carefully selected, dynamic instructors who teach at a fast pace but value individuality and have a genuine respect for students.

It seems incongruous to report that teacher style is important in an experimental situation and at the same time to assume that college work will provide stimulation merely because the subject matter is advanced, while neither measuring nor taking into account the characteristics of college teachers expected to provide the stimulation. My recent research on educational attitudes of college faculty members and my personal observations indicate that if college work stimulates the radical accelerant, it may do so *in spite of* the college teachers.

Students who take courses at a large university likely will be taught, initially, by poorly compensated graduate assistants with minimal experience and little incentive to dedicate themselves to the teaching task. Further, out-of-class faculty-student interaction is likely to be infrequent at a large university, at least in the lower division program. Lastly, individual learning activities customarily are not optimal in colleges; with a few exceptions for personalized instruction experiments, the lecture method prevails.

Under such conditions one might look to the small college that prides itself on the teaching role and on individual attention to students. Yet, in a current study of 287 faculty members in six liberal arts colleges, I have found that 76 percent believe that unless motivated by grades students will not study, 63 percent feel that students do not learn well when studying on their own, 60 percent do not expect students to dig deeply into topics in which they are interested, and 52 percent do not believe that students should pursue their own interests. These and similar attitudes common even among professed teaching faculty seem antithetical to the kind of teaching brilliant students might expect to receive in college courses. I would conjecture that many of the successful radically accelerated students who are at college full time have sought and found relationships with particular professors who have the characteristics necessary to keep lit the spark of learning and, further, that such students merely tolerate the other classroom professors who perform their roles lackadaisically. Developing such a relationship is more difficult if a student begins acceleration on a part-time, commuting basis. If appropriate professors can be identified, as I believe they can, one might assign intellectually talented students to work with such teachers as apprentices to give such students a meaningful anchor point in the university apart from just enrolling in a course or two.

My second proposal is related to the first. In general, our society does a poor job of preparing adolescents and young adults for the transition from school to work. This transition is a particularly crucial one for youths who finish college at the age of 16 or 17. We should not only study the difficulties that current accelerants might encounter but also seek opportunities to ease the transition in order to promote appropriate career choices. Our labor laws, originally designed to protect youth, now allow a mathematically precocious 15-year-old to lift heavy grocery bags in subzero temperatures but not to program a computer or plan an electronic circuit in an industrial setting where he or she might explore potential scientific careers. Staff members of SMPY have reported that the radical accelerants with whom they work have a meaningful self-image and are interpersonally effective, socially mature, and well-equipped to meet challenges.

One challenge that needs to be confronted is the opportunity to use one's skills in a setting other than the classroom. For example, the contrast between the collegiate investigative world and the work-a-day world where employees pace themselves to complete a minimum of tasks is a difficult one. But awareness of this contrast is a maturation experience that should not be neglected. Efforts to facilitate appropriate employment and the study of accelerants in such settings seem as important as facilitating year-round study, which may provide too little variation for the self-motivated accelerant. An important next step in investigating the progress of intellectually talented youngsters who pursue accelerated study would be the provision of planned work experiences and longitudinal case studies of adaptation.

STANLEY: All of the five seniors in our SMPY program at Hopkins have somehow managed to get high-level, meaningful work experience. They find it difficult to get paid even minimum wages for such work, as Dr. Stark pointed out. But by one way or another all of them have managed to do so during their undergraduate years. Gene Stark's problem was that he finished the sophomore year at Johns Hopkins while he was still 15. He did not become 16 until July 10, and yet he was ready to get into some research. He had to wait until his sixteenth birthday before he could go to work for a national organization. The next summer he had even more trouble. He was employed at age 16, but they had, as I understand it, to acquire him like a sack of flour on a purchase order, because they couldn't actually pay him as an employee at the age of 16 even though he had finished his junior year at college with a distinguished record.

The final viewpoint will be given by SMPY's greatest long-term advocate and friend, who has come to every paper presentation and meeting we have had for many years. I have known Al Kurtz for a long time. He has a distinguished background as one of the early specialists in measurement. He has been known to me ever since the beginning of my own graduate days, back in 1945, and we have been very pleased to have him so interested in our project. It's quite fitting that he be the final speaker. Dr. Kurtz:

ACCELERATION VERSUS ENRICHMENT
—THE TENTH RULE OF THREE-CUBED
Albert K. Kurtz

I shall quickly do what Dr. Stanley asked me to do—state my positions on acceleration and on enrichment. That's easy.

First, I'm for acceleration. Why? So that the greatest minds in our country can develop their talents to whatever extent they wish. I hope the teachers in our public schools will encourage these gifted children, enabling them to complete the twelve grades in what is for them the proper length of time. But at least, let us no longer allow the teachers to deter bright children from attaining what are for them simply normal and eminently reasonable objectives. What are these objectives? I'll give you an example. Let's say a boy with an IQ of 120 lives next door to a group of children all having IQs of 100. When he is 5 years old with a mental age of 6, his knowledge is equal to that of the 6-year-old. Every time a year goes by, he learns 20 percent more than the child next door. When he reaches 10 he has a mental age of 12. This process will continue until he reaches 15 (we have a little problem here over which Terman and Wechsler disagreed, concerning when mental ages reach their peaks). Until that time he will have continued to learn about 20 percent more each year and will have accumulated about 20 percent more knowledge than the 15-year-olds next door, whether or not he then has a mental age of *exactly* 18 years.

The Tenth Rule of Three-Cubed

The average child (and far too many bright ones) graduates from high school at age 18. We just saw that a child with an IQ of 120 could set graduation at age 15 as an eminently reasonable objective; he'd know as much as the average 18-year-old. But what about other bright students? The tenth rule of three-cubed gives the answer. It works this way. Take one-tenth of the IQ, subtract it from three-cubed, and get the eminently reasonable graduation age. Thus, when we subtract one-tenth of 120, or 12, from three-cubed, or 27, we get 15, just as we did before. This simple rule works for nearly all bright kids. For all IQs from 115 to 157 we either get the theoretically exact value or miss it by no more than a month or two.

Thus, as any of Dr. Stanley's mathematically talented youths long since have figured out, I feel that students with IQs of 120, 130, 140, or 150 should have no trouble in graduating from high school at ages 15, 14, 13, or 12, respectively. Yes, that says that Terman's gifted children could well have been graduated at 13 years, as some of them did. Many others could have and should have.

Now let us turn very briefly to my position on enrichment. I'm thoroughly fed up with this emphasis on agemates. I have a one-word comment on enrichment, the same one General McAuliffe gave thirty-three years ago: Nuts!

STANLEY: Thank you very much, Dr. Kurtz for your summation. There will be time for comments about your point of view from the audience. Feel free to ask questions of any person on the panel.

CONNIE STEELE:[22]   I'm delighted that everyone is concerned about those children who are accelerated into college and I can understand the concerns of the

---

[22] Audience questioner: Connie Steele, Texas Institute of Technology, Lubbock, Texas 79408.

Johns Hopkins University group. If we, however, are going to respond to the potential that might be possible for our children, as Ellis Page alluded to, in order to solve our problems, how can we identify them at very young ages? Shouldn't this early identification begin systematically from birth, rather than just by proud papas and proud mamas who say "Gee, my child is doing these great things?"

NANCY JACKSON: I would like very much to take on that question. We are working on the problem of how to identify children with advanced intellectual abilities before they reach age 5, the usual age of public school entrance. We have been working first in a small-scale, pilot way within a large-scale, longitudinal study. We are beginning to see what I think are going to be some very important trends. We have not been successful in doing any large-scale identification of precocious children before the age of 2. When we look back retrospectively at children who later show signs of extreme precocity, we can see many remarkable things that they did during infancy, but when we have tried to solicit from parents in the community a large group of children who are less than 2 years of age, we have discovered that almost every infant looks extraordinary to his or her parents. Beginning at about age 2, however, such children appear to be more successfully identified. This also is the age at which a standardized assessment first is possible. By this age we can get extensive reports from parents by means of lengthy questionnaires about various aspects of a child's intellectual development, including what things a child is interested in, when the child first started to do various things, and so forth. What we seem to be finding is that at age 2, or perhaps 3, information from parents, proud though they are, actually is at least as good and possibly in the long run a better predictor of what the child will be like several years later than is a test score alone. Standardized tests take such a small sample of a child's behavior. If a child does very well, then we know something, but if the child is noncommunicative or highly active during the test session and simply not interested in our games, we don't know whether it is a case of can't or won't. What we have been doing is taking information from parents of the children with whom we deal. Rather than have the parents answer directly the question "Is your child extraordinary?" we have raters read through the questionnaires and make judgments about the child in a variety of intellectual dimensions on a three-point scale. These points include whether the child seems to be developing at an average rate, an advanced rate, or an extraordinarily advanced rate. To date our findings are that these judgments can be made reliably by two independent readers and that they contribute significantly to the long-term predictions of the child's accomplishments.

STEELE: Is your material available?

JACKSON: Yes, and if you would write to us I would be glad to send it to you.[23]

KEARNEY: One of the things that kept coming up in the various discussions

[23]EDITORS' NOTE: Professor Halbert Robinson conducts the Child Development Research Group at the University of Washington in Seattle, Washington 98195. Dr. Jackson is on the staff of that study.

concerned the possibility that some negative emotional developments might occur if we fail to identify these children and provide for them. The only study that I recall, is one that was done as a doctoral thesis by Dr. Richmond Barbour, who was the assistant superintendent of the San Diego schools. He did a twelve-year longitudinal study in which he took three groups: one group just went through school; one group was isolated from peers; and the other group was matched for a portion of the day according to members' particular levels of precocity. The study concerned both achievement and emotional development. Dr. Barbour found out that by doing nothing for them (group 1) you actually *cause* major emotional problems. So great was this study's impact, that administrators set up a clinic for emotionally disturbed gifted children in San Diego and found that the children without special provisions tended to end up with some type of need for counseling prior to the end of the twelfth grade, if they got that far. The other students seemed to do well, especially those in the group that was totally iso-lated. Those in the other group did almost as well, but those in the control group seemed to have developed serious emotional problems.

KEATING: I want to go back to a brief comment about what Nancy Jackson mentioned a moment ago in terms of early identification. As Nancy and the other people on her project well know, one of the problems has been the difficulty of using infant intelligence-type measures and the notorious unpredictability of such measures among anyone under 4 or 5 years old. There is a book by Michael Lewis that addresses this issue and tells why that might not be the case.[24] If we are going to be successful at all in terms of prediction for long-term development, we need to look for functional equivalences. I think this is the kind of research that is being conducted at the University of Washington.

EHRLICH: We have in New York City a program that we have been direct-ing for children who are 4 at the beginning of the year when they are admitted to kindergarten. This means that frequently we test them at the age of 3½. We have had considerable success using in part identification by parents. Parents do a very good job of recognizing the giftedness of their very young children. Of course, we follow through by a psychological testing and an interview. We do use the Stanford-Binet. Three-and-one-half years later we have found that the youngsters we located originally were identified correctly. I think we had only one child in all of that time who we felt should not have been included in our program. I would like to add the point that we are doing an intervention study in conjunction with Teacher's College of Columbia University under Dr. Harry Passow. The study compares the youngsters whom we selected with a control group of young-sters who applied to the program but for various reasons could not be accepted (mostly because we did not have space). Perhaps soon we will have some answers to the question of what happens when there is, or is not, intervention of the type we advocate at an early age.

[24]For those persons interested in reading Michael Lewis's book, the citation is as follows: 1976. *Origins of intelligence.* New York: Plenum Press.

STANLEY: Dr. Stark wants to make a comment. I recall that her son, Gene, was tested on a Binet-type instrument quite early, and scored quite high, so she probably has observations about her experiences with an extremely bright youngster from preschool years. Dr. Stark:

STARK: I was going to try not to be as anecdotal as that. The instance occurred when Gene was 4 years and 5 months old. When the school informed me, I went to find out what I should do. Should I send him to kindergarten because he was reading at, I think, around the sixth or seventh grade level? He read the *New York Times* regularly at that point. I was told, however, that he should be put into the normal program, and by fourth grade he would be like everyone else. I think that probably would have been the case except that he skipped the second grade due to a very diligent teacher who saw the matter in a different light than did the kindergarten teacher. I could give you a whole bunch of anecdotes about kindergarten, but what I wanted to suggest is that I think there is a very simple way of identifying these children at about the second grade level, maybe even the first grade level. Preferably it should be done early, and certainly it should be done because what these children discover very quickly (because they do use some logical reasoning) is that it is better to hide their light under a bushel basket. They will quickly find out that their peers do not have the same interests that they do, and therefore they will sneak away into back rooms to read what they want to read, or play the piano, or do whatever they want to do. I would hypothesize that at about the second grade level one could, after establishing some trust and confidence with the child, ask him or her two questions: "What is it you like to do the most when you are alone?" and "Why don't you do that in school?" And you can easily find that the child has discovered that it is not wise to be smart.

STEVE CHRISTOPHERSON:[25] I have a question for Ellis Page. I'm curious about justifications for separate programs for the gifted in the public schools. The practice of separate programs seems to imply a belief that there are two bodies of knowledge to teach, one for the gifted, one for the others. I am confident that ultimately there is only one body of knowledge to draw from in each of the subject areas, but is there evidence that the nature of the intellectual development of gifted children is different or simply more precocious?

PAGE: This is a very big question. You spoke of separate programs not being appropriate, and (if I understand you correctly) you are saying that the gifted 10-year-old who has an IQ of 150 is like the average 15-year-old. Is that what you are saying?

CHRISTOPHERSON: That is what I'm curious about.

PAGE: The point that I was making is that, as well as having this common *g*, there are differences that separate that 10-year-old from the 15-year-old. That is the implicit justification for those who defend enrichment over acceleration.

[25]Audience questioner: Steven L. Christopherson, Department of Education, Trinity College, Hartford, Connecticut 06106.

CHRISTOPHERSON: So you think that the nature of the development is different but that their minds don't follow different rules. Their age differences or backgrounds and experiential differences might justify separate programs.

PAGE: My own opinion agrees with what you seem to be implying, that cognitively the gifted 10-year-old is not very different from the average 15-year-old. This is one of the very central issues in the whole discussion.

JAMES: I would like to comment on this question. One of the papers delivered here suggested that the child at a given age who is gifted will have acquired everything that any other child at that age is likely to have acquired and more, since the potential for learning 20 percent more each year carries that child on at a faster rate. It is not a question of learning different bodies of knowledge; rather, it is a question of the gifted child's learning it faster, at an earlier age, and continuing to learn more as he or she grows older.

GOLD: I'd like to make two points. The first is one that James J. Gallagher has addressed, the issue concerning the qualitative versus the quantitative differential. Suppose it is really a quantitative differential, point by point and characteristic by characteristic, but would not the interaction in the summation indeed lead to a qualitatively different individual? The second point is that it seems most of us today have been talking in terms of curricula and programs that have been. We haven't addressed a very important issue, programs that could be. Now if education is just the acquiring of bits and pieces of knowledge, if we go no higher than 2.00 in Benjamin S. Bloom's *Taxonomy of Educational Objectives,* then maybe indeed acceleration is the answer and we have the 10-year-old sitting with 15-year-olds. But as we said, we are dealing with a different kind of individual with a different potential undoubtedly. Perhaps we could start moving this type of youngster into the 3.00 through the 6.00 levels and go beyond what we have been doing for the last couple of thousand years.

KEATING: The second part of the question was I think rephrased appropriately by Tom James. The question as to whether the difference is qualitative or quantitative is a very difficult one to answer, because we have to define very clearly what we mean by a "qualitative" and what we mean by a "quantitative" difference. It seems to me that a very careful review of the literature would indicate that it is difficult to come up with criteria that could be put forth noncontroversially as qualitative differences. As I mentioned in my talk, the most compelling evidence is for a quantitative or rate difference. That doesn't necessarily mean, however, that we wouldn't want to improve curricula. If we look at qualitative differences in terms of different patterns of intellectual development, different kinds of reasoning, and so forth, it is relatively difficult to come up with evidence. It is much easier to come up with quantitative kinds of differences. As Ellis Page mentioned, however, this question is still unresolved.

OWENS: There is a political dimension in what we're discussing now, one we have run into directly in Alaska, concerning whether or not there is a difference at all. We have assumed one, and we have established programs that differentiate and treat students differently on the basis of giftedness, however we define it. I think we have opened the door, in the same way as we have done in special education, to a rash of court cases that will require that we serve students whom we have already identified as being exceptional. Once we have defined a class of students, we are bound morally, legally, and ethically to serve them as individuals in a manner appropriate to them.

GIBB: I am concerned that we *do* have to tackle this issue of quality versus quantity, difficult as that task is. In speaking of mathematics in particular, the mainstream (regardless of where it is, even at the collegiate level) can be so narrow. After shopping through that, it seems like these youngsters have lost a lot of the creativity they could bring to knowledge and leadership.

GEORGE: I would like to respond to both Dr. Gold and Dr. Gibb. One supposed problem or question that keeps coming up when you mention educational acceleration is as follows: "Are there gaps? Are these students missing something if we do not spread out or enrich their education?" I recently asked a couple of SMPY early entrants to comment on this issue. Both have been through fast-math programs. The first person, Mr. Kevin Bartkovich,[26] said the following: "The main flaw that is apparent in these arguments from the start is the assumption that mathematically talented students should become mathematicians. I view the applications of mathematics as the more important aspect. In my development math has been a tool, providing a base on which to build. Some people propose that creativity can be stimulated best by enrichment. I believe from personal experience that acceleration is a better method of enhancing creativity. A gifted student is always looking ahead, hoping to proceed further once a concept is understood. Math always is building on the preceding topic, and a gifted student is curious as to what is the next step. This is the essence of creativity, probing further ahead into the material. This creativity is motivated by acceleration, whereas enrichment can be the method that stifles it. I believe the assertion that programs of acceleration leave gaps in understanding is not valid. If the standards for proceeding in a sequence of courses are stringent enough, a student must have a good knowledge of a subject in order to proceed. Learning something quickly does not necessarily mean superficial knowledge. In fact, some concepts (e.g., limits in calculus) do not become clear until a year or two after the initial presentation. Mathematics always is applying previous knowledge in learning new concepts. It is this building and application, and not enrichment alone, that creates deeper understanding. In fact, I have learned precalculus well enough in an extremely fast-paced class to be able to tutor other talented students." The other young man noted that by being allowed to go through the material rapidly he had a much better chance of learning other subject matter as well. In fact, he felt that his divergent production and creative potential were stimulated by his being challenged with a lot of topics that he learned one after another. From what these students said and hundreds more like them I don't

[26]Kevin G. Bartkovich entered The Johns Hopkins University in the fall of 1976, one year early and with sophomore standing. He presently is an outstanding student in a B.A./M.A. program in electrical engineering and one of SMPY's chief mentors.

think acceleration results in learning that would be considered at the lower end of Bloom's taxonomy.

Not all enrichment programs are bad, however. There are many excellent programs at the elementary school level, as pointed out in Julian Stanley's article in the *Phi Delta Kappan*.[27] Many are individualized and challenge the student's special talents. The danger lies in the transition from elementary to secondary school. One Michigan coordinator for the gifted and talented explained it in the following way. She has a class that was accelerated through algebra I by the end of grade six. She then was told to slow down and enrich them because these students would run out of curriculum. This was devastating to the students' willingness to learn. Thus, appropriate enrichment leads naturally to some form of educational acceleration. The University of Washington group commented earlier in their position paper that we should forget the terms *acceleration* and *enrichment* and consider whether actually we are decelerating the potential of the student. Are we allowing him or her to learn at his/her natural rate in areas that are challenging and interesting? Are we really decelerating the intellectual challenge that the student has? This should be even a bigger concern than enrichment versus acceleration. The two blend together; often, a program of enrichment ends up with some form of acceleration, but deceleration may be the aspect at which we need to look.

STANLEY: One of the most powerful bits of evidence about the effectiveness of fast-math classes, skipping grades, moving ahead quickly in math, and getting into high-level college courses quickly in math and related areas is simply the satisfaction felt by those who do it. Those who are *eager* to accelerate some of their educational experiences and are able to do it are almost invariably thrilled, pleased, and delighted that they have done so. They do not prefer to plod through any kind of enriched curriculum of any feasible sort within the typical school, nor would that program usually be feasible unless it was extremely expensive. It is cost-effective for them to move ahead. We have not had a single youngster who has come to college early who said, "I'm sorry I did it." When we ask them at the end of the first year, "Would you rather have been back in high school this year?" they turn rather pale at the thought of having had to stay in high school. These are the ones who wanted to move ahead, of course, so we must keep in mind that we are talking about extremely able youngsters who are eager to do these things. We are not talking about reluctant kids. We are not even talking about Norbert Wieners or John Stuart Mills who were programmed and pushed unusually strongly by their parents.

A second observation concerns defining ability broadly to include a number of different types of cognitive style assessment techniques. Participants in SMPY, even those who finish college at barely 15 with tremendous records in pure math, are not a species apart. They are not different from other mortals,

[27]For those persons interested in reading Dr. Stanley's article see chapter 11. Also see his 1978 Educational non-acceleration: An international tragedy. *G/C/T* (Gifted, Creative, and Talented Children) 1(3, May–June): 2–5, 53–57, 60–64.

except in the incredible speed and complexity with which they can work. There is an extreme rate difference, a difference in degree but not in kind. On the other hand, we have to keep in mind that this would have to be a multivariate model, because the single-score IQ model is inadequate. The Binet IQ is simply the average of a lot of different abilities, some high, others low. There is not a single simple continuum, but instead the aggregate of different abilities. For instance, it is not at all uncommon to find a youngster who excells on most cognitive tests but is relatively inferior on some one, such as mechanical comprehension. There is a young man at Johns Hopkins, one of SMPY's current twenty-six radical accelerants there, not one of the seniors, who is extremely able except that he can hardly do even the sample items on a mechanical comprehension test. We do not know why he is poor at that, but he took physics and had trouble. He had trouble with chemistry lab and so forth. So he is different from someone whose strongest ability is high mechanical comprehension. We have another youth who scored incredibly high in mechanical comprehension at age 13, the highest score we have ever had. He is a computer hardware specialist today, which is not surprising. There is a cognitive difference.

I don't like the magic theory or the "gee whiz" approach so dear to the hearts of many of the journalists who write about gifted youths in the popular press. "Math whizzes" and "genius" are the typical expressions they like to use. There are some questions about details of cognitive styles that are very important. Even among mathematicians there have been quite different cognitive styles, as those of you who have read Eric Temple Bell's somewhat inappropriately titled *Men of Mathematics* know. Some mathematicians aren't good with geometry, and some aren't good with algebra, but they can still be great mathematicians. There are many modalities that should be studied. Individuals are complex mentally, but we have no reason to suppose some sudden qualitative "jumping off" (that's what I call the pre-Columbus theory— suddenly you come to the end of the world and fall off). You don't suddenly come to a different type of person as far as math ability is concerned. It is just some kind of multivariate set of continua that one must study: cognitive differences between individuals and within them.

NINA LIEBERMAN:[28]   I want to relate my comment to what Dr. Stanley said about one of the presenters, Mr. Daurio. He commended him for finding the time to go over the literature. (I do believe my comment refers both to enrichment and acceleration.) I am wondering, based on my own research and the theoretical model with which I am working, whether we give enough time, time to reflect, time to ingest knowledge. We have been talking about acquisition of knowledge, but in my books at least to become familiar with what you know is really basic to creating the new. At that point, as I have found in my own research, combinatorial play comes about. I am wondering as we are looking at the gifted and as we are planning for curricula for the gifted, how much consideration we give for

---

[28]Audience questioner: Nina Lieberman, Brooklyn College, 21 Lewis Place, Brooklyn, New York 11218.

time to reflect, time to digest, time to be comfortable with the familiar. My concern also relates to the feeling of joy over one's own accomplishments, and it might also serve to contribute to a global concept called mental health.

STANLEY: We are trying to help these mathematically talented youths move ahead quickly to a first-rate graduate degree from a major university, which is what most of them want, at the highest possible level and the earliest feasible time. That gives them the years of early maturity in which to be highly creative and energetic rather than waiting until they are 26 to 30 or more years of age. We are trying to help them get Ph.D.s early—19, 20, 21, 22—as for instance Dr. Anastasi did. I believe she had her Ph.D. at 22, and a great deal of nice creative work came from her shop in the early years when she might otherwise have been hacking away at routine teaching or turning someone else's research crank as a doctoral student. For philosophy or creative writing, the situation *might* be rather appreciably different. SMPY operates in math and related areas, instead. Most of the youngsters with whom we work will not become pure mathematicians. I think we have to emphasize that there are less than 500 Ph.D.s a year in the whole country in pure mathematics, less than 500 out of a population age group of three and a half million people, so actually we are talking little about pure mathematicians. We are talking about computer scientists, mathematical statisticians, physicists, electrical engineers, operations researchers, and so forth.

LIEBERMAN: If I may just respond to this. I spoke also as a developmental psychologist, because I think these things have to be socialized early. My own research was propelled by something that was said about Einstein. He thought that one of the most important things is combinatorial play, and play occurs only in a kind of relaxed setting.

STANLEY: He was so relaxed that he quit the gymnasium at 16 to get away from that boring setting and go on to the university. Then he did have a good deal of time, while a patent examiner third class (a lowly occupation), to conceive of and write about special relativity and to publish three papers that made him famous by age 26.

FOX: One thing to think about in planning programs for the gifted is related to your point—how we schedule their time. One of the things that we did early in the Study of Mathematically Precocious Youth, at the time with some trepidation, was to set up a class that met only once a week for two hours. The student had that whole week in which to work over the material and move ahead. While there was some required homework to be turned in, the students knew that they had to determine whether or not they needed to work more problems in a particular section. While it doesn't work perfectly with all students (and we had to do a little counseling and to encourage them to pace themselves rather than to save up all the home work until the night before the next class), that model seems to be much better for these kinds of students than a daily class where they tend to sit and daydream and get extremely bored. This way they get very excited and turned on in this intense two-hour period, and then at their leisure, when the mood strikes them during the week, they have time to pull out the mathematics. We see them coming back to class responding to something that the instructor threw out as an "Oh, by the way, why don't you see if you can prove this problem?" They come in excited and compare notes with the other students, because they have spent a lot of time during the week working on it. So I think for the highly gifted a different kind of course scheduling would make better sense, thereby allowing them longer periods of time for intensive concentration on their own.

GOLD: A discussion as to what should be included for gifted kids strikes me as almost a discussion about religions. Your own always is the best and the others are inferior. This approach leaves something to be desired. One study that was not mentioned today would do us all good to recollect; I vaguely remember a lot of it, but the results were most important. That is the work Ruth Martinson did in California back in the late 1950s, comparing the effectiveness of the variety of approaches for gifted students in that state. There were fourteen or eighteen different kinds of programs—ungraded primary, Saturday seminar, enrichment activities, acceleration, etc. She doesn't make the result as blatant as I am making it, but somehow she conveys the message that no matter what you do for the gifted, it is almost as good as anything else you do for the gifted. Each of those kinds of approaches is a whole lot better than doing nothing for the gifted. This is something that we might want to look at when our own biases get in the way of what is better, acceleration, enrichment, segregation, or 105 other kinds of terms that could be employed. If any of you remember "Fiddler on the Roof," Tevye was having a discussion with a couple of men and one man makes a point and he says, "You know something, you are right," and then another man makes a point which is diametrically opposed and Tevye says, "You know something, you are right, too!" The third man says, "If he's right, and he's right, how can they both be right?" and Tevye replies, "I'll tell you something, you're right, too."

KEATING: I just want to make the brief comment, that one particular connotation of the term *acceleration* probably is an undesirable one and not an appropriate one. That combination is one of being harried and rushed, sort of whipping right through all the stuff without time to think about it. Our observations within this particular study (SMPY) would not support that kind of interpretation. Self-selection helps prevent such hurried progress. If a student feels that he or she is just going too fast, he/she always has the option of exiting a program at a variety of different points. I've never had the impression that the kids with whom we work (observing them in a variety of situations and talking with them at some length) felt harried or pressed. Instead they feel that they finally have gotten to do something at a pace normal for them, rather than having to sit through a lot of boring, irrelevant material.

KEARNEY: Something that bothers me about today and about all the other meetings I've attended is that we are here because we are interested in the gifted. Hal Lyon's research report a few years back indicated that 57 percent of the principals who responded said they had no gifted children in their schools. I think that leads us to an important fact; education at the university level for teachers should require one course, at least, not just in the exceptional child but specifically concerning the gifted child.

Fox: I just want to pull together what Dan Keating, Joan Stark, and Marv Gold said: there are a variety of ways to do things. All may not be equally good, but each may be differentially good for different students. As Joan said, certainly by ages 11 and 12 the students are good at picking out which ways meet their needs, which fit their styles and their time designs. We found in working with these gifted students that after they found out we had written a book, some of them went off, read it, and came back to see us and said, "I want to do it this way." They had all the arguments. Someone else came and said, "I want to do it another way." So I think you are right. There are multiple approaches, and the important thing is to keep all the options open and let the student have a choice as to which options suit him or her at that particular time.

STANLEY: Unfortunately, many school systems have at most one option for the gifted, and that is grossly insufficient. Thank you very much for your long-term patience here. We are delighted to have had a chance to talk with you.

[THIS CONCLUDED THE SYMPOSIUM]

As a final summation of the discussion on enrichment and acceleration, Dr. Dorothy S. Sisk, then Director of the Office of Gifted and Talented in the U.S. Department of Health, Education, and Welfare, was asked to present her viewpoint. The following position paper was solicited after the symposium.

ACCELERATION VERSUS ENRICHMENT: A POSITION PAPER

Dorothy A. Sisk

High ability and potential are served best by an education that is more than rigorous and academic. Indeed, education for our nation's gifted and talented must be more than an accumulation of successive concepts, ideas, and facts. Education for the gifted and talented must deal with activities that nurture and develop individual motivation and that produce wisdom.

For years the standard answer to educational programming for the gifted was enrichment. This was true regardless of the research available. Investigators such as Terman and Oden (1947), Gallagher (1975), and Reynolds, Birch, and Tuseth (1962) clearly stated that early admission was to the advantage of the gifted, and that social and emotional difficulties were not synonymous with acceleration.

With the current emphasis on mainstreaming the exceptional child in the regular classroom and the fear of segregation, coupled with the continuing concerns and anxieties of both parents and teachers regarding acceleration, there is a real danger that programming for the gifted and talented will become a group-directed enrichment travesty. In these kinds of activity-oriented projects, the material to be learned often is extended in quantity rather than depth, all in the name of enrichment.

The passage of public law 94-142, with its emphasis on individual educational planning (IEP) for the handicapped, has led many educators to reexamine enrichment as an answer to IEP for gifted youngsters. They are finding that enrichment often increases breadth of information, that it emphasizes variety and exploration, but that it lacks experiences that call for precision and intensive work.

In fact, much of the so-called enrichment of many programs for the gifted and talented is being found to exist only on paper. Many of the programs lack comprehensive planning and organization; the "enrichment" exists only in the verbalizations of the teachers and administrators who describe such programs.

Where acceleration and enrichment are concerned, the answer to programming for the gifted and talented clearly is not an either/or proposition. No one can deny that some type of educational readjustment is needed to reduce the extended period of education required for a professional career. Making our best minds and talents mark time until age 29 or older is denying both the individual and our culture the benefit of their gifts and talents.

Part of the problem is lack of understanding on the part of both parents and educators that acceleration and grade-skipping don't mean the same thing. Indeed, rapid promotion can damage gifted students if they skip important sequences in a curriculum. However, equal or even greater damage is done to gifted and talented students who repeat materials and are forced to progress slowly with a group.

Optimum education for the gifted and talented should blend enrichment and acceleration for an emphasis on excellence in education. Perhaps a new word such as "exceleration" needs to be coined. That would afford the gifted and talented both the breadth and exploration of enrichment and the rapid progress and telescoping of work of acceleration.

No two gifted individuals are alike. Their variability arises from their creativity, interest, and capacity for problem-solving. The uniqueness of gifted individuals makes it impossible for educators to develop and prescribe any single curriculum for "the" gifted, but their education can be planned so it will provide for total development, including intellectual, emotional, and character aspects. More and more educators are realizing that there is an inherent relationship between intellectual growth and emotional welfare (Howe and Howe 1975, Glasser 1966).

To program for the gifted, all that is needed is the courage to examine what is appropriate for each gifted student and the willingness to make the administrative arrangements to accomplish it. A rapprochement between acceleration and enrichment very well may be the solution.

References

Gallagher, J. J. 1975. *Teaching the gifted child.* Rockleigh, N.J.: Allyn and Bacon.
Glasser, W. 1976. *Positive addiction.* New York: Harper and Row.
Howe, L. W. and Howe, M. M. 1975. *Personalizing education.* Hart.
Reynolds, M., Birch, J., and Tuseth, A. 1962. Review of research on early admission. In *Field demonstration of the effectiveness and possibility of early admission for mentally advanced children.* Reston, Va.: Council for Exceptional Children.
Terman, L. M., and Oden, M. H. 1947. The gifted child grows up. *Genetic Studies of Genius,* vol. IV. Stanford, Calif.: Stanford University Press.

NAME INDEX

9295-4
5-40